STRUGGLES FOR AN ALTERNATIVE
GLOBALIZATION

For Connie Birchfield

Struggles for an Alternative Globalization

An Ethnography of Counterpower in Southern France

GWYN WILLIAMS

Routledge
Taylor & Francis Group

LONDON AND NEW YORK

First published 2008 by Ashgate Publishing

Reissued 2018 by Routledge
2 Park Square, Milton Park, Abingdon, Oxon OX14 4RN
711 Third Avenue, New York, NY 10017, USA

Routledge is an imprint of the Taylor & Francis Group, an informa business

First issued in paperback 2018

A Library of Congress record exists under LC control number: 2007041404

Notice:
Product or corporate names may be trademarks or registered trademarks, and are used only for identification and explanation without intent to infringe.

Publisher's Note
The publisher has gone to great lengths to ensure the quality of this reprint but points out that some imperfections in the original copies may be apparent.

Disclaimer
The publisher has made every effort to trace copyright holders and welcomes correspondence from those they have been unable to contact.

ISBN 13: 978-0-8153-9722-9 (hbk)
ISBN 13: 978-1-1386-2069-8 (pbk)
ISBN 13: 978-1-3511-4848-1 (ebk)

Contents

Acknowledgements

This book was written while I was the Leach/RAI Fellow in 2005 and 2006, a position funded by the Royal Anthropological Institute, the Esperanza Trust and the University of Sussex. I would like to thank everyone at Sussex University who welcomed me and provided a friendly and stimulating intellectual environment in which to work. Thanks especially to Jeff Pratt, Simon Coleman, Geert De Neve, Peter Luetchford and Neil Stammers for their comments, criticisms and encouragement. The book emerged out of doctoral research carried out at Cambridge University and funded by the New Zealand Foundation for Research, Science and Technology. Thanks also to Maryon McDonald, Paola Filippucci and others at Cambridge who provided advice and support.

Some of the material presented here has been developed elsewhere. An article I wrote for the journal *Nature and Culture*, entitled 'Cosmopolitanism and the French anti-GM movement' (vol.3, no.1, 2008), explores activists' opposition to genetic modification. Another article in vol.28:1 of *Critique of Anthropology* (2008), 'Cultivating Autonomy: Power, Resistance and the French Alterglobalization Movement', expands on the book's overall argument concerning autonomy.

Bits of this book have also been tried out in various forms at conferences in the UK and the US and in seminars at Cambridge and Sussex. I have benefited much from the feedback I received from participants. Thanks to David Graeber for kindly sending me his book draft and to the anonymous reviewers for their time and feedback.

I owe a great deal to the colleagues and friends who have been there for me over the years. Gisa Weszkalnys has commented on various versions of this book and been a excellent source of support. Laura Jeffery has been wonderful in lots of ways. Thanks heaps to Paul Husbands and Alan Latham for being good to talk to about pretty much everything and for sharing food, hospitality, elbow grease, laughs and so on. And thank you, too, to Jim, Theresa, Louise, Katy, Judy and Philippa.

Biggest thanks, however, go to all the committed activists who collectively form the subject of this book. I hope I have not done them too much injustice in these pages. I will mention only a few by name. Pierre Vuarin provided me with early introductions, a place to live and ongoing encouragement. Christine Thelen was a source of much help and enlightenment on what was happening around me. She ferried me around in her car on many occasions and was my entry point for much of the activist world. And Jeanine Boubal was always there to tell me the other side of things. As much as she drove me crazy, her poker face, spontaneous poetry recitals, cursing and mischievous grin all helped make my stay on the Larzac a pleasure.

Chapter 1

Introduction: The Voice of the Street

In the summer of 1999, a group of activists 'dismantled' an uncompleted McDonald's restaurant in the town of Millau in southern France. They removed prefabricated walls, doors, light switches, bits of roof and, after loading everything onto trailers, paraded through the town and delivered it all to the sub-prefecture.[1] Often described as a 'nonviolent' and 'symbolic' protest, the dismantling was carried out by members of the Confédération Paysanne, a farmers' union, and by activists from Millau and from the Larzac plateau, which rises above the town. It was led by José Bové, Larzac activist and Confédération Paysanne spokesperson, against what he calls a symbol of 'economic imperialism' and 'anonymous globalization' (Bové and Dufour 2000, 29, 98). Following extensive media coverage of the events and of his subsequent imprisonment, Bové became a household name and one of the most celebrated figures of what is now known as the *mouvement altermondialiste*, the alterglobalization movement.

The McDonald's dismantling was triggered by US import tariffs imposed on a hundred or so European products, among them Roquefort cheese, which Bové described to me as 'the most local product possible and the most symbolic of local products'. The tariffs, which were approved by the World Trade Organization (WTO), were a retaliation for a European Union (EU) refusal to allow the importation of hormone treated meat from the United States and angered local farmers who sell ewes' milk to the Roquefort firms. But the McDonald's action was much more than a corporatist protest against the US by farmers concerned with their livelihoods. McDonald's came to symbolize everything that the activists involved, many of whom were not farmers, consider wrong with neoliberal globalization. McDonald's epitomizes standardization and the effacement of local diversity, the commercialization and the commodification of the world, the privileging of the private over the public good, and the liberalization of the global economy being driven by the WTO. Against such neoliberal forces, activists assert that 'the world is not a commodity', a phrase popularized in the title of one of Bové's books, *Le monde n'est pas une marchandise*,[2] and which has become the catch-cry of the entire French alterglobalization movement.

In addition to making Bové into something of an activist superstar, the 'McDonald's affair' helped to cement the Confédération Paysanne at the forefront of the movement and it reinforced the reputation for resistance which the Larzac had acquired thirty years earlier. The Larzac became famous during a decade of protest in the 1970s

---

1 For accounts of the events see Bové and Dufour (2000, 16ff.), Alland (2001, 169ff.), and the *Spécial Anti Mac Do* in the Larzac's activist newspaper (GLL 1999).

2 *The World is Not for Sale* is the English title (Bové and Dufour 2002).

when local peasant farmers fought the extension of the plateau's military camp and the expropriation of their farms. Their struggle, however, was not waged alone. They formed an alliance with thousands of outsiders, many of whom were the children of May '68 determined to oppose what they viewed as a centralized, authoritarian and militaristic state power whose will had been imposed on the provinces. A few settled on the plateau, occupying farms the army had managed to purchase. Others helped the farmers in the summer months and participated in regular meetings and protest actions – demonstrations, occupations, fasts, festivals, illegal construction projects and marches – which were inspired, indirectly, by Gandhian nonviolence. As the struggle continued throughout the decade, the Larzac itself became a 'symbol of resistance'. It provided an inspiration for social movements elsewhere and furnished, in the words of an English pacifist and regular visitor to the Larzac in the 1970s, 'arguably the most important model in Europe for the successful conduct of a Gandhian-style struggle' (Rawlinson 1996, viii). For Jean-Paul Sartre, 'the Larzac struggle [was] one of the most beautiful of the twentieth century' (quoted in Martin 1987, 24).

Over twenty years after the Socialist government of 1981 cancelled the camp extension, 'the Larzac' is still considered a symbol of resistance by many, even *the* symbol of resistance in contemporary France. Local activists, amongst whom I conducted fieldwork in 2002 and 2003, affirm its symbolic importance and the leading role the Larzac plays within the French alterglobalization movement. They consider it a place where people actively struggle against the forces of capital and neoliberal globalization, where 'citizens' assert their rights to engage in a politics of protest in defence of the public good. Through their tireless political engagement activists continue the tradition of protest that began over three decades ago. They participate in meetings and demonstrations against a range of foes, neoliberal globalization, the Israeli occupation of Palestine, genetic modification, the US invasion of Iraq and state repression of the social movement being the most salient.

For many activists, however, it is the WTO that is the greatest single cause of the world's injustice and its wrong. In 2003, activists from the Larzac and Millau, with the assistance of activist groups in Paris and elsewhere, organized an enormous gathering on the plateau 'against the WTO'. Known as Larzac 2003, the gathering was held over three days in August and attracted an estimated 300,000 people to a series of concerts and political forums. Participation was diverse. In addition to the highly visible presence of the Confédération Paysanne and Attac, one of the major alterglobalization organizations in the country, the gathering involved the stalls and displays of 150 activist associations and unions from across France. There were forums and debates on the WTO, agriculture, state repression, nuclear energy, genetic modification, colonialism, racism, Palestine, Kurdistan, fair trade, the liberalization of public services and numerous other topics. Despite the diverse range of their interests, many different activists and political groups find a place within the alterglobalization movement, or within 'the social movement' (*le mouvement social*), as it is often called. Their various struggles have in common the fact that all oppose the domination of the meek by the powerful. It is the perceived division of the world into those 'above' (*d'en haut*) and those 'below' (*d'en bas*) – to cite a distinction infamously defended by then French Prime Minister Raffarin – to which activists most object (cf. Berglund 1998, 101). They express their objections by taking to the streets, by making their collective voice heard, in flagrant rejection of another of Raffarin's assertions that 'it's not the street that governs'.

Other worlds are possible

This book is about the politics of protest in which the activists of the Larzac and Millau engage. While the Larzac is always a central focus, I am also concerned with the alterglobalization movement more generally, a movement which, in some sense at least, is very much a global one. Through an in-depth exploration of activism in a rural area of southern France, I aim to offer a point of entry into an ostensibly worldwide movement to create alternatives to neoliberal globalization.

The emergence of this movement is often thought to have two key moments: the Zapatista uprising in Chiapas, Mexico, in 1994; and what is sometimes called the 'Battle of Seattle' in 1999. On 1 January 2004, the day the North American Free Trade Agreement came into effect, three thousand mainly indigenous members of the Zapatista Army of National Liberation took control of four major cities in the state of Chiapas. The Zapatistas sought local autonomy and control over their own lives and the natural resources to which multinational corporations were gaining increasing access. Significantly, they managed to gain the support of people around the world and to create large solidarity networks through the use of the Internet. Their struggle inspired Western activists to question neoliberalism, and the kinds of grassroots democracy they established encouraged experiments elsewhere in truly democratic and participatory forms of social organization (Johnston and Laxer 2003). By 1999, the WTO, which had been established four years earlier, had come to epitomize neoliberalism and antidemocratic decision-making for activists around the world. Thousands came to Seattle in November of that year with the aim of disrupting the WTO Ministerial Conference taking place in the city and putting an end to The Seattle Round of trade negotiations. Present in Seattle were NGOs, labour unions, anarchists, environmentalists, students and others, all somehow united in a loose coalition against multinational capitalism, WTO policies and neoliberal globalization. The protests involved various peaceful marches, blockades, lockdowns and street occupations, but also some destruction of corporate property, violent confrontations with the police, the deployment of the National Guard, hundreds of arrests and three deaths. Importantly, the protesters prevented many conference delegates from travelling between their hotels and the Convention Center, forcing formal negotiations to be abandoned. For activists, Seattle was a major success in an ongoing struggle. It demonstrated that ordinary people, if sufficiently organized, could constitute a major political force and that neoliberalism was far from the 'only alternative'.

In early 2001, a little more than a year after Seattle, the first World Social Forum (WSF) was held in Porto Alegre, Brazil, in opposition to the World Economic Forum (WEF) held at the same time in Davos, Switzerland. While the WEF assembled political and economic elites from around the globe – the 'self-proclaimed "masters of the world"' hidden 'behind armoured vehicles and barbed wire', as the Larzac's activist newspaper put it (Gesson 2001, 7) – the WSF aimed to give voice to those excluded from such elite deliberations. Organized by a committee of eight Brazilian organizations and with an International Council of over a hundred, its Charter of Principles states that the WSF

> is an open meeting place for reflective thinking, democratic debate of ideas, formulation of proposals, free exchange of experiences and interlinking for effective action, by groups and movements of civil society that are opposed to neoliberalism and to domination of the world by capital and any form of imperialism, and are committed to building a planetary society directed towards fruitful relationships among Humankind and between it and the Earth.

'The World Social Forum is a world process', the Charter continues. The aim is to develop alternatives to neoliberalism and multinational capitalism in the interests of participation, solidarity, diversity, human rights and social justice. 'Another World is Possible' is its slogan. It is not a decision-making body and 'does not constitute a locus of power' but is rather designed as a forum for interaction, discussion and debate. 'The World Social Forum is a plural, diversified, non-confessional, non-governmental and non-party context that, in a decentralized fashion, interrelates organizations and movements engaged in concrete action at levels from the local to the international to build another world' (WSF n.d.).

The first WSF was attended by 10,000 registered delegates from 123 countries. Larzac activists considered Porto Alegre to be an ideal location given the backing the WSF received from the Brazilian Workers' Party of soon-to-be president Lula and the support of the local Porto Alegre administration, which had been experimenting in forms of participative democracy. Later WSFs attracted many more people and in 2004 the Forum moved to Mumbai, India, before a 'polycentric' edition was held in Mali, Venezuela and Pakistan in 2006. The WSF also spurned a whole series of regional and local forums, from the African, Asian, European and US Social Forums, to social forums centred on Italy, Aotearoa/New Zealand, Liverpool, Boston and, indeed, Millau.

Many of these forums have seen the participation of activists from the Larzac and Millau area. Ten attended the first WSF in Porto Alegre, including José Bové who had been invited by the organizers as spokesperson of the Confédération Paysanne and 'figurehead of the struggle against neoliberal globalization'. As part of one of the larger delegations from France – along with South Americans, the French were amongst the best represented in Porto Alegre – Larzac-Millau activists visited small farms, participated in a 'march for life and against neoliberalism', and attended just some of the 400 workshops on offer at the Forum itself, with the aim of 'developing an alternative to the neoliberal dictatorship', as one activist writes (Gesson 2001, 1, 7). Most memorably, they helped members of Brazil's Landless Peasant Movement destroy three hectares of transgenic maize planted by Monsanto, an action which subsequently saw an arrest warrant and expulsion order issued against Bové, an unsuccessful police attempt to 'kidnap' him in the underground car park of a hotel, and his eventual 'triumph' at the Forum's closing ceremony, where he received a standing ovation from 5,000 delegates.

Porto Alegre was neither the first nor last time Larzac activists had travelled beyond French borders to join thousands of others in the global struggle against neoliberalism. In 1999, shortly after the dismantling of the Millau McDonald's, the Confédération Paysanne sent a delegation to Seattle which six activists from around Millau joined. Each member smuggled a Roquefort cheese into the US – 200 kilos somehow made it in all – and Roquefort was handed out all week at press conferences and in the streets. Roquefort, Chaia Heller writes, 'continued its career as a potent non-human actor in the anti-globalization network', symbolizing diversity and quality in opposition to standardized junk food, and the resistance of 'culture against transnational capital' (2004, 93–4).

Through their participation in mass political events, Larzac activists consciously aim to forge links and build solidarities with activists elsewhere and to strengthen 'civil society' around the world. Their intention is to create a 'citizens' offensive against globalization', an offensive which began, at local level, with the McDonald's dismantling in 1999 (Gesson 2000, 1). Following the McDonald's affair, Larzac activists felt a certain obligation 'to be represented at the citizens' counter-summit in Seattle' and to help in creating a global movement against neoliberal globalization. In an editorial entitled *Think globally, act locally*, Bové writes that their trip to Seattle allowed them to 'federate revolts, unify people, develop projects, live a hope' in a place that saw 'the birth of a planetary movement linking the local and the global' (2000). All over the world people opposed to the WTO's policies and to multinational capital were beginning to talk, share ideas and unite across boundaries of geography, wealth and culture. As put by the president of the American National Family Farm Coalition, in words of welcome to visiting French activists just prior to Seattle, 'We share the same goals, we have the same objectives. We have understood that we will not succeed in attaining them unless we unite and fight together' (quoted in Gesson 2000, 7). Small local protests, mass demonstrations in major cities such as Seattle and Paris, and Social Forums large and small are all integral to the effort to unite, to create activist networks, to share analyses and to struggle against global domination and injustice. And in slogans that reverberate in different languages across the world – from 'think globally, act locally' to 'another world is possible' – it indeed seems that activists from Brazil to France, China to Mali, are newly linked into one great global movement of resistance.

This vision is, perhaps, a bit deceptive. Globalness is certainly key to the way 'the movement' is imagined. But a global movement remains 'in process', something to build rather than an existing reality, and action on the ground and ways of understanding the world remain somehow as 'local' as they ever were. The movement for 'another world' or for 'other worlds' – variously known as the antiglobalization movement, the globalization movement (Graeber 2004), the globalization-critical movement (Mueller 2002), the global anti-capital movement (Lacey 2005), the world citizens' movement (Polet 2004), or the alternative world movement (Hayes and Bunyan 2004) – is marked, to the extent that it can be understood as a single movement, by its diversity. Activists in different parts of the world – from the relatively affluent French men and women I shall discuss to landless Third-World peasants, from indigenous peoples to ecologists, from New York anarchists to the working classes of Latin American – have, given the concrete specifics of their existence, different concerns which they address in different ways. Forging solidarities between such varied and widely dispersed groups of activists is often problematic. The problem is partly practical. The Internet certainly helps in this respect, although activists in Paris have greater access to it than their counterparts in rural Africa. Even Larzac activists seemed, on my arrival on the plateau, to be remarkably unconnected to the World Wide Web. Money, or rather the lack of it, provides another major obstacle. While the French are fairly visible at World Social Forums in Brazil, Chinese and Africans are notable by their absence. The WSF is largely a forum for the mobile middle classes, for a few less-privileged individuals who receive funding from donor organizations, or for those who live nearby. And despite the rhetoric of a global movement, organizing at a local or national level, and an understanding of the 'local' or 'national', often remain vitally important. Even the Zapatistas, whose use of the Internet to cultivate worldwide support for their struggle, depended fundamentally on long-standing local solidarities. Indeed, the supposedly transnational 'Zapatismo' their struggle engendered – a grassroots, democratic philosophy and global sense of solidarity shared in by Western activists – drew extensively, Johnston and Laxer argue, on a certain Mexican nationalism (2003, 70; see Collier and Collier 2005, 452–3; Doane 2005). Frequently, local and national connections with people who share language and experiences in common remain more central to everyday struggles than do transnational networks (Johnston and Laxer 2003).

The task of creating a single movement, a global civil society, thus also encounters problems associated with stitching together independent movements with contrasting visions of the world, styles of organization and ideas about how best to confront forms of domination. The understandings, aspirations and tactics of those who associate themselves with the fight against neoliberal globalization are often awkwardly compatible. Old style labour movements and left-wing political parties remain highly hierarchical, to the dismay of those who fight for democratic and consensus-based forms of organization. NGOs have become increasingly professionalized and increasingly lack any real grassroots membership or a desire for the sort of mass mobilization that others consider essential (Cmiel 1999, 1243). 'Reformists' are quite willing to negotiate with political elites while 'radicals' seek only fundamental change, whatever that might mean, through forms of direct political action.

Strategies for bringing about change through protest action also vary. The anarchists of the Direct Action Network, discussed by David Graeber (n.d.) in what, at the time of my writing, was an unpublished ethnography, 'abhor the corporate media', while for activists of the Larzac the mass media provide a vital tool. 'Direct action' in the US is not really a question of 'visibility' or 'spectacle' in which the aim is to influence 'the public', although all these are crucial to the French activists I shall discuss. US direct action is not intended to be 'symbolic' as it is in France, it is not media focused and not a question of 'civil disobedience'. French-style civil disobedience – although one of its greatest proponents, José Bové, would insist that the tradition is not French (see Bové and Luneau 2004) – is about pressuring the state into reform by making visible to 'the people' the injustice of laws. Direct action, on the other hand, 'proceeds', Graeber writes (n.d.), 'as if the state does not exist'.

Direct actionists often enter into confrontation with state authorities but they refuse to recognize the authority of the state's representatives as a legal one. They judge it solely on moral, not legal, grounds and are concerned with directly acting to stop the powerful exercising their power, not just having them exercise it more justly. Seattle, where WTO negotiations were brought to a halt, provides an example of successful direct action.

The problem, for many activist groups, is to find some commonality amongst the diversity. It is this focus on commonality that characterizes both Graeber's anarchists and Larzac activists, as well as participants in World Social Forums. One point of common ground is found in opposition to multinationals, the WTO and their agenda of free trade, which has a concrete and adverse impact on people all over the world. Another exists in the desire to create new forms of democracy, truly participative and egalitarian ways of organizing based on a rejection of all hierarchy. Creating something new, a real alternative, is an ideal shared by everyone.

'Newness' is a central theme in both scholarly and activist discussions of social movements today. In a recent book called *Globalizing Resistance*, the principal editor, François Polet, who describes the book 'as a crossroads between the militant and the academic', refers to 'the emergence of a "world citizens' movement" that seeks new forms of collective and democratic regulation' and which is based on 'new forms of organization' and 'solidarity' (2004, x, vii–ix). Writing on the World Social Forum, the sociologist Boaventura de Sousa Santos similarly argues that the WSF is a radically new political phenomenon. 'The WSF is not an event', 'not a social movement', 'holds no clearly defined ideology', 'rejects the concept of an historical subject', 'is not structured according to any of the models of modern political organization', is neither reformist nor revolutionary and is inclusive despite the great political and ideological diversity of those who participate in it (Santos 2004, 165–6). What unites participants is an insistence, against the neoliberal claim that there is no alternative, that 'other worlds are possible'. Rather than a rigid belief in a 'closed' and universal model of a future socialist society, they consider it essential to engage in the 'constant search' for a plurality of alternatives that are capable of sustaining different people in their daily lives (173). Rather than accepting hierarchical organizational structures, 'the WSF is a large collective process for deepening democracy' and seeking the participation of all (181). In all this, the WSF contrasts with left-wing movements of the past.

Hardt and Negri's concept of the 'multitude', 'the living alternative that grows within Empire' (2005, xiii), gives a name to the radically new collective activist subject of the twenty-first century. Composed of 'singularities', the multitude is a 'social subject whose difference cannot be reduced to sameness' (99). Unlike entities such as 'the people' or 'the masses' whose internal differences easily collapse, the multitude has no single identity. Unlike the working class, it is inclusive (xiv). Difference is thus fundamental to it, and yet it acts on the basis of what its singularities have in common. The multitude produces the common, while remaining different (100).

The novelty such authors assign to contemporary political movements does describe certain aspects of the politics in which French alterglobalization activists engage and in the following chapters I explore various of these themes in detail. In some respects, however, the radical newness is overplayed. In the next section

I consider some of the historical continuities and discontinuities relevant to an understanding of the alterglobalization movement. I shall discuss, in particular, the importance of protest to France's political tradition, the nation's revolutionary beginnings, the anarchists of the nineteenth century, and the mass demonstrations of May 1968. My aim is to sketch the historical context of alterglobalization activism and a framework of ideas on which activists draw.

Power and the people

France has frequently been seen in academic circles as a country of protest and resistance (Duyvendak 1995, 3). The titles of three influential scholarly works are indicative of this tendency: *France: nothing but opposition* (Grosser 1966), *The ruled: protest as a national way of life* (Hoffmann 1974) and *The Contentious French* (Tilly 1986). But if France is described as a nation of protest, it is also described as a nation in which power is concentrated in the state and centralized in Paris (Tilly 1986, 396). Indeed, for some, it is this fact that explains protest. Jan Duyvendak (1995, 39ff.) argues that the French state is relatively 'closed' politically, allowing few legitimate channels for the articulation of political concerns by ordinary people. Such political exclusion has meant the periodic eruption of radical, disruptive and sometimes violent protest on the part of social movements and unions. People protest because it is the only way to get themselves heard.

Protest, however, is more than just a consequence of limited opportunities for political participation. There is a strong tradition of radical politics in France, one rooted in a long-standing organized communist left, in an enduring anticapitalist culture, and 'in the "theoretical" productivity of the far left' (Raynaud 2006, 8–10). A politics of protest and resistance has considerable legitimacy for those whose aim is to overthrow the bourgeois order.

In addition, resistance is perceived as somehow written into the very 'identity' of the nation (Abélès 1999; Braudel 1989). The French Revolution provides both activists and the political orthodoxy with a source of legitimacy. If the existence of the French state is based on and legitimized by revolution, the revolutionary tradition also lends legitimacy to protest against the state. In the 1970s, one of the protesters against the Larzac military camp extension, in a letter explaining why he was refusing military service, wrote that '[h]istory shows salutary examples of disobedience: General de Gaulle on 18 June 1940, the seizure of La Bastille on 14 July 1789 which has become our national day' (quoted in Rawlinson 1996, 72). French politics is characterized not just by a rigidly prescribed and centralized state political apparatus but also by a 'continual effervescence and ferment' from below, a diverse political culture of 'ideological assertion and political activity ... usually regarded, even by conservative circles, as creative and culturally legitimate' (Cerny 1982b, 99–100).

Such ideas of the legitimacy of protest stem not just from the fact that France's origins lie in revolution, but from the particular understanding of power and politics to which the Revolutionary period gave rise. With the Revolution, 'the people' became the subject of politics and the central referent in the legitimation of power

(Mény and Surel 2000, 14; E. Weber 1991[1974], 301). In Republican political theory, influenced by the writings of Rousseau and given a certain reality by the Revolution and the inauguration of the Republic, it is the people who assume power: sovereignty lies with the people, with citizens, whose right it is to actively participate in its exercise and, particularly, in the formation of laws (Sewell 1988, 105). 'Law is the expression of the general will', states Article 6 of the Declaration of the Rights of Man and of the Citizen of 1789. 'Every citizen has a right to participate personally, or through his representative, in its foundation'.

This document continues to inspire Larzac activists today who consider themselves to be citizens who, through various acts of resistance, exercise their right to participate in political life. Such acts are often aimed, as I shall later discuss, at influencing the formation of laws. But resistance itself is also explicitly referred to in the Declaration of 1789. Article 2 guarantees what it refers to as the 'natural and imprescriptible rights of man: ... liberty, property, security and resistance to oppression'. Not only, then, does Republicanism make the people sovereign (Cranston 1988, 98), paving the way for democratic government by and for the people, it also assures the possibility of resistance to any form of power that is corrupt, that violates the general will, the laws of the nation or the rights of man. Article 35 of the Declaration preceding the French Constitution of 1793 guarantees the legitimacy of 'insurrection', which it calls 'the most sacred of rights', in the case where the government ceases to express the general will of the nation (Raynaud 1988, 143). Thus there emerges the possibility of a power which is *not* legitimate, and faced with such a power citizens are entirely within their rights to resist (Taylor 2002, 92).

Such a view of power and resistance was influenced by Rousseau whose *The Social Contract* is a response to the political theory of Hobbes (Cranston 1988, 100). Hobbes' view of things contrasts markedly with the one that emerged with the French Revolution. Like Rousseau and the French Revolutionaries, Hobbes' *Leviathan* connects sovereignty to the people and to a secular contract as a substitute for the divinely sanctioned power of Kings (Mény and Surel 2000, 186–7). But Hobbes, writing in the context of civil war, taught absolute obedience to the sovereign who had absolute power, not participation in that power (Weiler 1997). Men 'Authorise and give up [their] Right of Governing' to the sovereign. 'And ... this Person, is called SOVERAIGNE, and said to have *Soveraigne Power*; and every one besides, his SUBJECT' (1985, 227–8; ch. 17 pp. 87–8 of original edition [1651]). As subjects, men abandon any rights they may have had to resistance prior to entering into a covenant with other men. They renounce that part of the 'Fundamental Law of Nature' – the 'Right of Nature' – to 'seek, and use, all helps, and advantages of Warre' as are in their interests 'to defend [them]selves' (190; ch. 14 p. 64, emphasis removed). In return for protection, they offer absolute obedience. The sovereign makes laws, but only 'subjects' are subject to them (313; ch. 26 p. 137). The sovereign is 'a single transcendent power' (Hardt and Negri 2000, 85).

Law, power and sovereignty, for Hobbes, stand opposed to 'the people' and their obedience as subjects. Resistance, in such a logic, cannot be legitimate because sovereign power is absolute. Resistance is not part of a theory of power as it has become in the modern world. The French Revolution did away with the absolute power of the sovereign and turned subjects into citizens. It gave people the right to participate in the exercise of sovereignty (Sewell 1988, 106). And, in so doing, it also gave them the right to resist. With the Revolution, the legitimizing principle of power – the people – becomes the same principle that legitimizes resistance.

It is precisely this Republican and Revolutionary notion of power that underpins the political activity of Larzac and Millau activists. They consider even the purportedly democratic power of the state to be illegitimate to the extent that its laws, which, in principle, are 'the expression of the general will', fail to express the will of the people, respect their rights and represent the common good. Most citizens, activists will argue, are excluded from the process of law-making by the very system of representative democracy by which they supposedly participate in the exercise of sovereignty. They echo Rousseau's concern that '[s]overeignty cannot be represented for the same reason that it cannot be alienated; it consists essentially in the general will, and the will does not admit of being represented' (1997, 114; III, 15, 5). If democracy is government by the people for the people, there is no system of democracy that is worthy of the name (Rousseau 1997, 91; III, 4, 3). When the touchstone of just and democratic functioning is the people, and when, in practice, most do not participate in government and the formation of laws, then the 'democratic' exercise of power is always in danger of being perceived as unjust. Elected representatives are not 'the people' (Mény and Surel 2000, 185ff.). Democracy – literally, the power of the people – becomes just a 'pompous word for something that does not exist' (Sartori 1976, 3, quoted in Mény and Surel 2000, 215).

In saying this, it is worth pointing out that activists' conception of things differs significantly from that of the enlightened minds of the Revolutionary period. The general will was not, for Rousseau and the Revolutionaries, the will of 'the people' as activists conceive of this latter, highly abstract, category. Nor did it emerge from the addition of individual wills. Political representatives produced the general will just as they decided on the 'common good'. Determining both was, and really remains to this day, the prerogative of the state (Rosanvallon 1992, 164ff.; Hardt and Negri 2000, 85). For activists, however, the people exists independent of the state and somehow opposed to it. The people is the collective term for the many individual citizens who make up 'civil society' and who are the democratic source of the state's power. The term 'civil society' in the eighteenth century, in contrast, tended to refer to the state (Kumar 1993, 376).

The role of the citizen in public life, or, rather, the notion of citizenship itself, is of key concern in this context (Wallerstein 2003, 651). Excluded from power, in their view, by the very mechanism of democracy, activists assert their right as citizens to engage in politics by other means: from the street. That the social movement is often referred to as a citizens' movement (*mouvement citoyen*) is significant. It is a movement struggling for political inclusion. When Prime Minister Raffarin declared in 2002 that 'it is not the street that governs' (ironically parroted back at him by his detractors), he was asserting the right of elected representatives to ignore the voice of the unelected activists. He was affirming their political exclusion except by 'democratic' means of the ballot box, and their otherwise *passive* role as citizens. Activists, for their part, assert their right as citizens to *actively* participate in power.

This battle over citizenship and the relationship between power and the people is again the inheritance of the French Revolution. The distinction between active and passive citizenship was first made by Emmanuel Joseph Sieyès in his *Reconnaissance et exposition raisonnée des Droits de l'Homme et du Citoyen* shortly after the seizing of the Bastille. 'Active citizens' (essentially propertied men) had full rights ('active rights') to participate in public life. 'Passive citizens' (women, children, foreigners, domestic servants and non tax-payers) had the right to protection alone ('passive rights'). In a sense, however, passive citizens are not citizens at all, they are merely subjects. The term 'passive citizen' is an oxymoron because it contradicts the Revolutionary and Enlightened notion of what a citizen is: someone who actively participates in public affairs (Sewell 1988, 105). Yet the notion of passivity remains a means, or marker, of political exclusion (Wallerstein 2003).

It is the contradiction between inclusive Revolutionary ideals of equality, democracy, citizenship and political participation for all, on the one hand, and processes of exclusion, whereby the full rights of citizenship and participation in power become the province of a few, on the other, that gives rise to the social movements of the nineteenth and twentieth centuries, whose principle aim is to seek greater political participation (Wallerstein 2003). In the nineteenth century, there was an important shift in the form that 'resistance', as we tend to categorize it, took. Previously peasants may have indulged in James Scott's (1985) 'everyday forms of resistance', motivated by the 'the sentiment of their interests' (E. Weber 1976, 255), but such acts were more matters of survival, honour or daily life, than they were explicitly 'political'. As Charles Tilly says of seventeenth century France, 'contentious action' took place in the context of daily routine and local life, in contrast with that of the nineteenth century which tended to break with everyday routine, to be deliberately organized and to be oriented towards national politics (1986, 75). In the nineteenth and especially twentieth centuries, 'the social movement – the sustained, organized [and legally recognized] challenge to the existing structure or exercise of power ... – took shape' (76). As part of the social movement, activists seek to act as full citizens, to be accorded the rights of Sieyès' *citoyens actifs*. And they seek to challenge any power that is illegitimate, exercised for the private and not public good, in the interests of some and not all. They attempt to enact the Republican ideal whereby members of 'civil society' – citizens – participate in political life (see Wilder 1999).[3]

Anarchy and revolution

The French Revolution provided a new framework for understanding political life, new ideas of power, resistance, injustice, participation, citizenship and rights. And it gave birth to a new kind of politics, both the democratic politics of the ballot box and a politics of resistance. It provides a sort of myth of origin for many activists today, as it does for the French state. Most importantly, the Revolution furnished

---

3 See Comaroff and Comaroff (1999, 5, 12) on the polyvalent and slippery 'Idea' of civil society which becomes particularly 'good to think' when conventional connections between the political and the social, the state and the public, appear to be unravelling.

activists with a set of ideas and principles – ideals that, today, many consider to have been betrayed by the powerful whose position depends on ignoring people's rights and trampling on their freedoms. These ideas provide the foundations on which an alternative global order might be built, one of equality, solidarity, autonomy and fundamental rights.

In a sense, the French Revolution is not seen as a 'bourgeois revolution', as it was for generations of Marxists seeking a new revolution of the working class. Indeed, there is an inversion of the Marxist scheme here. For many alterglobalization activists (the communists among them being the exception), virtue lies in the values of the French Revolution, and particularly in ideas of autonomy and rights, not in revolution itself. Marx, in contrast, famously argued in *On the Jewish Question* that rights play an important role in capitalist forms of domination. He wrote that 'none of the so-called rights of man goes beyond the egoistic man, the man withdrawn into himself, his private interest and his private choice' (1967, 236–7). Liberty, as a right of man, has as its practical application the right of private property and the right of self-interest (235), he argued, and equality is merely the 'equal right to liberty' (236). Rights, for Marx, serve to depoliticize economic domination, to justify capitalist forms of power, to encode the conditions of our unfreedom, to naturalize the egoism of capitalist society, to disguise the collusion of the state with capital by legitimizing the state as the neutral representative of the people (Brown 1995, 106–14).

But for Larzac and Millau activists, human rights are absolutely fundamental to the creation of 'other worlds' (see Raynaud 2006, 178–9). Revolution, however, is not. Few consider themselves to inherit a revolutionary communist or socialist agenda. Indeed, in recent decades there has been a marked change in the general flavour of activist politics in this respect. The students who took to the streets during the mass demonstrations of May '68 sought the revolution of the working class (Seidman 2004), and during the early days of the Larzac struggle against the extension of the military camp, ideas of revolution were similarly in the air. Pierre, an outsider who assisted in the struggle, spoke to me of his involvement with a Maoist movement. Their aim in participating in the Larzac struggle, he said, was 'to awaken the peasants to the revolution'.

> We advocated a socialist model, a revolutionary model ... a change at the level of the means of production. ... One no longer hears talk of revolution as such because, in effect, the reference is obsolete. ... Activists in the region of the Larzac and Millau don't use the word 'revolution' ... they are for 'other worlds'. ... We're for the respect of a plurality of worlds with a strong will for social change.[4]

Activists are much more likely to consider themselves 'evolutionaries', with the stress on continuity and gradual change, than revolutionaries. Indeed, most are openly dismissive of the very notion of revolution. Revolutions are violent while the Larzac struggle quickly adopted tactics of 'nonviolence', they are based on an 'obsolete' alternative reference (the Soviet Union), and they replace one form of domination with another rather than doing away with it all together.

---

4 All translations from the French are my own.

As they have abandoned the revolutionary model, Larzac activists, like many around the world who struggle against neoliberal globalization (Santos 2004, 165), have also abandoned the insistence on the historical importance of the working class. According to Michael Seidman, even the student movement of May '68 was notable for its *ouvriérisme*, its overwhelming focus on the workers as the true revolutionary class. Many believed that only the workers could make revolution, while, for anarchists and Situationists especially, students themselves were the passive products of the university which trained bureaucrats to ensure the continued functioning of capitalist society (Seidman 2004, 29–30). For activists today, however, the paradigmatic political subject is the individual, citizen or human being – the general subject of rights – not a worker or social actor marked by their relationship to the means of production. Participation in political life, as I shall discuss in detail, is imagined to depend on desire, choice or right understanding, not objective criteria of class. In fact, today there is little place for class in alterglobalization discourses (see Ancelovici 2002, 447). Whether worker, student, intellectual or peasant matters little, a lesson well-learned on the Larzac during the military camp struggle.

But even this idea that desire, not social position, is the key to political participation has roots in May '68. Kristin Ross, whose interpretation of events differs somewhat from that of Seidman, argues that in May politics became the 'concern of each and every individual' as students refused their identities *as* 'students', workers their identities as 'workers', and people refused to leave politics to the politicians (Ross 2002, 11, 188). The movement of May was a 'flight from social location ... [and] eroded particularities ... of class and age' (p. 207, emphasis removed). It was marked by the convergence of people of diverse backgrounds and a desire to 'invent a name that might encompass ... [all those] excluded from the affairs of government' (188).

This 'erosion of particularities' and the search for commonality, I shall argue, is a major characteristic of the movement today. And although many of those who today live on the Larzac plateau and who came to help in the struggle of the 1970s were slightly too young to have participated in the mass protests by students and workers of a few years earlier, May '68 remains, for them, a defining moment in recent political history and in their own lives. They remember it as a period that promised, but failed to deliver, radical social change and aim to continue its spirit. Through the way they organize the alterglobalization movement, they attempt to enact the horizontal and bottom-up politics of the action committees (*comités d'action*) of May, whose goal was to institute a 'true' democracy based on ideas of participation and equality and a refusal of political representation and the delegation of power (Ross 2002, 76ff.). They are inspired by ideas of *autogestion* or self-management, something often associated with workers' control of their factories but which also constituted a more general demand for 'control of oneself and everything that concerns oneself' (Mouvement du 22 Mars 1968, quoted in Seidman 2004, 176). And they embrace May's anti-authoritarianism and its emphasis on autonomy and choice.[5]

Much of this places Larzac and Millau activists within the anarchist tradition rather than the Marxist one, though undoubtedly Marx remains an inspiration to

---

5 See Seidman (2004, 4–7) and Ross (2002, 182ff.) on the highly disputable claim that the enduring legacy of May '68 was its individualism.

many, and only some link themselves with anarchism, José Bové being one (Moran 2000). Jeff Pratt (2003, 64–5) remarks that 'what is striking is how many features [of anarchism] have re-emerged in contemporary politics ... [to become] core themes in the "new social movements"'. The list includes a stress on autonomy", equality, rights, voluntary association, small-scale organization, federation, direct democracy and direct action. David Graeber, in *Fragments of an Anarchist Anthropology* (2004), argues that such principles mark out anarchism, and today's 'globalization' (or alterglobalization) movement, as a fundamentally different sort of project from the Marxist one. Marxism, he states, 'has tended to be a theoretical ... discourse about revolutionary strategy', while anarchism 'has tended to be an ethical discourse about revolutionary practice' (2004, 6). What distinguishes the anarchists from the Marxists, Graeber continues, is, among other things, an emphasis on broad principles and ideals, general consensus and concrete questions of action, as opposed to high theory and scientific understanding (7–8). In many ways, Graeber's description of anarchism fits with the activist world I shall explore. This re-emergence of old anarchist principles and practices in contemporary politics is not just a question of conscious influence. Nor are such things unique to anarchism – indeed, for Graeber, people in a range of societies have put 'anarchist' ideas into practice throughout human history (2004, 3). But a look at anarchism in late nineteenth and early twentieth century Europe is, perhaps, instructive.

Anarchists, though diverse in their political beliefs, were united in their opposition to the 'authority principle'. They aimed to destroy all authority, which was exemplified by the state, and build a society without government (Kedwood 1971, 6). For some, such as Max Stirner, this implied the 'freedom of the will' and the discovery of self. Stirner's focus was the individual and he aimed to put anarchist ideas into practice immediately rather than waiting for society to change (Guérin 1998, 4; Kedwood 1971, 14). While the individualist current of anarchism was strong, social change was the primary concern of others, albeit without neglecting the liberation of the individual. French anarchist Pierre-Joseph Proudhon, the 'father of anarchism' famous for his 1840 claim that 'property is theft', sought a federalist society based on the free association of autonomous regions, workers' associations or communes. It would be organized in a 'bottom-up' manner in which the higher units of society were subordinate to the lower and each unit sovereign (Marshall 1992, 252–3). Mikhail Bakunin similarly insisted that every individual, association, commune, province, region and nation enjoy the absolute right of self-determination. An anarchist society would see free individuals form associations and autonomous communes, which would form autonomous provinces, which would make up regions, which would freely form countries, which would combine into a world-wide federation. Complete autonomy and the right of secession at each level he deemed inalienable (Guérin 1998, 134, 140).

Like Marxists, Proudhon and Bakunin wanted, by means of revolution, to overthrow the bourgeois state and emancipate 'the people', the labouring masses (Guérin 1998, 136). But Marxists and anarchists differed on how this was to be achieved. In his *Confessions d'un révolutionnaire* of 1849, Proudhon wrote that 'any revolution, to be effective, must be spontaneous and emanate, not from the heads of the authorities but from the bowels of the people' (quoted in Guérin

1998, 52). This sort of anti-authoritarianism was at the root of the disagreement between the anarchists or 'revolutionary socialists', on the one hand, and the Marxists or 'authoritarian communists', on the other, both of whom participated in the First International (the International Workingmen's Association) launched in 1864. Communists, led by Marx himself, wanted to take over the state and install a dictatorship of the proletariat, before the state eventually withered away. The anarchists and revolutionary socialists, of whom Bakunin was the most influential, wanted the immediate destruction of states. For Bakunin, communists support the authority principle and want to impose a new order, while anarchists trust only liberty and want human groups to 'organize themselves and federate spontaneously and freely from the bottom up, on their own initiative and in accordance with their real interests, but never according to some pre-ordained plan foisted upon the ignorant masses by a handful of superior intellects' (Guérin 1998, 127).[6] The division came to a head when the London conference of 1871, comprising mainly Marx loyalists, did away with the autonomy of the International's branches and federations, awarding authority to the General Council in order to centrally organize the 'working class's political action'. The Jura federations, however, reasserted their autonomy in a circular, asking: 'How could one expect an egalitarian and free society to emerge from an authoritarian organization?' The International must 'in faithful reflection of our principles of liberty and federation ... eschew ... any principle tending towards authority and dictatorship' (quoted in Guérin 1998, 120).

The early twentieth century saw the establishment, in different parts of France, of anarchist 'communities', 'libertarian islands' where people attempted to put their principles into practice by living autonomously and close to nature, promoting equality and liberty, and sharing everything in common. But few communities lasted long. André Nataf, in his study of turn-of-the-century anarchism, speculates on the reasons for their failure: problems of money, incompetence for things of the earth or for management, jealousy, personality conflicts, the taste for power, the authoritarian character of some, or the utopian nature of communes in general (1986, 317ff.). Whatever the reason for their decline, it was not until the 1970s that communities based on ideas of equality, cooperation, simplicity, autonomy and respect for the individual re-emerged in numbers. Two (though not explicitly anarchist) were established on the Larzac at this time. Both, interestingly, abandoned their communal organization in the early twenty-first century for a variety of reasons, which I shall address later, although the perceived problems that led to their dissolution are not too dissimilar to those Nataf mentions.

Anarchists were also a force in workers' movements early in the twentieth century. The French anarcho-syndicalists attempted to implement their social ideals in the way they organized themselves. The Confédération Générale de Travail (CGT) was based on principles of federalism and autonomy, in which the right of each member syndicate to self-determination was recognized. It also distinguished itself from other unions by insisting on autonomy from political parties and refusing to participate in conventional politics. Direct action – involving boycotts, sabotage, propaganda,

---

6 The quote comes from Bakunin's *The Paris Commune and the Idea of the State* of 1871.

workers' education and, most importantly, the general strike (as opposed to armed insurrection) – was the means for bringing about revolution and the collapse of the state (Kedwood 1971, 61ff.; Marshall 1992, 441–2; Nataf 1986, 267ff.). The CGT abandoned its anarchist principles after 1914, however, and ultimately the Marxist authoritarian model was more influential. Only in Spain did anarchists become dominant in workers' movements (Kedwood 1971, 78). The authoritarian model was inscribed in the state socialism of the Soviet Union and in the structure of unions and parties in the West. Capturing the state, possibly by revolution but increasingly through electoral democracy, was the predominant aim of the radical left. Parties and the authority principle became central to radical political aspirations. In France, the Communist Party came to dominate the parties of the left and, as elsewhere, there was an 'overall domination of party politics over social movements', as Duyvendak puts it (1995, 208; see Eley 2002, 6, 24ff.). Not until the 1950s and 1960s was there a revival of the anti-authoritarian, federalist, autonomist nineteenth-century ideals. The left began to espouse, although in new language, the old anarchist principles of autonomy, mutual aid, participatory democracy, decentralization, workers' control and direct action, and called for an end to hierarchy, domination and an authoritarian state (Marshall 1992, 541ff.).

Many of these anarchist themes are a feature of alterglobalization activism today. Like anarchists of the nineteenth century, Larzac activists place great emphasis on principles and ideals. They attempt to organize in a way that is participatory and 'horizontal' and reject all hierarchy and authority. They affirm the importance of autonomy, particularly that of individuals and of the social movement as a whole. They engage in forms of direct action, including an educational activism, and have no pretensions to seize power or take control of the state. There are differences, of course. Revolution, as I have said, is no longer a goal, and activists firmly oppose the violence that marked much so-called anarchist activity late in the nineteenth century (Kedwood 1971, 35ff.). They are, perhaps, not entirely against the state, which can be an essential aid in the struggle against neoliberal globalization, but keep their distance from it. And they do not aim primarily for the emancipation of the working class, but seek, rather, the autonomy of all. But even if the working class was somehow the privileged political subject for many nineteenth century anarchists, their simultaneous emphasis on human and individual liberty, which authority denied, allowed some to affirm that all had the potential for revolutionary political action. Where Marxists saw fundamentally different social categories, anarchists saw commonality. The revolutionary socialists, as Bakunin remarks (in Guérin 1998, 127), think 'they can only achieve [equality] through the building-up and organization, not of the political, but rather of the social and thus anti-political power of the laboring masses of town and country alike, including all men of goodwill from the upper classes ... willing to join'.[7] The ability to bring about fundamental change is here limited by desire, not class membership. The reference to an anti-political power echoes today's alterglobalization claim that the movement is a 'social' and not 'political' one, a 'counterpower' with no interest in political power itself. And like the Larzac activists of the 1970s, Bakunin saw virtue in the alliance of town and

---

7 *The Paris Commune and the Idea of the State.*

country. Indeed, many so-called 'anarchist' ideas Larzac activists trace back, not to the nineteenth century, but to the 'exemplary struggle' of the 1970s, as I shall explore in the next chapter.

Anthropology and the study of social movements

Since the 1990s, anthropological studies of social movements have been dominated by a concern with questions of identity, discourse, meaning and culture. Arturo Escobar, one of the most influential anthropologists in this field, argued that it was 'crucial ... that social movements be seen as cultural struggles in a fundamental sense, that is, as struggles over meanings' (1992a, 412). Escobar helped to focus attention on the way social movements resist, challenge, appropriate and redefine dominant cultural meanings. He drew explicitly on the literature on New Social Movements (NSMs), dominated by sociologists and political scientists, which made 'culture' and 'identity' central in explanations of collective action, as opposed to questions of class and socio-economic inequality which supposedly motivated 'old' movements (see Edelman 2001; Pichardo 1997). Class no longer seemed to provide a framework for understanding new political realities. Instead of two blocs – capitalists and working class – facing off against one another, each with its own clear vision of the world, attention turned to how social movements were unique and to how activists practised 'cultural innovation' (Escobar 1992b, 70). Social movements thus came to be seen to propose 'significant discourses of difference' (Escobar 2001, 158), to have 'alternative visions' (Nash 2001, xviii), to 'speak a language that appears to be entirely their own' (Melucci 1996, 1), to 'foster ... alternative modernities' (Alvarez et al. 1998, 9), to 'construct a place of their own, a specific arena of action and meaning' (Coleman 2000, 5), to create 'alternative spaces "from below"' (Doane 2005, 188).

Some, of course, go against this turn away from class. Jeff Pratt's *Class, Nation and Identity* (2003) combines the analytical focus on identity with an emphasis on organization and economic and social processes. Class is often central to the European movements he discusses. Winnie Lem (1999), similarly, looks at protest and identity among small-scale French wine growers defending their class interests, while Sharryn Kasmir (2005) explores the mobilization of class identities in a US car factory whose 'new world' labour-management partnership aimed to put an end to discourses of class and 'shed the "us/them" attitude' that opposed capital and labour. But, in general, the emphasis has not been on class but on meaning and difference, reflecting the postmodern and globalized world in which, according to many, we now live. NSMs are considered to belong to a world from which the certainties and order of the past have been abolished. For some, this is a world of 'reflexive modernization' in which individuals are supposedly liberated from the social structures of industrial society, such as class, kinship and gender, and set free to actively shape the modernization process (Beck 1992, 2, 87; cf. Giddens 1991, 19–21). It is a new world of circulation, flow, uncertainty, possibility and openness (see Tsing 2000, 331ff.). Arjun Appadurai (1996), to take an influential anthropological example, casts the global and postmodern age as one of disjuncture, unpredictability, instability, flow, mobility and the imagination of possible futures. Such a world is ripe for new forms of political action that depart from the rigid 'historical' opposition between the bosses and the working class and in which there is no privileged political subject (see Laclau and Mouffe 1985). NSMs have somehow been liberated from the stabilities and necessities of old. They have found a new autonomy.

Globalization, however, provides new challenges, not least being how the 'local' and the 'global' are articulated. Fox and Starn thus describe movements as the 'product of the alchemy of the local and the global' (1997, 10; cf. Coleman 2000, 70). But, for others, the global represents something altogether more sinister: homogenizing and antidemocratic force, or destroyer of meaning and culture. For Douglas Holmes, many movements are a 'cultural' reaction to the homogenizing, individualizing and destabilizing forces of globalization and 'fast capitalism' which are responsible for the 'flattening of meaning' and the undermining of identity, difference and autonomy (2000, 9–11). Social movements, by focusing on such things as locality, culture and identity, aim to create a stable, meaningful base to life, to reverse the 'degradation of significance' and restore the meaning that fast capitalism threatens to efface (Holmes 2000, 9; see Castells 1997; Calderón et al. 1992; Escobar 2001; Sklair 1995). Marc Edelman's book *Peasants Against Globalization* also addresses the reactions of Costa Rican peasants to the '*homogenizing* tendencies inherent in contemporary capitalism' (1999, 5), though he warns against an overemphasis on discourse and identity at the expense of political economy and material processes (1999, 4; see also Nash 2001). Responses to globalization may, as I have said, involve the mobilization of connections at a transnational or global level (see Cunningham 2000; Della Porta et al. 1999; Johnston and Laxer 2003; O'Neill 2004), and many social movements engage in a 'politics of democracy' against the antidemocratic practices of multinational corporations and states.

The global has thus been conceived of in both optimistic and rather more sombre terms. It is cast as a world of innovation, where ideas freely circulate and in which individuals and movements have been liberated, or as one in which meaning, identity or democracy are threatened by newly oppressive social forces. In both cases, the 'global age' is considered markedly different from the one that preceded it. No longer a world of class struggle, it is, however, one of autonomy, agency and the potential to imagine change. Social movements, many affirm, provide their own, locally-based, creative solutions to the problems of globalization, due to their ability to propose alternatives.

It seems to me, however, that anthropologists are sometimes a little optimistic about the extent to which movements are autonomous or present cultural alternatives (see Edelman 1999, 28). It may be true, in a sense, that social movements occupy a 'space of their own' and exploit the 'new role' that today's globalized world supposedly offers 'for the imagination in social life' (Appadurai 2000, 13). Undoubtedly, they are involved in an active production of cultural meaning. And when activists march in Geneva against the G8 summit, stating clearly that they will not accept the G8's 'illegitimate' neoliberal agenda, they undoubtedly express a vision of the world that is alternative to that of the world's leaders. But one must not read an excess of autonomy into the practice of cultural innovation, nor concentrate on the 'alternative' alone (Gledhill 1994, 190–94). Although they aim for an alternative globalization, Larzac and Millau activists draw on an established French Republican and Revolutionary tradition, as I have outlined above. They participate in and learn from a world in which production, exchange and communication are dominated by the agents of the state and of capital. Like all French citizens, they attend, ideally, the same schools, assume the same formal political rights and responsibilities, are subject to media influence and participate in a market economy. They may reject aspects of these structures of 'domination', but this is also the context in which they themselves have been formed. The ideological basis of protest is not therefore one that can be confined to an autonomous realm of alternative ideas.

Autonomy is, however, a goal for which movements everywhere struggle in the neoliberal age (see Nash 2005, 22). For Hardt and Negri, the potential of the 'multitude' for autonomy is central to the possibilities for liberation from the forces of 'Empire' (2005). In many ways, the struggle of Larzac activists is a struggle over autonomy – over the power to choose, to act independently, to be free of domination and dependency. Autonomy is central to their political discourse and aspirations. They see it as something power denies. But autonomy is more than just something to be won. It is problematically tangled up in many aspects of their lives and is of constant concern in their efforts to resist. In a sense, the protest in which activists engage requires a certain autonomy from power. But this autonomy can never be taken for granted because power in the form of ideology always has a tendency to contaminate people's minds and the power of multinationals or the state has a tendency to dominate their lives. Resistance thus becomes a matter of producing autonomy in various forms. This book explores the way activists resist by cultivating themselves as 'autonomous' political subjects and organizing a movement considered to be an 'autonomous' counterpower. I shall argue that autonomy is produced in the process of resisting through particular social practices and that these practices help to create an opposition between power and resistance.

Activism, anthropology and 'the field'

This book is based on fifteen months' ethnographic research between the summer of 2002 and the autumn of 2003. In solid anthropological tradition, I spent much of my time 'hanging out' with the activists I studied, participating in their general routine. I passed many hours in meetings, on marches and helping to organize protests and other events. On the Larzac, I got involved in other activities that might give me insight into activists and their lives. I taught English at the local primary school, helped prepare its thirtieth anniversary, went walking on the third Sunday of every month with the Larzac's mostly activist hiking group, sang in a choir with activists, offered comments on the design of an Internet site about the plateau and the struggles in which its inhabitants had engaged over the last thirty years, drank coffee at 5pm each day (other things permitting) with two of my elderly activist neighbours. At many of the meetings and gatherings I attended, I managed to slip into the background. People seemed to forget I was there or why I had come. They appeared to take me for just another activist, an activist foreigner with a funny accent, of which I was not the only one.

This view of me as an activist was not unfounded. New Zealand, where I have lived most of my life, had something of a reputation as a neoliberal paradise amongst activists, and Mike Moore, who'd had a brief stint as New Zealand Labour prime minister in the early nineties, was even head of the WTO at the time. I would make it clear, however, that I was not one of the neoliberals. I would often tell of how successive New Zealand governments had privatized public assets, sold off the bulk to foreign interests, how the rich had got richer and the poor poorer, and how the general rot of commercialism had set in. In particular, I had much to say on the commercialization of education in New Zealand – against which I had organized a symbolic protest at my old university – and I was asked to give two public talks on the subject, one in a small café in Millau and the other at the anti-WTO gathering Larzac 2003.

The fact that I'd had a grandmother who was a communist and unionist also helped to establish my activist credentials. At the end of my fieldwork, I wrote a letter of thanks, sent out to various people on the Larzac, in which I spoke of my grandmother and how she had influenced me as I was growing up. She used to tell me about the rise of capitalism, the appropriation of surplus value, class struggle and revolution. None of these things are really of central concern to alterglobalization activists today, but, like them, my grandmother was motivated by an abhorrence of injustice and domination and a desire to fight for a better world. In the letter, I cited a translation of her favourite poem, written early in the twentieth century by Ralph Chaplin, one of the 'wobblies', a member of the radical American union the Industrial Workers of the World which struggled for working-class control of the means of production (see Dubofsky 1988). The poem, I thought, expressed well the importance of *acting* upon one's sense of injustice, an idea of fundamental importance to Larzac activists. It was also pertinent because José Bové had recently been in prison for destroying genetically modified (GM) grain, the victim, for many, of political repression. The poem, *Mourn not the Dead*, goes like this:

Mourn not the dead that in the cool earth lie
Dust unto dust
The calm sweet earth that mothers all who die
As all men must

Mourn not your captive comrades who must dwell
Too strong to strive
Within each steel bound coffin of a cell
Buried alive

But rather mourn the apathetic throng
The cowed and the meek
Who see the world's great anguish and its wrong
And dare not speak.

I listened many times to my grandmother recite this poem and to her stories of social struggle. On the Larzac, I at times felt strangely at home. But this book does not have an activist purpose. Indeed, the point of the letter I wrote was to explain that my intentions were anthropological not political. My grandmother gave me both a desire for justice and change, and a desire to understand. Unlike Marx, these are not things I can reconcile with ease. Studying a bunch of activists with who I am sympathetic is, perhaps, the source of the problem. If corporate capital and neoliberal domination were my subjects, I would find it much easier to look on things as activist and anthropologist all at once. Studying activists as an anthropologist with activist sympathies, however, I feel obliged to maintain a scepticism that sits uncomfortably with the certainty of activists. When you identify with those you study, the problem is always distance. Closeness and a feeling of 'understanding' come too readily and are things of which you need to be wary.

There is another problem of distance here. Since Marx, the histories of activism and social science have been tangled up in one another. As a consequence, there is a huge overlap between activist and academic languages of analysis. In my case, activists understand the world today in terms of notions such as the social movement, the activist network, power, resistance, domination, globalization, capitalism and so on. In fact, one Confédération Paysanne activist even used the term 'rhizome' in reference to the activist movement while quoting another activist quoting Gilles Deleuze (Herman in Herman and Bové 2003, 16–17). All these are terms that I could conceivably use to analytical ends. But they form part of 'the field' for me. Such notions are part of what I am studying and this makes for the possibility of all sorts of confusion. A solution might just be to offset the problem, as does Annelise Riles (2001), by approaching things using notions that are more or less alien to the activist world, by taking, for example, an 'aesthetic' approach to activist politics. But I am reluctant to do this because I am, indeed, interested in power and resistance as theoretical notions. The problem seems, then, to be one I am stuck with. I can only try to be clear when I am talking of the 'network', 'power' or whatever in an 'ethnographic' sense. When I discuss the 'activist network', it is first and foremost in order to get at the sense in which the network exists for activists, not just the ideas they have of it but also the way they enact it. I am interested in the network's social reality, in the logic in which it participates, in the way it is relevant to activists – as a tool, a means, an idea, or as a set of relations – as multifaceted, complex and contradictory as it may be.

The interpenetration of the activist and academic worlds is, according to popular wisdom, greater in France than elsewhere, given the highly visible role of intellectuals in public life. Some well-known social scientists actively take a stand on the issues addressed by the social movement. In a recent book on politics and globalization, Alain Touraine, who was a young university professor in Paris in May '68, argues that we must move 'beyond neoliberalism' and that this depends on the action of autonomous social actors and social movements (2001). Pierre Bourdieu was much involved in the early days of the antiglobalization movement and in the creation of Attac, one of the most influential alterglobalization organizations in France. Attac counts many public intellectuals among its members and is explicitly intellectual and pedagogic in orientation. Its scientific council publishes pamphlets, articles and books on neoliberal globalization which are intended for a popular audience.

Writing is thus central to the alterglobalization movement in France. Newspapers such as *Le Monde Diplomatique*, noted for its anti-neoliberal editorial stance, are widely read by the activists I knew and bring complex social analyses of world affairs to a broad left-wing audience. Books, written by journalists, scientists, sociologists, historians, philosophers or unionists provide important sources of information on the problems of neoliberal globalization, Palestine, GM agriculture and other topics. 'Ordinary' activists also write for newspapers, journals, pamphlets or Internet sites. Many texts circulate widely. Many certainly emanate from outside the Larzac-Millau area. Like the texts they write, activists themselves are highly mobile. They travel, as I have said, to political events across France and around the globe, and their concerns are far from parochial. On many occasions during my fieldwork, we would set out by bus at 3 o'clock in the morning for a protest in Paris, the Pyrenees, Marseilles or other parts of France, but I also accompanied activists to Geneva, Florence and, for the World Social Forum, to Brazil. All this forms part of the movement I discuss here. The boundaries between 'local' and 'global' are anything but clear.

The alterglobalization movement tends to be stretched out in networks rather than bounded in space. This is true not just of the global activist network but also of the Larzac plateau. Although the Larzac is considered an 'activist place', people's activism cuts across place in complex ways. Activists do not collectively and straightforwardly constitute a spatially defined, local 'community'. This was pointed out to me by Pierre, from whom I rented the house in which I lived in the small Larzac hamlet of La Blaquière. Pierre lived in Paris but maintained the close ties to the Larzac he had developed during the 1970s when, as a young man, he participated in the struggle against the extension of the military camp. He had many fond memories of the plateau, spoke of the place and 'the struggle' with great feeling and excited eyes, and considered the Larzac to be an activist land. But he once remarked to me that the Larzac could not quite be considered a simple activist community. He said that everyone in La Blaquière lived quite separate lives and were involved in independent 'networks', a term he used often, according to their interests and occupations. One of La Blaquière's residents, Gilles, knew Bové well, Pierre told me, and spent much time on the local activist newspaper and with those involved in a couple of associations, but he had little to do with his farming neighbours or the other residents of the hamlet. Everyone lived in their own world, Pierre said. They moved in their own social networks and these different networks did not necessarily touch, despite the fact that people lived within the same tiny hamlet and on a plateau that you could drive across in half an hour.

My interest was the 'activist network' and this interest meant that 'the field', for me, was constituted in a particular way. People's activism and their identity as activists often appeared to stand apart from their lives as farmers, workers, students, parents and so on. Although the Larzac is a farming area and many activists were farmers, I had little to do with farming. I visited farms and was shown around on numerous occasions, but when I asked to help out, I was told that I would be in the way, or that my help just wasn't needed, or that the farmer in question preferred to work alone. Nor did I regularly participate in the daily routines of others on the plateau except in so far as those routines were 'activist' ones. Most often I saw activists at meetings, protests and various 'social' events. In a sense, this book is an ethnography of 'public' life (cf. Green 1997, 11–15; Navaro-Yashin 2002, 1–3), of the activist world open to anyone willing to turn up to a protest or meeting.

Many of the pages in this book explore the logic of the activist world and the assumptions and rhetoric that motivate people to construct an activist life for themselves. Each of the chapters deals with an aspect of the lives of Larzac and Millau activists. My focus is 2002 and 2003, although I often use the present tense. Chapter 2 lays out the terrain and gives an overview of the place, the people and the activist movement. Chapter 3 looks at the way the social movement is organized. Chapter 4 explores what it means to engage oneself as an 'activist' in the movement and at the way activism is lived in everyday life. Chapter 5 is concerned with what activists struggle against and describes their conceptions of power. Chapter 6 looks at the way forms of resistance are acted out in public space, and Chapter 7 discusses the moral frameworks of rights and truth on which activists draw. The Conclusion then considers the theoretical implications of the preceding ethnography.

Chapter 2

The Larzac and Millau

Located, predominantly, within the *département* of Aveyron in the southern *Massif Central*, the Larzac is a *causse*, a limestone plateau which rises close to a thousand metres. There are several *causses* separated by deep, often forested, gorges. Sheep farms dominate the Larzac, which is rocky, arid and windswept, its soils thin and relatively infertile. Although often presented as isolated, the region has long been connected with the wider world. The Graufesenque potteries, at the foot of the plateau near present-day Millau, flourished in the first and second centuries A.D. and exported their wares all over the Roman Empire (Goody and Whittaker 2001). In the twelfth century, the Templar and Hospitaler religious orders established a series of fortified villages on the Larzac and welcomed pilgrims on route to the Holy Land. And from the nineteenth century, Millau was the centre of a major tanning and glove-making industry which reached its peak in the 1960s before competition from Asia provoked a sharp decline. Millau glove-makers supplied both ordinary people and fashion houses in Paris and abroad.

Since the 1880s, the Larzac's economy, and that of surrounding rural areas, has been dominated by the production of ewes' milk for the Roquefort cheese firms (Rogers 1991, 61; Da Silva and Laurens 1995). Roquefort ensured relative prosperity for southern Aveyron during a century of economic crisis. Between the 1880s and the 1960s, the entire *département* experienced a rural exodus which saw farms abandoned and a huge demographic decline (Jones 1985, 15; R. Béteille 1979, 378ff.). The Larzac was no exception. Of the plateau in the 1950s, regional historian Henri Enjalbert writes that it was in such a state of neglect that 'one could doubt whether a renewal was possible' (1979a, 478–9). The 1960s, however, did bring economic recovery as young, well-educated farmers moved in with their modern farming techniques (Enjalbert 1979a, 474). The modernization of agriculture, financed by loans from the Crédit Agricole, was stimulated by the increasing commercialization of Roquefort (Martin 1987, 22–3). Since the nineteenth century, production methods have aimed at ensuring uniformity, and the premium prices farmers received for ewes' milk have seen the progressive specialization of agriculture (Rogers 1991, 60–64). In 1904, there were twelve Roquefort dairies on the Larzac alone to collect milk from local farms and to ensure milk quality and the standardization of production (Enjalbert 1979b, 364). Interestingly, Roquefort is today often presented as the epitome of an authentic regional diversity, the antithesis of standardization.

Roquefort still forms the backbone of the local economy, although over-production and the imposition of milk quotas have resulted in a certain agricultural diversification on the Larzac. Recent decades have also seen the development of the tourist industry. The Millau region is well-known for adventure tourism, particularly hang gliding and rock climbing, while the Templar-Hospitaler fortified village circuit has been much promoted by the local council. There are also farm-stays and other holiday accommodation on the Larzac, which farmers use to supplement their income.

The Larzac struggle

Protest activity on the Larzac has its immediate historical roots in the decade-long struggle, beginning at the end of 1970, against government plans to extend the military camp on the plateau. This struggle, and the evolution of the 'Larzac movement' into the 1980s, has been subject to anthropological analysis by Alexander and Sonia Alland (2001) who focus on the invention of tradition, the use of symbols and the formation and evolution of community as central aspects of political struggle.[1] While in this book I focus on present-day activism, 'the struggle' of the 1970s, affectionately referred to in French as *la lutte*, remains very much alive in activists' imaginations.

The government's decision to extend the military camp, which threatened local peasant-farmers (*paysans*) with expropriation, was made without consultation and suddenly announced one evening on the television. The necessity of 'fighting' the government's plans, however, was not initially clear to many peasants. Although keen to keep their land, many, particularly those born in the area, were deferential to authority, and it was the recently-settled 'modernizing' farmers who, along with local *notables* and union delegates, took a leading role in opposing the extension by attempting to counter the government's argument that the Larzac was a 'desert' unfit for agriculture. Quickly, leftist radicals from elsewhere – 'strangers' whose ways many peasants regarded with suspicion – adopted the Larzac cause as part of a broader, often revolutionary, anticapitalist struggle. In May 1971, activists from the far left (*extrême gauche*) organized the first march in protest at the camp extension, without, however, the complete support of the peasants. The march was dominated by young Occitanists, a group struggling for regional autonomy against the 'internal colonialism' and militarization of the French state (Holohan 1976). But the peasants were against neither the state nor the army. They just wanted to keep their farms. Later that year, Maoists instituted a 'long march' on the plateau in an attempt to get to know the peasants, to raise their political awareness and to help them in their daily lives. Despite their efforts, the Maoists' 'liberated' sexual habits, poor work discipline and occasionally violent methods of 'defending the Larzac' provoked anything but approval on the part of the peasants (Vuarin 2005, 17ff.; Alland 2001, 117).

Importantly, the peasants, who were staunchly Catholic, had the support of more than just young radicals and revolutionaries. Church leaders began to speak out against the camp extension. Catholic Action movements the Jeunesse Agricole

---

1 See Holohan (1976) and Martin (1987) for sociological analyses of the struggle. There are also various popular accounts (e.g. Rawlinson 1983, 1996; Galtier 2000) and theses on the subject (Fabre 2000; Vuarin 2005). The Larzac peasants themselves contributed to a book on the struggle (Bonnefous et al. 1984) while Lebris (1975) was often cited as the best book on the period by activists I met.

Catholique and Chrétiens dans le Monde Rural introduced the peasants to a discourse of peace and made them reflect on the objectives of their struggle. March 1972 saw the arrival on the Larzac of spiritual leader and Gandhian disciple Lanza del Vasto who, during sermons and a fifteen day fast in which numerous peasants participated, encouraged those threatened by the camp extension to adopt a strategy of nonviolence. Before the end of the fast, 103 peasants signed a pledge confirming their opposition to the extension, affirming their solidarity and swearing never to sell their land to the army. They decided that nonviolent tactics furnished them with a certain moral authority and the most effective way of challenging the state. As the decade wore on, this core group increasingly affirmed its autonomy against the demands of public authorities, union leaders and local *notables*, and against the attempts of radical leftists to appropriate the struggle for their own ends. Nonviolence and respect for the wishes of the 103 became the conditions for outsiders' engagement in the Larzac struggle, and all decision-making regarding goals, strategy and means remained in the peasants' hands (Alland 2001, 30ff.; Vuarin 2005, 27ff.).

The struggle mobilized people from all over France who formed 'Larzac committees' in order to organize various forms of resistance and support in consultation with the 103. Thousands bought shares made available by specially formed agricultural land corporations called GFAs[2] in order to purchase plots on the plateau that might otherwise have been sold to the army. Many more refused to pay three percent of their income tax – the portion reckoned to go towards financing the military – and donated it to the Larzac peasants. A small number of outsiders, José Bové among them, settled on the plateau, occupying farms the army had managed to purchase and putting the land to agricultural use. Others assisted the farmers in the summer months and participated in regular meetings, marches, occupations, educational initiatives, festivals, illegal construction projects and other actions of protest and defiance. Perhaps the most impressive protest events of the struggle were the three gatherings (*rassemblements*) held on the plateau during the 1970s, the largest, in 1974, attracting 100,000 people. The most enduring monument to this alliance of outsiders and local farmers is today considered to be the sheepfold in the hamlet of La Blaquière where I lived for most of my stay on the plateau. Its existence affirms, for the Larzac's inhabitants, the victory of 'sheep over canons', of farming as a life-sustaining activity over a military machine whose business is death, of solidarity over a concern for one's own private good, which supposedly prompted some farmers to sell their land to the army (see Alland 2001, 101ff.). The sheepfold was built illegally – all planning consent having been denied for buildings within the proposed camp boundary – with the assistance of thousands of volunteers in the early seventies and symbolizes the struggle and its legitimacy more that anything else on the plateau (see Alland 2001, 37–40). In its stone walls you can still see today the names and emblems of the people and organizations involved in its construction.

The struggle inevitably involved many internal conflicts and difficult moments, although these are seldom highlighted when people talk of the period today. Shepherds and agricultural workers were of low status, paid meagre wages for the essential labour they provided, and often felt excluded from decision-making

---

2 Groupement Foncier Agricole.

processes and marginalized in the struggle. The 103 were not always in agreement and tensions emerged, particularly between those from large modern farms, who dominated the peasant leadership, and those who farmed on a smaller scale. A few broke their pledge and sold out. In addition there were tensions between the 103 and their outside supporters. Those outsiders who came to help out on the plateau found the peasants suspicious of them and less than welcoming. There was disagreement, furthermore, over the means and ultimate aims of struggle. Many extreme left organizations were committed to class struggle and revolution. They sometimes agreed a little reluctantly to subordinate their cause to the nonviolent struggle of the peasants for their land. Indeed, one of the key early supporters of the struggle, the Paysans-Travailleurs (Peasant-Workers), who organized the first mass gathering on the plateau, was absent from the third gathering four years later, ostensibly because the Larzac peasants lacked a class analysis of their situation (Vuarin 2005, 47, 97). The peasants also engaged in various discussions with the public authorities with a view to resolving the struggle through a negotiated compromise. Such deliberations, which might have involved their acceptance of a mini-extension of the military camp, were dominated by the wealthier peasants from large farms. Some farmers suspected that their own small farms would be sacrificed in order to save the larger, while the Larzac committees vehemently opposed any partial resolution of the conflict negotiated with the authorities (Vuarin 2005, 76–7, 107; Alland 2001, 115ff.). But in spite of the tensions, the struggle was fought on the basis of wide-spread cooperation, the mobilization of thousands in the face of perceived injustice, and the cultivation of links with struggles elsewhere. Finally, in 1981, newly elected Socialist President Mitterand cancelled the camp extension. The struggle was won.

Activists today often refer to the struggle as a model one, an exemplary struggle which broke with the past in important ways and stimulated people to new forms of resistance. Unlike revolutionary movements, it was nonviolent and the means of struggle were thus 'coherent' with the end sought. Refusing the authority of those who claimed to know better, the 103 managed, moreover, to maintain a certain autonomy from the various political parties and radical organizations involved. The solidarities forged during the struggle and the sense of common cause further made it exceptional. It involved the participation of Maoists, anarchists, socialists, hippies, ecologists, revolutionaries, pacifists, intellectuals, the clergy and notables, people whose ways of life and views of the world were diverse. Under the influence of the Paysans-Travailleurs, the farmers built new ties with workers who had previously tended to look on farmers as the owners of the means of production and therefore as their class enemy (see Lambert 1970; Martin 2000; Vuarin 2005). And central to the whole struggle was the unlikely alliance of highly conservative, authority-fearing Catholic peasants and liberated outsiders who accepted not the hierarchies of the rural world. Together this relatively powerless bunch of farmers and outsiders fought the state for ten long years and won. They won because they were the weakest, it is sometimes said (see Alland 2001, 101). Weakness is considered the great strength of nonviolent protest.

With the cancellation of the camp extension the land the army had purchased was again made available for agricultural use. This hardly meant, however, that the inhabitants of the Larzac abandoned their political engagement. In a conscious attempt to 'return the solidarity' and support received from outsiders during the struggle, they turned their attention to political battles in other parts of the world. The Fondation Larzac was set up to raise funds in order to assist in a variety of struggles against domination and oppression bearing some imagined link with the Larzac, the most notable of which was the Kanak independence movement in New Caledonia. Today the political activity and this turn to the outside world continue. The struggle of the Palestinians and the Kurds to self-determination and the plight of peasants in the underdeveloped 'South' are of special interest to local activists.

It is the struggle of the 1970s which confers on the Larzac its 'mythic' and 'symbolic' status (see Alland 2001, 101ff.; Martin 1987, 159ff.). Through the 1970s, the Larzac itself became a symbol of protest and resistance. Activists today continue to affirm what they call the 'symbolic' importance of the Larzac. In the process of setting up a registered association called Construire un Monde Solidaire (Constructing a United World) to organize the anti-WTO gathering Larzac 2003 and to coordinate political protest within the region, there was an animated discussion on whether the name of the association should have the suffix 'Larzac-Millau' attached. While those against considered that the suffix served to make the association exclusive to those living on the Larzac or in Millau, those in favour argued that the name 'Larzac' was 'symbolic', an inspiration to people elsewhere. In a sense, the Larzac is considered not so much a place as a symbol of struggle and victory. It represents a movement of resistance against power in general, not just a particular struggle or geographical location. It is certainly the case that the Larzac as a place is synonymous with activism, both for those from the plateau and those from elsewhere. When activists use the term 'Larzac', they are often referring just to the activist north-east corner of the plateau and the areas surrounding the extended military camp boundary. This is the Larzac of political activism past and present. But while an exemplary type of activism is firmly linked to the Larzac as a place, the Larzac symbolizes a form of nonviolent resistance that is generalizable and extendible beyond the plateau (cf. Escobar 2001). As I discuss in the next chapter, the political activity of those from the plateau merges into that of a social movement imagined to be global.

The Larzac's status as activist 'symbol' is contested by some. A couple of non-activist inhabitants of the plateau I met expressed great annoyance at the way activists used the name 'Larzac'. The Larzac, the couple told me, is an ordinary, if beautiful, area of rural France and I shouldn't believe everything Bové and others told me about the place and its people. Amongst those who define themselves as activists, some think the Larzac 'myth' serves the interests of local activists rather than 'the social movement' more generally. The Larzac today is less important to the movement as a whole than people would like to think. One woman spoke to me of what she called the 'Larzac cliché' in which the rhetoric of an exemplary struggle – nonviolent, egalitarian, uniting peasants and outsiders – hid a reality of conflict, hierarchy, secret deals with the authorities and other things that failed to live up to the ideal. For her, activists too often clung to a romantic past and refused to confront today's realities.

But such criticism is seldom heard in public in activist circles. In the collective activist memory, the struggle remains a model one. Often referred to, the struggle is viewed as a foundational period which made the plateau and its inhabitants what they are today. It turned the obedient and authority-fearing peasants of the 1960s into the politically critical ones, enlightened in their awareness of power and domination of the 1980s. Similarly, the struggle saw the end of hierarchy on the Larzac and the beginning of equality, autonomy, nonviolence and solidarity as principles of social organization. It provides, as does May '68 for many radical French trends, a 'metaphor of origin' (McDonald 1989, 81).

The struggle is commemorated and kept alive in numerous ways. It lives on in the name 'Larzac' itself and in that of the bimonthly activist newspaper *Gardarem lo Larzac*,[3] founded during the struggle and today serving to keep its 750 outside readers informed of the Larzac's continuing political involvement. Plans tabled in 2003 to redevelop the plateau's activist restaurant and museum, La Jasse, focused on developing a theme that would celebrate the continuity between the activist past and present. The gathering Larzac 2003, similarly, was timed to honour the thirtieth anniversary of the first mass gathering on the plateau, while in speeches at protests the military camp struggle is often presented as an inspiration to today's activists. The Larzac often also hosts meetings and conferences of groups of activists from beyond the plateau – Kanaks, Kurds, pacifists, unionists, civil servants, teachers and others – who come to the Larzac explicitly because of its activist reputation and to share in the wisdom of those Larzac residents who lived through the 1970s. By connecting the activist period of the seventies and the activist twenty-first century the Larzac is produced and reproduced as a symbol of resistance.

The struggle also serves to divide the inhabitants of the Larzac into two main categories: the *purs porcs* ('pure pigs'), and the *néo-ruraux* or *néos* (neorurals). The *purs porcs*, from families who have lived on the plateau for generations, are born of the land and are considered, in some sense, to be authentic peasants. The *néos* are newcomers who hail from cities all over France and even other parts of Europe.[4] During the 1970s and 1980s, dozens of outsiders came to the Larzac and established themselves as part of the agricultural community. In the seventies, they came to participate in the struggle. They considered their agricultural activities to be simultaneously political ones, illegally squatting army land both in order to farm it and in order to fight off the French state. In the eighties, they came to settle the 6,300 hectares of land that the cancellation of the camp extension had opened up. Some had themselves been engaged in the struggle and came as activists to live in a land of activists. Others came for a life close to nature, for the open spaces, the beauty, the quiet. Like their counterparts of the 1970s, many came from the cities inspired by by back-to-the-land ideals (cf. McDonald 1989). Following the struggle it was, with some notable exceptions, the *néos* who kept the tradition of political activism

---

3 'We shall keep the Larzac'. The language is Occitan, a regional language I heard occasionally at poetry recitals and 'cultural' evenings but which few now speak. The Occitan movement never gained the strength of the Breton nationalist movement (see McDonald 1989). Although the Larzac farmers adopted an Occitan name for their newspaper as a symbol of their resistance to the state, they resisted Occitan participation in the struggle in order to protect their autonomy (Holohan 1976).

4 These categories can be further refined. The category '*néos*', for example, subdivides into those who came during the struggle, those who came to settle and farm shortly after, and the more recent non-farming arrivals of the 1990s.

alive (Alland 2001, 69–70). Today few *purs porcs* are regularly involved in activist associations.

The Larzac today

I arrived on the Larzac in July 2002, hitch-hiking up onto the plateau from the McDonald's – eventually completed following its dismantling – on the outskirts of Millau. The plateau's northern end lies 450 metres above Millau, a town of just over 20,000, and the whole plateau is roughly 20 km wide and 30 long. There are several villages, the largest with a population of about a thousand. In the north-east lies the military camp, which still exists in its non-extended form, its boundary marked by large, regularly spaced signs declaring 'Entry Prohibited'. A narrow winding road, about 15 km in length, passes just north of the camp from which a few side roads lead to isolated farms or small hamlets with their activist inhabitants. There are no villages in this area and no shops. The hamlet of La Blaquière where I lived has a population of about eighteen and none of the other hamlets is much bigger.

It was early evening when I arrived at the camp ground at Le Cun that would be my home for the first month. Le Cun had been established by conscientious objectors in 1975 (originally in another location where its members squatted until their eviction by the army) as a centre for research on nonviolence. It has a small library and since its inception has regularly run seminars and training programmes to outsiders on nonviolence, respect for the human person, renewable energy and the environment. Until recently it functioned as a *communauté*, a community or commune, with decision-making, budget and work collectively organized. In my experience, however, Le Cun exists as a place – buildings and grounds – used by various independent associations. It serves as a camp ground, hostel and community centre run by a young couple from northern France, but is also the base for a story-teller and for an association called Conflict, Culture, Cooperation. This association was set up by Hervé, one of the original founders of Le Cun, and runs courses around the country on nonviolence, conflict management, cooperation, intercultural communication, decision-making and personal growth. In July and August, Le Cun hosts summer camps for children, self-development courses, and throughout the year welcomes teenagers in difficulty and activist associations from elsewhere wishing to use its dining hall, kitchen and outside tables for workshops and conferences. The facilities are also regularly used by Larzac activists for meetings, film screenings and parties. If events are held outside, Le Cun can cater for hundreds.

Immediately after my arrival at Le Cun, I was taken by the couple who ran it to a farmers' market in nearby Montredon, one of the hamlets squatted during the struggle in the 1970s. The market consisted of around twenty stalls selling local produce: cuts of meat, dried sausage, cheese, honey, pottery, pastis, bread, vegetables, fruit from the valleys, cakes, salads, pizzas, an Aveyronnais potato and cheese mash (*aligot*), and drinks. There was a grill on which to have your meat barbecued and a field to picnic in. In addition to the food stalls, there was also a stand belonging to the Larzac's activist newspaper, GLL, and stalls providing information on neoliberal globalization, the Israeli occupation of Palestine and genetic modification. You could buy anti-GM stickers, Palestinian solidarity tee-shirts, and shirts celebrating the June 2000 gathering in Millau in support of those on trial for their part in the McDonald's dismantling, emblazoned with the words 'The world is not a commodity (*marchandise*)', and on the back 'nor am I'. Towards nightfall a band played where the stalls had been. The market, which only ran over the summer, was regularly attended by locals and activists from Millau, as well as by tourists, many of whom came because of the Larzac's activist reputation or because they themselves had participated in the 1970s' struggle. The market struck me as remarkable for the way it sold both agricultural produce and political awareness.

Agriculture dominates the local economy and is central to the political concerns of local activists (see Woods 2003). Many farmers have attempted to escape dependence on Roquefort. The majority still produce ewes' milk, but many use it to make cheeses which they sell direct to the consumer. A number belong to a successful cooperative, Les Bergers du Larzac, which markets its own cheeses and even sells in Holland and Germany. Some produce lamb instead of milk and many have gone organic and tried to de-intensify production. The vast majority of farmers from this corner of the Larzac are members of the Confédération Paysanne, affectionately known as the 'Conf'. Founded in 1987 (by Bové among others) and the second largest agricultural union in France, the Conf led the dismantling of the McDonald's in 1999 (see Martin 2000). At the time of my fieldwork, Bové and one other Larzac farmer worked for the Conf at national level, regularly spending two or three days a week in Paris.

The Conf argues for a small-scale peasant agriculture (*agriculture paysanne*) in which farmers are numerous upon the land and which rejects the excesses of 'productivism'. A productivist agriculture is much criticized by Bové and François Dufour in *Le monde n'est pas une marchandise*, the book which stands as the Confédération Paysanne's unofficial public manifesto, having at one time been advertised on the union's website as one way 'to get to know us better'. Productivist agriculture, as Bové and Dufour present it, is essentially an economic activity where the aim is to maximize production and profit irrespective of social need or environmental cost, 'to produce for the sake of producing' (2000, 106). It is an export-oriented agriculture, feeding a system of free exchange on the global market. The result of productivist practices, Bové and Dufour argue (110), is increased rationalization, specialization, standardization and the concentration of economic resources in the hands of a few as multinational agribusiness firms maximize their profits and small farmers are forced out of business. Just as productivism threatens the environment (fertilisers 'kill the earth', one farmer said to me), it also threatens the very existence of small farmers and the 'peasant' way of life. It 'completely devalues peasant know-how', Dufour claims (113), indeed specialization and standardization have been responsible for the disappearance of local systems of agriculture as the *paysan* ('peasant') has been transformed into a mere 'producer', his activity 'reduced to its economic dimension alone' (111ff., 204; Confédération Paysanne 2002). Productivism is considered a consequence of the neoliberal economic policies pushed by the WTO and it is here that the Conf fits into the alterglobalization movement more generally.

The Confédération Paysanne marks its politics in its name, as do the farmers of the Larzac who refer to themselves as *paysans*. In my discussion of the Larzac struggle, I have translated the term *paysan* (feminine, *paysanne*) as 'peasant', although I shall more often translate it as 'farmer'. Neither English term, however, conveys the richness of meaning associated with *paysan*. In a general sense, a *paysan* is someone of the land, someone who works the earth. It lacks, for the people I studied, the pejorative and anachronistic connotations of the English 'peasant', which it also had in French between the Revolution and the 1970s (Barral 1966; Jones 1985, 87). The term has been reappropriated by those on the Larzac and by the alterglobalization movement more generally. Activists associate it with a rejection of productivist agriculture and the word symbolizes resistance to hegemonic forces, those of the state or of neoliberal globalization (cf. Edelman 1999, 146).[5] In tales of the 1970s, it is *paysans* rather than *agriculteurs*, the 'modern' term for farmers, who fought the military camp extension.

Although agriculture is at the heart of the politics of Larzac activists, the Larzac is not just a land of *paysans*. With the new arrivals of the last twenty years, the activist population and the economy have diversified. A low-impact tourist industry has developed, as evidenced by the Montredon market, La Jasse restaurant on the main highway and the farm-stays and hostels (*gîtes*) that dot the north-east. In addition to those directly engaged in sheep farming there are now as many artisans and others who do not derive their income from milk or meat: potters, wood cutters, bee keepers, weavers, artists, herbalists and, in my hamlet, a hat maker, wood turner, journalist, lighting technician and a couple of cooks. A number of people also work in Millau and elsewhere in salaried employment.

Since the 1970s, there has been an important population of people aiming to live in accord with 'higher' principles. In addition to Le Cun, mentioned above, the struggle also saw the establishment of the Communauté de l'Arche at Les Truels. The Arche (Ark) communities, of which there are several in France, were founded by Ghandian disciple Lanza del Vasto on principles of nonviolence and simplicity. Members of the Arche, as explained in a brochure I was given, engage in a spiritual quest and a path of personal transformation with a view to deepening their 'own' religious tradition, however they may define it, and saying 'no' to all forms of violence, especially as encountered in everyday life (Arche n.d.). Work (gardening, milking, herding, cheese and bread making), money and prayer were organized communally at Les Truels until a few years ago when the several households decided to abandon the communal organization because of a desire for more 'autonomy'.

Autonomy is a key theme within the activist world and one that runs throughout this book. Many of the people who have settled on the Larzac since the 1970s claim to have done so out of a desire for greater autonomy in their lives. For Jean-Luc, a member of Les Truels, the Arche was about 'trying to be as autonomous as possible'. By this he meant an individual and spiritual autonomy – 'work on the self' (*'travail sur soi'*) is a central part of Arche philosophy – but also avoiding dependence on big business (Roquefort, for example, and supermarkets) and capitalist excesses of production and consumption. This latter desire is one shared by many who call themselves activists on the plateau. They aim, to varying degrees and in various

---

5 See Rogers (1987) for an anthropological discussion of the idea of the peasant in France.

ways, to escape what they call the 'society of consumption', to live relatively simply, in respect of the environment and their fellow human beings, and to maintain a control over their own lives that they feel an uncritical integration into the world of wage work and consumption would make impossible.

Living autonomously implies living critically, conscious of the way one acts in the world. It may mean a certain simplicity – a lack of materialistic excess – but rarely means going without. Many consider themselves relatively privileged to live on a clean and beautiful plateau, and while few are wealthy, most are far from the precarious position of the socially excluded (*les sans*) whose interests they often claim to defend. Most own cars, televisions, various home appliances and live comfortably in the well-restored stone houses that are a feature of the Larzac. Farmers receive EU subsidies and make use of the latest methods and machinery.

Many on 'the Larzac' consider themselves activists but they live their activism in diverse ways. Many engage themselves in the voluntary political associations established since the 1970s. A few participate in almost all associations but most restrict themselves to one or two. Others are rarely seen at the regular meetings held to organize protests. They express their activism in their non-commercial lifestyle, in their 'work on the self' or in their writing. Since the Larzac struggle and the establishment of the activist paper, GLL, writing and the attempt to inform have constituted an important part of local activism. Thierry from Les Truels is one person who considers the articles he writes for GLL to be his way of engaging in activist politics. He is rarely seen in meetings but makes his voice heard in print. Others write for newspapers, magazines or for the Internet site that was set up in 2003 by the association Construire un Monde Solidaire.

Yet others on the plateau mobilize only for important events. Their activism, in a sense, lies dormant until their support is required by their more active counterparts. The best example of this are the protests in solidarity with José Bové during his imprisonment for his role in the McDonald's dismantling and for sabotaging GM rice and maize. In June 2003, he was arrested by 80 armed police officers who, expecting resistance, arrived at his house at 6am with dogs and a helicopter, smashed in his door and flew him away to prison where he spent the next six weeks of a ten month sentence. Immediately, people took to the streets. Within an hour, the street outside the *gendarmerie*[6] was full of people from the Larzac and Millau, many of whom were not ordinarily present at meetings, angry at this act of 'repression'. In the days and weeks that followed, many of the Larzacians I seldom saw came out to protest in support of José.[7] Friends and neighbours became activists. On Sundays, they would drive the hour and a half to the prison to do the 'tam tam', banging on the road barrier outside with stones. They marched with others in the streets of Millau, dumped rubbish outside the courthouse, turned up to meetings to discuss what to do next. But any large protest always draws the less active activists onto the streets.

---

6 The *gendarmes*, part of the army, are responsible for policing small towns and rural areas.

7 Like the activists I lived with, I shall use both 'José' and 'Bové' to refer to the movement's most well-known figure.

This book is not simply about those from the Larzac itself but also about activists from Millau and the surrounding region. The majority of meetings and local protests are held in Millau, and political associations have Millau as their base. The Larzac and those who live there are certainly central to the activist world. Larzac activists play key roles in most associations, and meetings often involve as many people from the plateau as from the town.

Perhaps a few hundred people in the area consider themselves activists. There are equal numbers of women and men, judging by meeting attendances, and key figures are also likely to be of either gender. Those who are most active – perhaps only forty or so regularly attended meetings – tended to be those who had participated in, or remembered well, the Larzac struggle of the seventies. The core activist population thus tended to be over forty years of age. My first impressions were that young people, with a few notable exceptions, were lacking from the movement. I was wrong. Many young activists were the children of those who had been involved in the struggle. If they were reluctant to get too involved in associations dominated by the older generation, they did form associations of their own and participate alongside their parents in demonstrations and other large events. They played an essential role in the organization of the anti-WTO gathering Larzac 2003.

My first encounter with activists in Millau came while hitching down to the market one Friday morning. I was picked up by two men playing in the world *pétanque* championships in the town. Half a kilometre down the road they picked up a second hitch-hiker, an 82 year old woman called Jeanine. Jeanine was a colourful character of 'no fixed abode'. For five years in the 1970s she had occupied a farm on the Larzac and had also lived many years in India, Israel, Algeria, Morocco, England and elsewhere. Periodically she returned to the Larzac and this time had arrived a little before me. She was 'bourgeois', she later told me, a lesbian and one of the first women to wear trousers in Paris after World War II. She had worked in factories and as a teacher, had fought for the revolution, and she loved literature and poetry which she would often spontaneously recite to me. When she wasn't reciting poetry she would curse the soldiers in the military camp next to her house for blowing things up, the farmers for destroying the boxwood hedgerows, or anyone else to whom she took exception. On the trip down to Millau she firmly insisted that we come to the 'Hour of Silence for Palestine'. I came, the *pétanque* players did not.

The Hour of Silence had been running every Friday since early 2002 and continued until June 2004. It was to be the most regular demonstration in which I participated. It generally consisted of around twenty people standing more or less silently (Jeanine would sternly berate the talkers) in the centre of Millau. Placards and leaflets detailed the suffering of the Palestinians at the hands of the Israeli army and called for 'Justice and Peace in Palestine' and a UN peace keeping force for the 'protection of the Palestinian people'. The Hour of Silence was considered a 'symbolic gesture' and an expression of solidarity. But it was also thought important as a means of raising awareness amongst the public of the gravity of the conflict and of the need to act. Displays, it was hoped, would catch the eye and encourage people to stop to learn about the plight of the Palestinians. In the spring of 2003, one member brought along large photos depicting 'suffering' and 'massacre'. Usually, one or two people would hand out leaflets to passers-by to inform them of the Palestinians' 'daily humiliations', of their 'resistance', of Israel's 'crimes against humanity', of the efforts of Israeli pacifists and 'refusniks', of the need to boycott 'made in Israel', or of an upcoming talk by, for example, a visiting Palestinian on the situation in the Middle East.

The Hour of Silence was organized by the Comité Palestine 12, normally just called Palestine 12,[8] whose meetings I regularly participated in throughout my stay. While meetings served to keep people informed of what was going on in Palestine or in the activist network, their main aim was often organizational. We would decide who would hire the bus for the trip to Marseilles, who would collect the bus money, where and when we would meet, who would bring the banners, or who would paint the 'Boycott made in Israel' placard, print the leaflets, write the announcement for the newspaper, hire the hall for a public debate, investigate whether a particular supermarket stocked Israeli products so that we could protest outside it on a Saturday morning and stick 'boycott' stickers to offending cartons of grapefruit juice. Certainly there was discussion of ideas and philosophy, about whether a boycott was an effective political strategy, whether to take the protest inside the supermarket or not, or whether the Hour of Silence should be converted into an 'information hour' to allow activists to talk with the public. But the general tenor of meetings was practical. The important thing was always to *do* something about injustice.

The activists I knew were concerned with acting and meetings are the place where political action is organized. Activists exhibit what van Vree calls a 'compulsion to meet' (1999, 9). They were constantly arranging meetings, checking their diaries to find a free evening, and much of their time they spent *en réunion*. Typically meetings were held in the evening (9pm was a favourite time, although they habitually started 20 minutes late), lasted between one and a half and three hours and involved between 15 and 30 people, although Larzac 2003 and Bové's imprisonment drew from 40 to 80. Even an unexceptional week might be punctuated, for those who are particularly active, by several meetings of various associations, and during the organization of Larzac 2003 it was not uncommon for people to attend three meetings of different committees in a single day and sometimes in succession, at, say, 5, 7 and 9pm, with no time for dinner in between.

Meetings were generally held in one of several places. For most we would go to the premises of an agricultural cooperative on the outskirts of Millau where a couple of activists worked. They would open a largish modern room which could accommodate up to eighty if tables were pushed back allowing everyone to cram in. Otherwise the Formica-topped tables would be arranged in a raggedy circle and people would sit on plastic moulded seats facing each other. Large meetings saw a constant flow of bodies in and out of the room as people went outside to smoke or to take calls on their mobile phones. During the organization of Larzac 2003, meetings were also held at the shared premises (called *le local*) of various activist associations and unions near Millau's market square or, in the summer, in one of the cafés in the square itself. *Le local* consisted of three small offices and although a sympathetic landlord allowed free use of a couple of rooms above the main offices in the months

---

8 12 is the number of the *département* of Aveyron.

leading up to the gathering, there was never room for more than about 25. Meetings on the Larzac itself, most of which concerned only the plateau's inhabitants, were sometimes held at La Jasse, occasionally in someone's house, but more often at Le Cun. While those from the Larzac normally went down to meetings in Millau, Le Cun often welcomed local associations for Annual General Meetings and other special events.

Many of the people who attended meetings of Palestine 12 also belonged to other associations, and I was thus able to follow them as they moved from Palestine to genetic modification to the repression of the social movement. Pierre and Suzanne, a retired couple who had lived on the plateau since the 1970s, and Christine, who also came to the plateau during the struggle, were well-known figures who participated in almost all associations. Christine, in particular, I got to know well. Pierre and Suzanne used to run *le local* in Millau. The office, which I would regularly visit, opened to the public on Wednesday and Friday mornings during markets. It held information on a range of struggles – GM crops, Palestine, privatization, state repression, the WTO – and sold books, videos, tee-shirts, badges, and the like. For much of 2003 it was the bustling headquarters for the organization of Larzac 2003 and served as a centre of coordination between local associations and those elsewhere in France.

Construire un Monde Solidaire

'Associations', embodied in meetings, are at the centre of activist politics. Activists talk about the importance for them of 'associational life' (*la vie associative*). The most important association of all was Construire un Monde Solidaire (CUMS), established in early 2003 after many meetings to discuss its charter and purpose. It was formed for two main reasons. The first was to ensure more effective communication and better coordination of political action between otherwise separate associations within what is known as 'the social movement'. Secondly, CUMS was established in order to be able to employ people and open a bank account for the organization of Larzac 2003. Its creation formalized and provided juridical status for what sometimes appears to be a fairly nebulous movement, involving many collectives, such as Palestine 12, that have no legal existence. Membership of CUMS is open to individuals, unions and associations but not to political parties who, in meetings, people frequently accused of being concerned more with power than the social good. The association, to cite its Charter, situates itself within the framework of the 'autonomous social movement ... outside political parties'. Parties threaten to use the social movement for their own purposes, according to activists, to appropriate (*récupérer*) its ideas and actions, to take control of the movement for party-political ends. They seek to 'get into power', while the social movement seeks a better world through direct action, a world of justice, basic rights, freedoms and equality for all. The movement is often described as a 'counterpower'. The control of power is its aim.

The stress on autonomy from political parties is a feature of much grassroots political organizing in the world today which aims, in Appadurai's phrase, for some sort of 'deep democracy' and a 'globalization from below' (Appadurai 2002). A politics without parties is the ideal clearly expressed, for example, in the charter of the World Social Forum and characterizes, as Appadurai discusses (2002, 28), the fight of NGOs and the urban poor in India for access to land, housing and services. As I have outlined in the introduction, however, the anarcho-syndicalists early in the twentieth century similarly refused to participate in party politics, and autonomy was always a broad anarchist principle of political and social organization. But activists generally trace the scepticism of political parties and the emergence of an autonomous social movement back to the Larzac struggle of the 1970s when the peasants refused to allow the parties that dominated left-wing politics to determine the course of the struggle, its strategies and objectives. This autonomy from parties is what permitted them to unite with a diverse array of actors who agreed to put aside their differences.

Along with the organizations I have mentioned above – Palestine 12 and the Confédération Paysanne – CUMS regroups a number of other associations, unions and collectives, each with specific interests and aims. Shortly after Larzac 2003, the Collectif des Faucheurs Volontaires (Voluntary Cutters) was set up by a member of the Community of the Arche and the Confédération Paysanne to oppose the surreptitious entry of genetically modified organisms (GMOs) into French agriculture, the economy and the consumer's shopping basket. During much of my field research it was CUMS itself that coordinated the fight against GMOs, taking over from the now defunct Collectif OGM Danger. Its efforts were focused on educating the public and organizing protests in solidarity with José while he was in prison. The Faucheurs Volontaires collective aims to increase the level and visibility of protest by cutting down GM crops.[9] Such self-declared acts of 'civil' or 'civic disobedience' are not targeted at scientific research on GMOs, as the collective's charter explains (Faucheurs Volontaires 2003), but at field trials which pose the risk of 'irreversible contamination' to the environment. The charter denounces the unknown effects of GM food on people's health, the patenting of living things, the domination of biotechnology companies and the logic of the market. Over 3,000 people across France had signed up to the collective by the summer of 2004, 6,000 three years later, and many subsequently participated in locally organized crop destructions. In early 2006, GLL reported that there had been seven trials in the space of two months to prosecute at least some of those involved (Gesson 2006).[10]

Two associations from the Larzac that are intimately bound up in the history of resistance on the plateau belong to CUMS. Larzac Solidarités (formerly the Fondation Larzac mentioned above) assists in the struggles of people elsewhere, often in the Third World, both financially and by creating 'solidarities' that involve visits and the sharing of experiences. Its members are particularly concerned with Palestine and many are actively involved in Palestine 12, although the war in Iraq and the plight of the Kurds were also on the agenda during my fieldwork. APAL represents the inhabitants of 'the Larzac' and acts in its 'cultural' role as guardian of the heritage and memory of the 1970s' struggle. Established in 1973 as the Association for the Promotion of Agriculture on the Larzac, APAL was financed by the 3 percent 'military tax' that people throughout France refused to pay and

---

9 *Faucheurs* comes from *faucher* which means to cut, scythe or reap.
10 Unfortunately, I was never able to participate in a GM crop destruction.

played an important role in the struggle. It helped organize the construction of farm buildings, such as the sheepfold at La Blaquière, and the installation of a piped water supply to farms (Alland 2001, 37). Following the struggle, APAL changed its name, keeping the acronym, to the Association for the development (*aménagement*) of the Larzac. Its current statutes define its aims in relation to the preservation of the Larzac's 'economic and social balance, its heritage (*patrimoine*), as well as its environment', and the promotion of 'solidarity' ('*une forme de vie plus solidaire*'). Members of APAL and Larzac Solidarités play key roles within CUMS and other associations.

In addition to the Conf, there is one other important union involved in CUMS, Sud (*Solidaire, unitaire, démocratique*), which has separate industry-based branches and forms part of a broader federation of unions, G10 Solidaire. Like the Conf, it is a highly visible part of the social movement within France and does not restrict itself to representing its members' work interests alone. Sud, one of its members told me, does not draw a sharp line between union or work matters and those of general social concern. It is opposed to today's neoliberal economic turn, the WTO, privatization of the public service, and the general commodification (*marchandisation*) of the world.

Attac,[11] another key member of CUMS, was established as a national association in France in 1998. Open to all, Attac France has 230 independent local committees. As stated in a book called 'Everything on Attac', it is opposed to a globalization which tends to the 'total freedom of capital to circulate', which is carried out in the interests of transnational companies and financial markets, and which results in increasing 'economic insecurity and social inequality' (Attac 2000, 16–17). Its aim is to contest the 'domination of finance in a world in which everything is progressively becoming a commodity' by providing an alternative expertise (22). To this end it possesses a scientific council whose role is to produce critical analyses of financial globalization and its consequences, published in the form of pamphlets, papers, books and Internet articles. While Attac's vocation is explicitly pedagogical, collective political action is also a prime concern. Attac is often described as a movement for 'popular education oriented towards action' (26). Activists of the 'Attac type' ideally inform themselves with the documentation that Attac's scientific council produces, but also protest in the street (28). Attac's best known concrete proposal for change is the Tobin tax, a tax on speculative financial transactions to be instituted at a global level to finance development aid, fight inequalities and protect the environment (53ff.). The local branch of Attac with which I was familiar was interesting in that its members, with the notable exception of a few, kept their distance from other associations. Attac meetings often struck me as more 'intellectual' than the majority I attended, veering away from practical organizational matters into philosophy. Many activists saw Attac as overly intellectual, a criticism to which I shall return.

---

11 Association pour une taxation des transactions financières pour l'aide aux citoyens (Association for a tax on financial transactions and for aid to citizens).

In contrast to Attac, Aarrg[12] is much more action oriented. Involving young people for the most part, its actions are, according to its national website, nonviolent and often spectacular, involving costumes, occupations, 'impertinences', 're-appropriations of the street', tagging and other acts of civil disobedience (Aarrg 2002). As Jérôme, a Millau Aarrg activist, told me, it is not too intellectual, has no lofty aims, and participating is fun. The point is to make some sort of symbolic statement of discontent. Often Aarrg members would produce a colourful array of posters on a variety of topics. During José's imprisonment they unfurled giant banners from the belfry in Millau against the 'repression of the social movement'. Frequently, they would arrive at protests in costume and stage a performance of some kind. To protest the Iraq war, activists, dressed all in white, prostrated themselves on the road while someone spray-painted round their bodies creating, once the bodies had been removed, the outlines you would find in a television a murder scene. The emphasis was always very much on doing, a vision of 'action' shared by the authors of its website. Aarrg, they claim, has no pre-existing programme or doctrine, no affiliation and is always 'in construction'. 'Our theories elaborate themselves through practice. Our arguments form themselves through struggle', its website states (Aarrg 2001). Aarrg operates through a network of independent local groups, and its field of action is unlimited, the aim being to assist any union or association in a wide range of struggles, be they anticapitalist, internationalist, antifascist, antiracist, antisexist, feminist or antihomophobic. Aarrg 'combats capitalist globalization and works towards the globalization of resistance' (*la globalisation des luttes*) (Aarrg 2001).

The Conf, Sud, Attac and Aarrg all have some form of national coordination – name, administration, charter – which unites and gives direction to otherwise autonomous local groups. The associations concerned with GMOs and Palestine are also affiliated with like-minded organizations at national level. Similarly, Paris-based organizations have a myriad of transnational links. The Palestinian solidarity movement is considered an international one and the fight against GMOs to be a global struggle. The Conf forms part of Via Campesina, 'an international movement' independent of all party affiliation 'which coordinates peasant organizations of small and medium sized producers, agricultural workers, rural women, and indigenous communities from Asia, America, and Europe' (Via Campesina 2005). Attac now exists in numerous countries in Europe, Latin America, Africa and Australasia. All of these associations participate in the World Social Forums which began in Porto Alegre, Brazil, in 2001.

In a sense, the alterglobalization movement thus exists at a global level and involves long-distance exchanges and solidarities. The term 'antiglobalization' is really a misnomer, although in English it is common to hear talk of the antiglobalization movement, and, indeed, the activists I knew used the term themselves. During the period in which I did my fieldwork, however, 'antiglobalization' (*antimondialisation*) seemed to become increasingly objectionable to people and to be used less often. Activists and the press started talking about *altermondialistes* (alterglobalists) and *le mouvement altermondialiste*, and over the course of 2002 and 2003 the appellation

---

12 Apprentis agitateurs pour un réseau de résistance globale (Apprentice agitators for a global resistance network).

was gradually adopted. *Altermondialistes* are for an alternative globalization to the neoliberal variety they currently see being imposed on the world, an 'alterglobalization', as I have termed it.

The guiding light for activists within CUMS and within the alterglobalization movement more generally, both in France and overseas, is the slogan 'other worlds are possible' ('*d'autres mondes sont possibles*'). The phrase is emblazoned above the door of the CUMS premises in Millau and is the unifying theme for people engaged in diverse political struggles. Neoliberal globalization is often considered to be the root of the world's problems. The term refers to a world in which everything is becoming a commodity, where the concern for profit outweighs a concern for people, where citizens' rights are denied by the forces of capital, and where the opponents of this globalization are repressed. CUMS is broadly concerned to fight, as stated in its charter, 'the harmful consequences of the commercialization of the world by transnational firms under the aegis of international institutions such as the WTO, the IMF and the World Bank'.

CUMS' charter, drafted by my sometimes neighbour Gilles and then refined after months of meetings and the input of all member associations, is sweeping. Thirteen headings cover 'all aspects of resistance to neoliberal hegemony'. The first deals with the social movement in general, calling for guarantees for the freedom of association and expression, promoting the practice of 'direct democracy' and aiming 'to cultivate and promote civil disobedience' as a political tool. Headings two to eight cover the defence and protection of union rights, the public service and social security, the right to work and a decent wage, the right to housing, women's rights, the rights of the socially disadvantaged, and the environment. Nine promotes a sustainable agriculture and healthy food, opposing all forms of agricultural pollution, patents on the living, and the use of genetic modification. Ten to twelve insist on the construction of a 'social' and fair Europe, the refusal of war as a means for resolving conflicts, and international solidarities with those struggling for recognition of their rights. The last heading deals with international rights and law (*droit international*), arguing for the subordination of the market to the great international charters on human, economic, social and cultural rights. It proposes a reform of the IMF, WTO, World Bank and other international institutions so as 'to put the economy at the service of humanity' and not the other way round (CUMS 2003). The most salient feature of this charter is the place accorded to rights. I shall discuss rights at length in Chapter 7.

Associations such as CUMS ensure a source of income that is used to finance activist politics. Subscriptions, however, tend to be low – between five and twenty euros – and the money does not cover much more than photocopying and mailing costs. Organizations such as Attac and the Conf have a broader financial base, drawing on a national membership and, in the case of the Conf, on government funding in proportion to the number of seats gained in national elections for the Chamber of Agriculture. Bové's activities were paid for by the Conf. Day to day, however, people pay for their activism, which mostly involves petrol costs, out of their own pockets. CUMS subsidizes bus trips to Paris or Marseilles. Expensive events are often partly funded by donations from activists or foundations. Donations – from the 3 percent 'military tax', for example – were crucial during the struggle of the 1970s. For Larzac 2003, the sale by CUMS of vouchers of support (*bons de soutien*) brought in 80,000 euros, the Conf provided €30,000 and Attac France €10,000. In addition, €30,000 was donated by the Fondation de France and a grant of €50,000 was received from the Regional Council. But the bulk of the €1.2 million raised came from the sale, during the gathering itself, of drinks (€680,000), of tee-shirts, CDs and other souvenirs (€170,000), plus about €100,000 in commissions on sales of food which were organized independently of CUMS.

I have tried, here, to indicate the variety of issues that are of concern to the activists I knew and the main associations (though not all) with which they are involved. It may appear that the activist world is tightly structured and highly organized. To an extent this is true. But parallel to the relatively formal organizational structure of CUMS, there is also a much more vague, informal and fluid 'activist network'. It is particular individuals who are at the centre of the activist network. The membership of many activist associations overlaps considerably. A small number of people – perhaps ten – play a large role in the organization of many activist events and in the running of CUMS. The network exists through the channels of communication which they enact and tends to function fairly informally. Decisions, in my experience, are often made outside meetings in conversations between key people, the telephone here being perhaps the most useful, and private, of all organizational tools. And despite CUMS being established to improve the flow of information within the social movement, communication about protests and meetings tended afterwards to happen by word of mouth, information circulating well in parts of the network and less well in others.

Active nonviolence

Larzac-Millau activists engage in a politics of protest. The aim of protest is often to bring to public attention a matter of social concern, to create debate and to influence government. In this the media play a key role. Protests, as I shall discuss later, are frequently targeted at the media and their success measured in the media attention they attract. Often protest is viewed as part of a long-term political strategy. Activists aim to bring about gradual change by first changing attitudes. But activists also engage in actions which have a fairly immediate, direct and concrete impact. Occupations may secure land or buildings for use as they did during the Larzac struggle. Arguing that rights in use take precedence over rights in property, the Conf recently supported the occupation by a young farmer of an unused tract of land on the Larzac, owned by a countess. The 'civilian missions' (*missions civiles*) to Palestine – visits by international observers intended to provide support for the Palestinians and to attract world media attention – also often have material benefits. The participants on one mission, several of whom I knew, provided a computer for a school, and one man began importing fair-trade olive oil and other Palestinian-made products for sale in France. He considered such concrete benefits to be essential to any political engagement.

Sometimes activists just want to annoy those in power, to make life difficult for them with the hope that they will reconsider their position on things. One biotechnology company is said to have withdrawn from France because its GM field trials kept getting ripped up. Following Bové's 'incarceration' for his anti-GM activities, the Conf announced it would engage in a 'minister hunt'. 'They prevent José from doing his job as a unionist, so we'll prevent them from doing their jobs as ministers', one Conf member said. For then National Secretary and Larzac farmer Jean-Emile Sanchez, the aim was to 'piss them off' (*les emmerder*) and to 'stop them from functioning' until, finally, the government 'cracked' and ceased its 'repression' of unions and the social movement.

Activists refer to their way of doing politics by the terms 'active nonviolence' and 'civil disobedience'. A commitment to nonviolence is the inheritance of the Larzac struggle. Nonviolent protest is always characterized by an inviolable 'respect' for human beings, I was told by Le Cun founder Hervé. It may occasionally involve the destruction of corporate or state property and the use of force, but in no circumstances may it menace people's well-being. Following an attempt to occupy the head office of Nestlé in Switzerland in which I participated – a protest organized by the Confédération Paysanne and its Swiss counterpart against Nestlé's dumping of milk products on the Third World, its exploitative employment policy and its GM research – I was told that our efforts at forcing the locked and guarded doors of the building were nonviolent because they had been directed at things, not people. Although one door was smashed, at no point were people our target. The security guards, in contrast, did use force on the protesters. One person described their 'violent' tactics as 'scandalous'. We came peacefully, he said, and were met with gas and batons. 'Nonviolent' protest thus allows any use of force by the authorities to be portrayed as morally reprehensible. Indeed, the tactic may be to provoke such a use of force on the part of the state. This idea of encouraging police violence was discussed explicitly during meetings to organize protests in the summer of 2003 calling for José's release from prison.

Active nonviolence is closely related to civil disobedience (*désobéissance civil* or *civique*), the political framework within which many activists claim to act. Bové explicitly places himself in the tradition of influential thinkers on civil disobedience such as Gandhi, Martin Luther King and Henry David Thoreau. Civil disobedience involves the deliberate transgression of laws that somehow sanction forms of injustice. The aim is to pressure government into modifying the law by creating debate and changing the weight of public opinion (see Bové and Luneau 2004; Mellon 1998, 8). Fundamental to the whole notion of civil disobedience is the distinction between legitimacy and legality. Activists judge breaking the law to be legitimate if carried out in defence of rights, the public interest or the common good, and against injustice and domination. It is considered justified 'when the law privileges the private interest to the detriment of the general interest', states the charter of Faucheurs Volontaires (2003).

Civil disobedience depends on an ethics of assuming responsibility (*assumer*), having the courage of your convictions and acting in accord with your beliefs. Because civil disobedience involves infringing the law, assuming responsibility entails accepting the legal consequences of your actions. You disobey the law to the extent that you consider it unjust, but accept its legitimacy to the extent that it is in accord with the common good. Disobeying means that you act openly, in good conscience and 'let society judge', as Hervé put it to me. Those who participate in the uprooting of GM crops thus do so in broad daylight and often submit their names to the police, demanding prosecution. By forcing the authorities to treat what is clearly a political act as a criminal one, activists aim to highlight the injustice of the situation and to provoke public debate in the hope that 'society' will eventually deem a change in the law to be necessary. Assuming responsibility is a much discussed moral imperative against which people's actions may be judged. Many consider José to epitomize this ethics of responsibility given that he has been imprisoned for his acts of disobedience.

It is also considered imperative that particular acts of civil disobedience and active nonviolence are well reasoned and well thought-out. Indiscriminate destruction of things or spontaneous actions are frowned upon. This became clear to me following an evening in which a protest got a little out of hand. The day following José's imprisonment in 2003, a call went out from CUMS for people to dump household rubbish outside the courthouse in protest at the 'rotten' justice system that had incarcerated a unionist for having acted in the public interest. For activists, José's imprisonment was a case of repression and the criminalization of legitimate political activity. The crowd of maybe 400 that gathered outside the courthouse was extremely animated, larger than at most protests in Millau and more lively. There were chants of 'Free José' and 'Police everywhere, justice nowhere'. People clapped in time to the chants, whistled and banged cans, bells and drums. After an hour or so, everyone marched down to the sub-prefecture. It was dark and the streets were empty apart from the protesters. Rubbish bags and wheely bins were recuperated along the way and rubbish thrown into the prefecture courtyard. Someone managed to force the gates and the crowd poured in. Rubbish bags were ripped open and their contents strewn everywhere. Then the riot police (CRS) arrived and formed a line across the street about fifty metres from the prefecture. Many in the courtyard took fright and ran out into the street. There was a great deal of confusion and heated argument amongst leading members of CUMS. Some wanted to stay and occupy the courtyard. They tried to get people to return and for everyone to stay together. Others wanted to provoke the police to violence. Others, still, thought we should leave as many amongst the crowd were not prepared for a confrontation with riot police, there were children present and we risked alienating the public. Finally, it was decided to abandon the idea of occupation and to return to the street. After negotiations with the police, the riot squad retreated, chased down the street by the cheering crowd.

At a meeting the next day there was much discussion of events from the night before. Christine, who had actively tried to persuade people to occupy the courtyard, said that the problems and disagreement stemmed from the fact that the protest at the prefecture was improvized and unexpected. No one had discussed the possibility of occupying the grounds of the prefecture, nothing had been planned, no one was clear on *why* the prefecture should be occupied. The call had not been to occupy, but to pile rubbish outside the courthouse. 'We achieved our objective. We must stay with the objectives we set', she proclaimed. She admitted she had been in favour of an occupation but it would have been the wrong decision. People were not prepared. The action had no common goal, no strategy, no rationale. It was based in emotion, not reason. Someone else added that there had been anger in the air during the protest. 'To act with rage', he said, 'is less good than acting with your head'.

Active nonviolence, as activists see it, must, therefore, fulfil a common goal and adhere to a strategy that has been discussed and agreed on for good reasons. When people break property spontaneously, when action is disorganized and not part of a strategy to achieve a particular end for the common good, it is thought wrong and possibly even violent. Some consider certain aspects of the McDonald's dismantling to have verged on the violent due, in part, to a perceived absence of organization (see Alland 2001, 188ff.). 'Free electrons', a commonly used phrase to describe people who are overly energetic and unpredictable during protests, are a worry for similar reasons. You never know what they are going to do and their actions often leave the frame of that which is considered controlled, organized, the result of debate. They sometimes stray into violence or appear to in the eyes of others. It is considered important to be able to justify collective action as being appropriate to the situation, born of a concern with the common good, and to be able to answer the question, 'why are we doing this, what is the aim?' These are marks of political action.

Chapter 3

Organizing the Movement

The period of my fieldwork coincided with efforts to organize the anti-WTO gathering known as Larzac 2003. Activists hoped the gathering would attract upwards of 100,000 people to the dry and windswept plateau and cement the Larzac as a focal point of the alterglobalization movement. It would be both a fun and festive celebration and have a serious political purpose, with free concerts complementing a series of forums, expert presentations and debates on neoliberal globalization and related topics. The gathering would also promote solidarities, demonstrate the strength of the movement and have concrete political effects. Eventually, activists' hopes were more than realized when an estimated 300,000 people converged on the temporary city of marquees that had been erected on a farm in the centre of the plateau.

The gathering dominated the time of many for over six months, during which 'organization' became an explicit concern. Larzac 2003 was made a reality by the mobilizing of the activist network, through ongoing meetings, the creation of independent organizational committees and through effective leadership and decision-making. Meetings became daily, and even thrice-daily, occurrences. Often they were held at night after work, but with the onset of summer the daytime, too, was consumed by meetings. People took annual leave to accommodate their organizational duties. Over the summer months, the CUMS offices in Millau were buzzing with people 'organizing'. A host of new faces appeared, many of them students home for the holidays or those from other parts of France who came explicitly to participate in the organization of the gathering.

This chapter explores this activity of organizing along with the more general organization of the alterglobalization movement, often characterized as horizontal, egalitarian and non-hierarchical. I begin the chapter with the way the activist world exists as a 'network' and then examine the role of meetings and leaders in its organization. The organization of the movement involves what Anna Tsing calls 'ideologies of scale' (2000, 347). A problem for activists is how to connect 'global' and 'local'. Network, meetings and leaders all serve to mediate the global and the local in some form. They involve practical techniques for addressing the problem of scale in the organization of the activist world.

The activist network and Larzac 2003

The concept of a 'network' is one that activists share with social scientists who use it for analytical ends. For the latter, the term has a long history (see Hannerz 1992, 37–42), although more recently it has been used to describe the kind of society in which we now live. Many consider a certain network quality to be a central feature of globalization. Manuel Castells speaks of the 'network society', one in which communication technologies promote the constant flow of ideas, information, labour and capital across the globe (1996). The thing about networks is that they allow us to 'escape the constraints of place', Ulf Hannerz writes (1992, 40). The vision is often one of cross-cutting and overlapping 'transnational linkages' through which space is somehow 'compressed' (see Harvey 1990; Robertson 1991). This network organization is one that can be exploited by capitalists and terrorists, honest folk and criminals, good and bad alike. If it heralds new techniques of capitalist domination, it equally provides social movements with a way to resist. Its dangers are matched by its 'emancipatory potential' (see Hardt and Negri 2005). Perhaps what is most significant about the language of networks is just how empowering networks are portrayed as being. They are described as potent, durable, open, and able to expand without limits (Edelman 2005, 32; Hannerz 1992, 40). They facilitate communication, cooperation, organization and the flow of ideas and things.

But, as Marc Edelman argues, networks also fall apart. They do have limits and often fail to work as, theoretically, they should. The activists he discusses, who participate in a Central American network of peasant organizations, 'feel the tug of disparate demands' from the regional, national and local organizations they represent. In reality, there are many reasons why ideas, information and resources fail to flow freely, and yet, Edelman writes, the 'network's representation of itself erases political, historical, and personal forces that might, in practice, impede the networking process' (2005, 36). Drawing on the work of Annelise Riles on networks of women activists and NGOs in the Pacific, he calls for attention to be given to how networks are experienced and enacted. Although represented in terms of formal links, networks are often based on personal ties, processes of exclusion and the 'network' often becomes an end in itself rather than a means (Riles 2001; Edelman 2005, 39). Riles and Edelman turn the network into an ethnographic category, something whose contingencies are open to exploration.[1] Like them, I am here unconcerned to squeeze much analytical mileage out of the idea of a network.

Larzac-Millau activists frequently speak of the 'activist network' (*réseau militant*) which allows the incorporation of both local people and those from further afield into a united social movement, one in which the range of participants are all broadly opposed to neoliberal globalization. 'The social movement', a term often used in the singular, is imagined to be both locally based and to extend worldwide. As such, it depends on networking, as the following passage from a Larzac Solidarités (2004) newsletter makes clear:

> Alterglobalization (*altermondialisation*) is organized through large gatherings such as Larzac 2003 and local, national and international Social Forums, but also through the coordination of struggles that are built everyday through a presence on the ground and the networking (*mise en réseau*) of organizations.

Irrespective of how specific and local a struggle on the ground may be, activists aim to come together to discuss the economic, social and political challenges common

---

1 Compare the approach to networks of actor-network theorists such as Latour (1991).

to people everywhere in a 'globalized' world. Larzac 2003 was intended to provide precisely such an opportunity and it was made possible by the activist network.

The network emerges most concretely through the activity of communication which takes place in meetings, protests, through mail, the Internet, word of mouth and the telephone. When activists telephone or talk to each other about activist matters, they put the network into practice. But the network often seems to have a reality for people independent of such actions. In a sense, it emerges as the 'effect', in Timothy Mitchell's terms (1999), of a particular organization of political action, an abstraction different from the casual, everyday, unorganized activity of communication. While José was awaiting a decision on when and where he would be imprisoned following his conviction for destroying GM rice and maize, his friends and neighbours discussed organizing some form of resistance to the 'forces of order' who would come to take him away. One idea was to block police access to his house. To coordinate this, they intended to rely on the 'telephone network'. The idea was simple. Someone would telephone five people to inform them of the immanent arrival of the police at José's house, each person would then telephone five others, and everyone would come to resist what many eventually described as José's 'kidnapping'. (In the end, the police got there first, although this didn't stop hundreds demonstrating outside the *gendarmerie* an hour later, along with the local press, and many thousands descending on the prison where José was later held.) Here the network was conceived to exist as a plan of action, an idea that could be enacted or of how information could be disseminated and people mobilized. It involved a designated set of people whose function was to pass on information to others. These people had to know their role and possess the telephone numbers of those they were required to ring. In such knowledge was contained an idea of the network. Periodically the network needed to be 'updated' (*actualisé*) – phone numbers corrected, people reminded of their role – to ensure that it didn't fail to serve its purpose. And sometimes it did fail, either because it wasn't up to date, or because people neglected to carry out their role.

My initial impressions were that some sort of failure was far from exceptional. There seemed to be no reliable way of widely diffusing information about meetings or protests in the Millau area other than word of mouth. The idea of an activist network certainly existed, but the way it actually functioned was vague and casual. Early in my fieldwork, I attended a meeting of the Support Committee for the Millau Accused, established to fight for those prosecuted for the McDonald's dismantling and against the general repression of the social movement, but which dealt with other issues as well. At one point, discussion passed to a recent meeting of the Collectif OGM Danger. Many people, however, had no idea that there had even been a meeting. The word had not got out, and, as people complained, it was often difficult to stay informed of what was going on. 'How better to ensure the flow of information?', someone asked. After much discussion, it was decided to establish a committee of four or five people to address the problem and consider the possibility of employing someone in the activist office in Millau for one day a week to take responsibility for the efficient flow of information.

But resolving the problem was not straight forward. The new committee proposed establishing a list of activists' contact details and sending out a regular newsletter containing general information, the dates of meetings and protests, and, maybe, meeting minutes. Suzanne, who already opened the Millau office to the public two days a week, noted, however, that a mail-out would have been prohibitively expensive. Most of the collectives in the area were skint, she said, and unable to contribute to postage costs. We would have to charge a subscription while, of course, avoiding any sort of commercialization. The telephone, on the other hand, seemed to be considered good for organizing a rapid turnout for extraordinary events, but as a means of informing everyone who might be interested in everyday affairs it was impractical. And while someone maintained an email list for Palestine 12, a majority of activists didn't have Internet access. Nor, for that matter, did the activist office.

Many of these practical issues remained unresolved and things continued as before until, months later, CUMS was finally established, taking up where the Support Committee left off. It was explicitly set up as a sort of hub to organize the flow of information, to improve the effectiveness of communication between local associations and, more specifically, in order to organize Larzac 2003. CUMS was registered with the prefecture and acquired formal juridical status, marking it out from most local activist associations which exist informally as *collectifs* or *comités* and have no clear membership, no subscriptions and no finances. Unlike them, CUMS was able to open a bank account, to charge membership dues and to go about raising funds for Larzac 2003. A 'CUMS' sign was placed above the entrance to the Millau office, and computers and an Internet connection were installed. A student, Catherine, was employed to work in the office until after the gathering (on an internship which contributed to her studies in community project management) and to deal with the day-to-day running of CUMS.

Despite its formal status as an 'association' under French law, CUMS, as Catherine once described it, was a 'network'. During meetings to set up CUMS and discussions over precisely what role it would play, people were adamant that it was not to be an 'umbrella' association (*un chapeau*) with authority over the associations that were its members. Like the activist network in general, it was to be open to all those organizations or individuals who wished to participate, but those who did so were to retain their autonomy to act as they saw fit. Ideas of openness, autonomy and participation are central to the very notion of a network, in this sense. In contrast to the structure of unions and political parties with which many were familiar – or, I might add, to the contemporary Bolivian social movements discussed by Sian Lazar (2004a) where participation in demonstrations is 'obliged' by an 'authoritarian' union hierarchy – the organizational ideal of the activists involved in CUMS entailed no chain of command, no hierarchy at all. CUMS served merely as a link or relay point between autonomous associations, unions and individuals.

As such, the network was a specific kind of organizational tool and key to activists' attempts to globalize resistance, an aim captured in one of Larzac 2003's slogans: 'globalize struggles, globalize hope'. In practice, this meant getting people involved in the gathering, especially people from elsewhere in France and from overseas. Like the telephone example above, the organization of Larzac 2003 was an exercise in what people called 'mobilization'. 'Networking' was the means to achieve this. Catherine and others at the CUMS office spent much of their time contacting people and 'putting them into contact' (*les mettre en réseau*). They made phone calls, sent emails and wrote letters to encourage the participation of those engaged in a range of social struggles and sympathetic to CUMS' anti-WTO position.

Central to this conscious organizational process were the committees (*commissions*) established to take responsibility for particular aspects of the gathering (food, drink, camping, parking, communication, volunteers, entertainment, forums and so on). The idea of committees was introduced to the Larzac by the outsiders who came to help fight the military camp extension in the 1970s, I was told by a *pur porc* involved in the struggle. They provided a practical means of dealing with the complexities of organization (cf. Jean-Klein 2003). For the preparation of Larzac 2003, a certain amount of centralized planning was deemed essential, given the reality of staging a gathering of over 100,000 people, in mid-summer, on a windswept plateau, far from sources of food or water. A five-member professional management team, with experience of organizing festivals and concerts, was employed. In meetings on what overall form the gathering would take, additional committees were established on the advice of those with experience organizing gatherings during the Larzac struggle or during the McDonald's trial in 2000. Each committee was given a clear idea of its responsibilities and how it was to work towards the realization of the gathering, and people were asked to sign up. In the interests of an 'effective' organization, committees were to function autonomously, in coordination with the others but without need for constant direction. In the stressful days immediately prior to the gathering, one of the management team reiterated at a meeting the absolute importance of committee autonomy. He and his colleagues could not hope to oversee everything. Committees had to manage on their own.

The Communication Committee, in which I participated, launched an Internet site to explain the issues concerning globalization and to encourage participation in the gathering. Often it relied on the personal contacts of committee members to spread information (cf. Riles 2001, 59ff.). One person who worked in radio enlisted the participation of tens of community radio stations for publicizing and broadcasting the event. Gilles, a Parisian journalist who now lived on the Larzac, mobilized press acquaintances of his own. The committee also drew on the Confédération Paysanne's national list of media contacts in order to extend the network throughout France and even internationally. Each contact had other contacts who, ideally, would spread the word of their own accord. Once the ball was rolling, the network would grow. To an extent, the network was imagined as a tool for creating a more extensive network (Riles 2001, 50). But the process of networking was never an end in itself. There was always a concrete aim: getting people involved, encouraging them to participate in Larzac 2003.

Many of the committees operated along similar lines, each enacting networks of their own and resulting in a 'network of networks', in Hannerz's phrase (1992). The Volunteers Committee (*commission bénévoles*) sent emails and letters to hundreds of unions and associations throughout France in search of volunteers for the gathering (an estimated 5,000 were needed). The Security Committee (s*ervice d'ordre*) did likewise. The Festivities Committee contacted politically-oriented bands and entertainers from home and abroad who they hoped might participate. The Forums Committee contacted well-known activists worldwide to speak to thousands at the major forums. They also contacted a diverse array of political associations to encourage them to set up displays and organize forums of their own. Overall, CUMS was to provide a structure within which participants could act as they wanted.

Setting up the temporary on-site infrastructure of marquees, tents, electricity poles, networked computers, car parks, camp sites, hardware supplies, ash trays, fire warnings, three huge stages and hundreds of metres of bar space for the sale of drinks took ten days. The gathering was eventually opened in sweltering heat to a crowd of thousands by François Dufour, farmer from Normandy, member of the Conf and Attac, and co-author, with Bové, of *The World is Not For Sale*. The stage was given over in turn to a range of speakers, indicating the gathering's diversity and its global nature: the Larzac farmer on whose land the gathering took place; Bové, who was fresh out of prison; Lori Wallach from Public Citizen in the United States; Yannick Jadot of Greenpeace France; Agnès Bertrand, author on the 'invisible power' of the WTO; Paul Nicholson, Basque farmer and Via Campesina spokesperson; a representative from an immigrants' movement in the Paris suburbs (MIB); and a Palestinian MP in the Knesset, Azmi Bishara, whose text was read by someone else because he was unable to attend.

The stalls and displays of 150 activist associations from across France – concerned with everything from human rights and corporate capitalism to housing, home-birthing and open source software – encircled the four huge open-sided marquees where the major forums were held. Most forums involved a panel of four or five people speaking, with the aid of microphones, to hundreds of attentive listeners, followed by time for questions and audience participation. Four forums were arranged by CUMS on the WTO, the liberalization of services, agriculture, and rights. Most of the speakers in the fold-out colour programme were from France, but some notable foreign activists were also listed: Andile Mngxitama from the South African Landless People's Movement; Evo Morales, later to become president of Bolivia; Indian academic and activist Vandana Shiva; and author Arundhati Roy. In addition to the CUMS' forums, there were many others run by different associations or unions on education, repression, health, water, nuclear energy, GMOs, colonialism, Palestine, fair trade, organics and other topics. There were film screenings, theatre performances, ample food and drink, but little shelter from the sun. Thousands wandered through the dusty city of tents, looking at the displays and listening to forums. As night fell, thousands more attended the free all-night concerts that ran simultaneously on three different stages, with Manu Chao and Asian Dub Foundation undoubtedly the highlights.

Larzac 2003 was made possible by extending the activist network nationally and, to an extent, globally from its local Larzac-Millau base. An imagined global network of activists was given a concrete reality in the process of organizing the gathering and connecting together people and associations seen to be involved in localized struggles of their own (Ferguson and Gupta 2002, 988). The gathering, in a sense, was the global network localized. It was localized in a space that, for many, symbolized resistance: the Larzac. CUMS activists reasserted the symbolic importance of the Larzac which re-emerged as a focal point in the alterglobalization movement, a place to meet, discuss, organize, and to put specific, local concerns in a global context.

Without the process of networking and the voluntary participation of thousands, the network would not have gained this concrete existence. The organizational problem was always how to mobilize, how to put people into contact and bring them together. Indeed, the network is often considered to be fragile, at risk of dissolving as soon as people lose the motivation to act. On many occasions, particularly during the Iraq war, activists bemoaned the French social movement's lack of 'strength', pointing to the unwillingness of people to come out onto the streets in protest (though unlike Britain and Italy, where demonstrations had involved millions, the French president had opposed the war). In the run up to Larzac 2003, people complained of fatigue, of being 'over-saturated' and of having their holidays eaten up. Their commitment was tested. In general, their activism competes with the demands of work, family and leisure (see Edelman 2005, 36). The movement depends on people wanting to participate and when they don't, it falls apart. Unlike the networks of scientific research discussed by Marilyn Strathern (1996), which have to be 'cut' through the technique of patenting in order to stop the flow of information and to establish ownership, the activist network is not without limit and cannot be taken for granted. For the activists in CUMS, the problem is not how to cut or limit the extent of the network, but how to build and maintain one.

Making the movement strong

The general purpose of the network, for activists, is to ensure 'action' – demonstrations, occupations, gatherings, forums, debates and the other modes of resistance I discuss in Chapter Six. Action is seen to require of the network a certain communicational efficacy (*efficacité*), although efficacy itself is not a goal. Communication 'must be effective' (*efficace*), someone said at the Inaugural General Meeting of CUMS, 'but the goal is action'. Ideally, effective communication will produce action that is well-coordinated, organized, publicized and involving large numbers of people. The point is always to have a public political effect.

Activists often speak of the importance of increasing the social movement's strength or of demonstrating that strength through collective action. This was one of the principal aims of Larzac 2003. Increasing strength was here a matter of forging one big social movement out of independent social movements, of merging Larzac and Millau activism into activism more broadly, or of incorporating activists from beyond the Larzac into a movement united and localized in the form of Larzac 2003. In early meetings held in Millau to discuss the gathering's aims, activists often mentioned the need to create what they called a *rapport de force*. This notion is important and translates, roughly, as relations of strength or of power. Activists aim to increase the strength of the movement in relation to the forces of power to which they are opposed, to shift the balance of power. In one meeting someone insisted there were two ways of creating a *rapport de force*: through violence, a path rejected by the bulk of activists who participate in the alterglobalization movement, and through numbers.

The numerical growth of the movement is a constant aim of activists. This aim contrasts with the general professionalization of activism since the 1960s in which political associations and parties have confronted declining memberships but continued to speak for large numbers of people (Skocpol 1999; Cmiel 1999, 1243; Eley 2002, 460, 485). Alterglobalization activists, however, take numbers seriously. They actively work to attract people to the movement, either by networking or through 'pedagogical' and 'symbolic' forms of activism (discussed in Chapter 6). In meetings prior to Larzac 2003, people often affirmed that the principal aim of the gathering was to assemble 'the greatest possible number'. Numbers and growth are considered a sign of the movement's strength and are indicative of its organization and unity, the worthiness of its cause, the commitment of its members (Tilly 1999, 261). Each year more and more activists from around the globe participate in the World Social Forum. The growth is considered impressive. 10,000 in 2001, 30,000 in 2002, 60,000 in 2003, 100,000 in 2004 are figures commonly cited to demonstrate the movement's increasing strength. Of themselves, numbers are considered to attract people to the movement. They are also thought key to ensuring the media coverage necessary to demonstrate strength to a broad audience. For the media, as one person said in a meeting on how to improve the effectiveness of political actions, 'nothing much is happening if there are not many people. ... The media are very quantitative'.

Numbers confer a certain democratic legitimacy (Rose 1999, 221). Large numbers are seen to bolster the movement's representativeness and are used to construct it as a 'democratic' force, one that represents ordinary citizens and that cannot be ignored by government. Activists always claim to be acting for the common or public good and the 'public' is often enlisted in the movement in the form of 'public support'. Support, demonstrated by statistics, is a sign that the movement is strong, that it represents the democratic interest and will of the people. '70% of French citizens of all horizons are opposed to GM food', states the charter of Faucheurs Volontaires (2003) in arguing that the social movement and civil disobedience can therefore 'count on important support amongst the collectivity'.

By invoking 'the public', the activist network is extended rhetorically, the movement made to grow and to include even those who participate merely through the support they are imagined to give. In the public reckoning of the numbers present at protests, activists and public authorities play a game of numbers. In contrast to the police, activists' estimates are far from cautious. Following the attempted occupation of Nestlé, Bové publicly proclaimed the participation of 400 when no one present to whom I spoke reckoned on more than half that number. During a public address after an anti-WTO march in Geneva the following day, the MC suggested there had been 8–10,000 participants while Bové spoke of 10,000. The other Larzac-Millau activists with whom I came, however, thought both figures clearly exaggerated. 3–5,000 was a better estimate, thought one. He laughed, recognizing the political value of such claims which would be reported in the media and would encourage others to join an ostensibly strong social movement. At Larzac 2003, CUMS organizers claimed 300,000 participants and perhaps 300,000 there were. But due to their presence on activist space they were portrayed as 'activists' within 'the social movement' when many came only for the free concerts and the festival atmosphere in the estimation of critics. Larzac 2003 became evidence that the movement was strong and a force to be reckoned with. In Geneva at anti-G8 protests, a key slogan, which pleased many with whom I went, was 'They are 8, we are billions'. The slogan illustrates that the interests of the powerful are opposed to the interests of the weak, but it also suggests that the weak are many and that the movement, which supposedly acts in their name, is strong. Billions of ordinary and relatively powerless people are on 'our' side.

At gatherings, marches and demonstrations, the movement emerges as thing-like, a collective subject capable of acting politically and having political effects (Weszkalnys 2004, 117). Like the crowds that so fascinated Elias Canetti (2000, 15ff.), its strength is measured in numbers. A large crowd of activists attracts people to participate in it, the police to control it, and the media who, through their coverage, demonstrate its force. The discourse on numbers also means, however, that the movement can be stretched to include more and more, to implicate even those who do not form part of the crowd, those members of the public whose support activists claim but who are not there. In this way the movement is made 'democratic' and 'representative' of the general interest. The social movement, in this sense, is a flexible and inclusive movement, one that can be expanded rhetorically to suit political ends.

But the movement is not infinitely flexible. Activists often refer to the social movement as a 'counterpower'. As such, the movement cannot be extended to include power, its opposite. 'The place the international antiglobalization movement must have ... is as a counterpower and not at all as a power', Gilles told me when I interviewed him for radio broadcasts that were to help advertise Larzac 2003. The movement, in a sense, is part of what Canetti (2000, 63ff.) called a 'double crowd' in which two enemies confront one another. Between the two, activists see a *rapport de force* which varies according to their relative strength and which separates them irrevocably. The language activists use is evocative of this opposition. Power and counterpower are seen to do metaphorical battle. Activists often describe themselves as engaging in a 'struggle' or 'fight' (*lutte*), or in a 'combat', and aim to achieve 'victory' over their political foe. At a forum at the 2003 G8 counter-summit in Annemasse, near Geneva, José spoke of the need to declare 'war' on Nestlé and on GMOs. Occasionally, such discourse is questioned. Following José's fighting talk, one young man got up and said, to much general bemusement, some applause and a little embarrassment on the part of some, that we had to abandon this 'warlike semantics' in favour of a discourse of peace. The movement, it must be said, is explicitly a nonviolent one. But if war doesn't provide an appropriate metaphor for political action, competition does. Often activists speak of 'winning' the political struggle. 'All together we will win', I have heard José say at various times in public addresses, and after six weeks of ongoing protests on the part of the social movement over his incarceration, José was released from prison to cries of 'We've won, we've won, we've won'.

At protests, the opposition between power and counterpower is enacted. Many are performed outside what are considered the symbols of the state such as prefectures, courthouses or *gendarmeries*. Other protests target capitalist power – the force of domination that Nestlé is seen to represent, multinationals who produce GM seed, McDonald's. In addition, power is always considered present at protests in the guise of security forces and the police, the 'forces of order', as people put it. The police are considered to possess a 'repressive' capability. They are able to turn political protests into a series of criminal acts (see Chapter 5). Before a huge march in Florence in 2002 against US plans to invade Iraq, there was a lively discussion between several Larzac activists over dinner about whether the police would provoke trouble to discredit the marchers. Yes, thought some, pointing to violent clashes between police and demonstrators in Genoa the year before in which one activist, Carlo Giuliani, had been killed. It was in the interests of the powerful to present marchers as troublemakers lacking in respect for property and order. In the end, the march was peaceful. But even in such circumstances, the police still constitute, for activists, a power opposed to the counterpower of the social movement. The opposition is often spatially represented and highly visible. At small demonstrations, police and protesters often face off against one another, while at large marches, riot police can be seen at the end of side streets, lined up intimidatingly across the road and effectively encircling the march. Activists fear that, if ordered, the police will act against them. When, as sometimes happens, there is confrontation at protests and the use of tear gas or batons, the opposition between power and counterpower is demonstrated all the more forcefully. We are in a 'logic of opposition' someone commented to me following an attempt to gain access to a GM research company that police and security guards foiled with gas and truncheons.

Illustrative of this logic of opposition, is the reluctance to admit a dissenting voice into the activist network. Public 'debates' (*débats*) or forums organized by activists almost never involve the participation of someone with a neoliberal view of the issue under discussion, never do they give power a voice. Exceptions appear to be few. The Larzac's activist newspaper, GLL, reported that a seminar at the 2003 European Social Forum in Paris, involved 'for the first time' the participation of representatives both of neoliberal financial institutions – the IMF and the World Bank – and of 'civil society' – Bové and Susan George of Attac (Gesson 2004, 1). But it is rare that activists even consider this possibility. One occasion on which they did so was during a meeting of Attac Millau in preparation for Larzac 2003. Attac was organizing a forum for the gathering on the commercialization of public health and someone had approached Attac asking to participate. But for various reasons people at the meeting suspected that this person was not entirely opposed to neoliberalism. They worried that he might hijack the debate. If this happened, power would enter where it ought not go and threaten to undo the work of 'decontaminating minds' that Jacques Nikonoff, President of Attac, considered it Attac's role to accomplish.

The notion that the social movement is a counterpower thus implies the categorization of people into activists and dangerous others, members and non-members. The activist network is selective and exclusive, in this sense, open only to those people and ideas that contribute to its strength. While activists imagine the network extending over the entire globe through ever expanding communicational links, and while they often describe it as open to all, as a network of activists it can never include the powerful. The idea of a network thus incorporates the idea of something contained. Communication takes place *within* the network, between activist insiders. Debate tends to involve only like-minded individuals and at workshops, forums and protests, the speakers very often find themselves preaching to the converted. Recognizing this, activists sometimes self-deprecatingly describe speaking events as 'masses' (*messes*). Some criticize activists for being uncritical with regard to themselves and for mutually confirming each other's point of view. Minds are already made up, one person told me. People know they are right and because of this, nothing is to be gained from listening to opposing views of the world.

The activist network and, indeed, activists themselves are sometimes described as 'closed', both by self-identified activists and by those who are somewhat marginal to the network. Importantly, the network is closed off from 'the public' – the very public that confers democratic legitimacy – to the extent that the public does not participate in the movement or support the positions articulated by its leaders (cf. McDonald 1989, 140). The aim of much of the educational activism I discuss in Chapter 6 is to extend the network to the public, incorporate people into the movement and thus increase its strength and its democratic mandate. 'We must win over the majority of citizens to these [anti neoliberal] ideas', said Nikonoff in a presentation at a Millau café, 'win the battle for public opinion'. The media and information evenings offer important tools for achieving this. The idea is to inform and, ultimately, to convert people to the right way of thinking. Paradoxically, information evenings fail miserably in this respect because the people who come are already informed and converted (cf. MacIntyre 1984, 71). When a Catholic organization invited a Palestinian to talk in Millau on conditions in Palestine under Israeli occupation, many activists considered that it touched more people and a wider variety of people than Palestine 12 ever did. This is a little ironic given that Palestine 12 sets itself the task of informing on this issue. But some activists to whom I spoke thought it entirely understandable as well. In order to touch the general public you cannot have a radical, alternative, activist face. The movement always risks being alienated from the very public interest it claims to serve (Clarke 2003, 132–3; McDonald 1989, 140).

The network is not just closed to those outside it, however. Some activists also perceive it as closed to activists themselves. If the network is considered a means to facilitate the flow of information, it is also considered a tool for its control. Clearly it is important to avoid 'leaks' to dangerous outsiders such as the police or unsympathetic journalists. But a common criticism of those who are ostensibly activist insiders is that certain people control the dissemination of information for their own personal ends, informing only those activists they wish to inform. The individuals who play the role of relay within CUMS are just as able not to relay anything, thus leaving others out of the loop, based on what is sometimes seen as a personal desire to stay in control (cf. Riles 2001, 50ff.; Polletta 2002, 213). The network in which information does flow freely is thereby reduced to a few select friends, closed to others and considered hard to penetrate (cf. Alland 2001, 122–5). It always has a tendency to break down due to what Riles calls an 'underbelly of personal relations' which is the counterpart to the publicly recognized network of activist associations, the network 'turned inside out' (2001, 68–9).

Meetings, associations and horizontal politics

One important feature of the activist network is what people call its 'horizontal', or non-hierarchical, organization. This horizontal political ideal is shared by many around the world who participate in grassroots movements and transnational activist networks. Appadurai, for example, in an article called 'Deep Democracy', discusses the 'transparent, nonhierarchical, antibureaucratic, and antitechnocratic organizational style' cultivated by an urban activist movement in Mumbai (2002, 31). Santos writes of the World Social Forum's concern to 'deepen' democracy and to change 'power relations into relations of shared authority' (2004, 181). And Robert Albro explores the 'inversion of the traditional vertical hierarchy' in a Bolivian movement against water privatization (2005, 252).

The contrast between a 'vertical' and a 'horizontal' organization was explained to me one night by several Millau activists in a discussion about associations and meetings. In a vertical structure, a president sits at the top of an association which is governed by a formal set of regulations. There is a delegation of authority and decision making, made possible by a series of hierarchically arranged offices. Roles are well-defined within a clear set of parameters. Meetings are governed by statutes and formal procedure, with agenda, minutes and voting. In a horizontal organization, in contrast, there is no fixed hierarchy, no president, no statutes governing meetings, no permanent chair, no formal rules, decision by consensus rather than vote, and minutes, as a formal record of proceedings, are rarely kept. Everyone, I was told, can contribute as and when they desire, and, in this sense, the movement and meetings are considered 'participative'. One man, Jean-Pierre, described this horizontal functioning as 'messy' (*bordélique*) (cf. McDonald 1989, 184), but he thought this meant things were more open to the possibility of change. Rules and formal hierarchy tend to function in the interests of those in positions of power and can be used to silence challenges to the status quo. But in the absence of such 'structures', as he put it, there were no tools to prevent change from occurring in the interests of the established hierarchy. I suggested that rules and offices serve to protect from abuses of power as much as they enable them and that messy meetings were also open to manipulation. While Jean-Pierre partially agreed, he considered a horizontal organization to provide a better alternative, despite the mess. The aim was to do away with hierarchy all together.

Another man present compared the activist network more broadly to the World Wide Web because it allowed what he called the 'democratization' of politics, its opening to all who chose to participate. As a general principle of political organization, CUMS activists often envisage some form of 'participative democracy' in which there is no 'delegation of power' to elected representatives and where decisions are made 'collectively' by the 'grassroots' (*la base*). 'We must put systems in place so that each citizen, there where he or she lives, has the right to speak and to give an opinion on all important questions', Christine insisted to me on one occasion. Decisions must never be imposed from above, she continued, but must emerge from below. Power, in a participatory system, remains with the people and politics involves the expression of the will of the people, another person told me.

Since the French Revolutionary ideal of citizens' active involvement in political life, notions of democratic participation have been a constant political force in the history of modern France. From the late nineteenth century, left-wing parties and unions provided the strongest organized attempt to extend democracy and the rights of citizenship to all sectors of the population (Eley 2002). However, the ideals of a truly participative democracy, in contrast to the parliamentary democracy that many parties saw as the route to power, are perhaps better traced back to anarchist thinking on social organization, such as the bottom-up, federalist politics of Proudhon. May '68, like the Revolution a period of considerable inspiration to activists, represents a recent reworking of the participative ideal and an attempt to put it into practice. The events of May are often seen, by scholars and activists alike, as putting 'an end to representation and delegation' and, to continue with the words of Kristin Ross, as marking the invention of 'politics as the concern of each and every individual' and of forms of 'direct democracy and collective self-organization' (2002, 11, 75).[2] Exemplary of this direct democracy were the small action committees that began to organize by profession, neighbourhood or factory in order to engage in anticapitalist combat and to materially support the general strike that began in mid-May (2002, 76). Committees were based on ideas of participation and equality. Their organization was 'supple', with no bureaucracy, no elections, no leadership, no imposed ideology. In the words of an activist of the time, their 'fundamental goal ... [was] to define a common political line from the bottom up (*à partir de la base*)' (quoted in Ross 2002, 77).

If the protests of May '68 gave rise to practical experiments in some form of participative politics, those I knew often cited the budgetary system of Porto Alegre, Brazil, as an example of participative democracy in action (see Baierle 1998). As explained to me by Gilles, who had thrice been to Porto Alegre for the World Social Forum, decisions are made at local level, within each neighbourhood, and from there they are taken for discussion in forums between neighbourhoods and, finally, the proposals from those meetings are taken for debate at the level of the municipality. The whole process of decision making begins with the grassroots. Ordinary people propose things and people higher up the 'hierarchy' are obliged to base all their decisions on what comes to them from below.

Another model which impressed the activists I accompanied to the G8 counter-summit in Annemasse in May 2003 was the 'Barrio system' in the tent villages. The counter-summit, held at the same time as the G8 summit of world leaders in Evian, consisted of a series of forums and discussions on a wide variety of issues relating to globalization and domination. Many thousands came from France and neighbouring countries and set up in the tent 'villages' on the outskirts of the town. The organizers encouraged the villages to adopt a participative Barrio system which functioned, as explained on a panel in one village, as follows. Small meetings feed into bigger meetings, which feed back to the smaller meetings, which have the task of considering, implementing and proposing changes to the bigger meetings. Each barrio (or even sub-barrio) has meetings and then there are interbarrio meetings whose decisions are taken back to the barrios. Anyone can act as 'messenger'

---

2 See Polletta (2002) on participatory democracy in American social movements.

between meetings and it is good if there is more than one messenger to take the pressure off a single person.

Loudspeaker announcements described the villages as 'common spaces' and as 'self-managed' (*autogéré*), an ideal prominent during May '68, and encouraged people to participate in the meetings which were an essential part of this self-management. Each village neighbourhood had meetings at set times to share out tasks such as cleaning and rubbish disposal. Of the couple of meetings I saw, much discussion centred, however, on organizing protest actions. At one, about fifty people sat facing each other on the ground to organize blocking the arrival of the Socialist Party secretary. (As I discuss below, activists are often distrustful of parties and the Socialists are considered to have abandoned their left-wing principles in favour of neoliberal ones.) People raised a hand and spoke in turn to express their opinion until agreement was finally reached, the making of banners organized, and a time and place set for beginning the march. Jean, who accompanied me to this meeting, was really impressed with the system of self-management (*autogestion*) and with the 'atmosphere of solidarity'. He thought wonderful one of the non-profit food stalls where everyone had to wash their own plates and cutlery. He kept remarking on how great it was to see people sharing, responsible, united, egalitarian, making decisions collectively and democratically, living out the world they were fighting for.

The political associations based in Millau also attempt to put into practice participatory and horizontal ideals. Many are open to all, have no president, secretary or any fixed offices, and, in principle, anyone can take on the tasks associated with such roles. Initiative is considered the key, the will to act. At meetings, an *animateur*, who often changes from one meeting to the next, will direct discussion, deciding who will speak next based on the order in which people raise their hands and ensuring that people remain more or less on topic. Someone always writes an account of the meeting (*compte rendu*), though this is not always distributed following the meeting and almost never subject to discussion at the next. It serves to remind people what they have to do. Often the meetings I attended took a round-table form. People sit in a rough circle and nobody is formally recognized as more important than anyone else. The concern, in general, is that formal structures not impede anyone's desire to participate and that all who speak receive equal recognition and attention (cf. Berglund 1998, 34). In a sense, the meeting is the place where public and private ideally cohere. Like Habermas's public sphere, meetings are understood as public spaces where private individuals meet to engage in rational-critical debate over matters of public concern (Calhoun 1992, 1; Habermas 1989). The private and individual should never be effaced in meetings, but rather given voice (cf. Heller 2004, 84).

The reality, however, is rather more complex and 'messy', as it was on the Larzac during the 1970s. Although, in many ways, the Larzac-Millau movement is remarkably non-hierarchical and activists indeed succeed in organizing along horizontal lines, an informal hierarchy is thought by critics to replace the formal one activists are concerned to avoid (cf. Alland 2001, 165–6; Alvarez et al. 1998, 20; Jean-Klein 2003). The organization of Larzac 2003 provides, perhaps, the best example of this.

CUMS organizers viewed the support and participation of associations and unions based in Paris as crucial to the success of the gathering. The Conf, Attac, Greenpeace, the suburb and immigrants' movement MIB, rights organization Droits Devant, No Vox, Sud and others would provide potential funds and expertise, serve to link the small Larzac-Millau community with a much broader population base, and publicize the event and mobilize support. Meetings to prepare the gathering were therefore held in both Paris and Millau, and both were supposed to contribute in equal measure. But many considered the relation between Paris and Millau to be hierarchical. From the start, all decisions regarding the organization of the 'political' and 'intellectual' side of the gathering – the forums and the text published explaining the gathering's aims – were made in Paris. Millau was responsible for the logistics, the practical task of ensuring adequate accommodation, water, food, volunteers, marquees, car parking and so on. This division of labour emerged under the guiding hand of those who attended meetings in both cities. It was never the result of a democratically-made decision to which activists in Millau were privy, and, if it had been decided in Paris, it was never made clear and explicit to those in Millau. Many in Millau quietly grumbled about the way they were sidelined in all that was 'political' (*militant*). They felt they were simply carrying out the hard task of putting everything in place according to a plan designed largely at 'national' level (cf. Jean-Klein 2003, 566). Paris appeared to occupy a higher position in a hierarchy that by rights ought not to exist, the sort of centre-periphery hierarchy that activists had fought in the 1970s when opposing government plans for the Larzac's military camp.

In Millau itself, a similar sort of hierarchy emerged. Following the establishment of committees for organizing different aspects of Larzac 2003, an 'intercommittee committee' was set up to which each committee was to send one or two representatives. Often, however, intercommittee meetings were overflowing. A committee known as the GOG was then created consisting of ten people to make the decisions that 'were necessary', as someone put it. The existence of the GOG became known before it was ever proposed, and agreed to, at a General Meeting. People began to refer to it as the 'politburo', suggesting, half-jokingly, that it would impose decisions undemocratically on the rank and file. Members of the GOG were sensitive to suggestions of this kind and insisted the GOG merely acted on collectively-made decisions. For some, however, reality did not always confirm this opinion. When the GOG decided to cancel completely the 'Kids village' that one of the committees had been organizing, it was roundly criticized because the decision was made without consultation with members of the committee. The decision, it must be said, was reversed at the following General Meeting following heated discussion.

Members of the committee responsible for organizing the 5,000 volunteers (*bénévoles*) required during the gathering were also very critical of the hierarchical mode with which they perceived the GOG to operate. Four of them resigned after the GOG effectively vetoed their plans for a hospitality village (*accueil bénévoles*) to welcome volunteers and provide them with food, drink, camping and parking space, and entertainment. In a letter addressed to members of the GOG, they summarized what they saw as the GOG's reasoning: 'Volunteers are activists who are there to give of themselves, and we do not have to worry about them, they're autonomous'.

The letter went on to speak of decisions 'imposed', initiative 'crushed' and opinions 'unlistened to' by a GOG committee which functioned like a 'court' (*tribunal*) and was bent on 'exercising its power'. The language was entirely opposed to that they used, in the same letter, to describe the mode of functioning to which, they claim, their committee attempted at all times to adhere and which remains, for all, an ideal: one based on principles of 'participative democracy', where 'power is horizontal' and 'shared', and where the ideas of all 'citizens' receive 'welcome and respect'. Following the gathering, in a meeting held to evaluate its success, a number of people asked, without reply, what the purpose of the GOG had been. For some, at least, the GOG left a bitter taste.

The problem with the GOG was that it made decisions which had a concrete impact on the way the gathering unfolded, but these decisions were made in a forum that was not considered public, and they were not subsequently returned to people at General Meetings for comment and approval. When defending the role of the GOG to me on one occasion, one of its members vigorously denied that the GOG did anything other than act on the basis of decisions made at General Meetings. Activists generally consider General Meetings to be the most democratic of all decision-making forums because, being open to all, they are the most inclusive. Because they figure lowest in the organizational hierarchy, they are highest in the democratic one.

But even General Meetings have an activist 'underbelly' where certain individuals have an authority they should not have. Echoing criticisms made during the Larzac struggle of the 1970s, it is not uncommon to hear people say that the 'real decisions' are made by a select group of friends in private discussions and telephone conversations (cf. Alland 2001, 122). Meetings are sometimes thought to involve a certain 'manipulation' by key people to get public and 'democratic' backing for their ideas. Decisions become democratic, they are not necessarily born so. The GOG, as I mentioned above, was thus known to exist in some form before any discussion of it had taken place in a General Meeting. In the meeting itself, a list of names was proposed, objections to the list were called for, none were forthcoming, and so the GOG came to be with little discussion of its role or purpose. Frequently, key members of CUMS hold sway in cases of disagreement due to force of personality or argument and the support they receive from other key people. One woman told me it was difficult to get up and say what you thought at meetings because if you said something that others didn't agree with, you met a bloc of disapproval and were talked down. You even started doubting the validity of the reasoning behind your own opinion, she said. The 'bloc' – consisting of well-respected and persuasive individuals – was too daunting. Another person described meetings as exercises in 'big mouth democracy' (*démocratie de la grande gueule*). Those who are heard are those who speak the loudest. Indeed, for him, meetings seemed to operate with a sort of logic of *rapports de force*. Activists get heard by being stronger than others (cf. Alland 2001, 144). This is always the way meetings function, he said, although others did tell me of the method of 'going round the table' that was formerly used on the Larzac, in which people are invited to speak by the *animateur*, rather than actively having to ask to do so.

Given both the horizontal ideal and the sometimes unsatisfactory reality, it is perhaps surprising that activists don't take practical steps to ensure that meetings always function democratically. The contrast with the direct action movement in the United States that Graeber (n.d.) discusses is marked. US anarchists share the concern of those on the Larzac with direct forms of democracy. But they put in place a quite formal set of procedures to make sure that no one dominates and that all contribute equally to decision making. Facilitators, especially trained for the purpose, keep strict control of meetings in the interests of fair and non-hierarchical process. Timekeepers oversee the length of discussions. There may even be vibes-watchers to ensure that nobody feels left out and that, say, men or middle-class activists don't dominate the meeting in spite of the rules. In addition, there are a whole series of clear procedural notions and steps – proposals, concerns, friendly-amendments, clarifying questions, stand-asides, blocks, modified consensuses – that are integral to meeting practice. There is nothing comparable, however, in the much more informal meetings held by Larzac and Millau activists. The absence of formality appears to be considered the important feature of meetings and to confer on them a certain democratic, non-hierarchical quality. Often criticism of current practice is made quietly behind the scenes rather than at meetings themselves, the case of the GOG providing an exception. But those critical of the GOG were not quite part of the core group of friends at the centre of CUMS and didn't quite command the respect of CUMS leaders.

José and the authority of leaders

Authority is evident within the activist network, but activists simultaneously find it worrisome if it emerges out of enduring hierarchies. The position of leaders, indeed the very notion of 'leader', is thus problematic, although leaders are an integral part of the movement. Activists often use the term '*leader*' (in French) to refer to someone who leads due to personal qualities and skills and not as a consequence of holding formal office (see Mény and Surel 2000, 102ff.). Unlike a *dirigeant*, which one might also translate as 'leader', a *leader* is not seen to have formal power of direction over others. A *leader* brings 'more power to the movement as a whole', as my landlord Pierre put it to me. Leaders (I shall cease italicizing the term) are thrown up by circumstance, experience and individual ability. At a conference I attended on 'social leaders', organized by Pierre on behalf of FPH, a Paris-based organization active within the alterglobalization movement,[3] a couple of the delegates described the qualities of leadership as 'natural' ones. The true leader is a leader 'by nature', nature and leadership here referring to personal abilities (*compétences de la personne*), in contrast to the powers inherent in the social role of a *dirigeant*. Such views echo

---

3 FPH, the Fondation Charles Léopold Mayer pour le Progrès de l'Homme, has important links to the Larzac due, in part, to Pierre's participation in the 1970s' struggle. The Foundation has financed such activities as the trips of Larzac activists to Porto Alegre and Seattle. Involving delegates from all continents, the conference focused on developing community leaders capable of confronting the problems of globalization (see Garcés and Betancourt 2001).

Max Weber's account of charismatic leadership which he also describes as 'natural' and opposed to the authority of bureaucratic office (1991, 245ff.; see Berglund 1998, 38). Nineteenth century anarchist Fritz Brupbacher held to a similar idea. 'They had no leaders and no led', he wrote of his anarchist colleagues, 'only men of greater or lesser resolution and initiative, naturally gifted to a greater or lesser extent' (quoted in Guérin 1998, 205–6).

Important amongst the perceived qualities of a leader is a desire to act and to encourage action. Leaders dare to lead and epitomize the *acting* activist. They are actors par excellence. José Bové provides the best example of this. Perhaps the most impressive demonstration of his leadership that I witnessed was during our attempted occupation of Nestlé's head office. From our rendezvous in the town square, we walked the 800 metres to Nestlé. José led the way, assured and marching quickly. When we arrived at the Nestlé building, we found security guards waiting for us inside. The element of surprise on which we had been counting was thus lost. José and those in front (the group of a hundred or so was well spread out) were met by a tall, suited gentleman, apparently head of security. There was heated discussion. After a short time, José and a few others elbowed their way past the man in the suit towards the automatic sliding glass doors of the entrance. They started to squeeze their fingers in between the doors to force them open. As soon as they got a certain amount of purchase on the doors, however, fingers were hit with batons by guards inside, who then sprayed José and others with what people said was tear gas (pepper spray according to the newspapers). Immediately, everyone rushed out of the covered entrance to get fresh air. But José remained in the entrance. He never left. Grimacing, with red face and teary eyes, he was visibly affected by the gas. He encouraged people not to retreat and to prepare for a second attempt. The result was the same: more gas; people running outside, holding their faces, coughing, eyes streaming; José waiting to try again. We did not get in. Finally, José managed to negotiate for seven people to be let in to speak with two Nestlé representatives, and we abandoned our efforts at occupation. Inside, José raised his arm in a victory salute.

During these events, most protesters kept back from the action and watched, almost like passive bystanders (cf. Sennett 2002, 195ff.). Those trying to force the doors were a small minority. José was always at the front, the only one to be there throughout. He always appeared cool and calm. He did everything: planned, encouraged, negotiated, tried the doors and took the punishment meted out. I was certainly impressed with what I saw, as were many others. One person remarked on José's incredible mental strength, his determination and his experience of protest. Most importantly, however, he demonstrated leadership and what Richard Sennett calls the 'superior personality' necessary to engender a following (2002, 229). He was *seen* to lead and his legitimacy as a leader was 'proved', in Weber's terms. When authority cannot be derived from codes or statutes, Weber writes, the 'charismatic leader gains and maintains authority solely by proving his strength in life' (1991, 249).

José is the son of scientists and, as a child, spent several years in the United States where he learnt English. He came to the Larzac in the early 1970s, having dropped out of university, to participate in the struggle. He squatted a farm in Montredon and, with his partner Alice, established himself as a sheep farmer and cheese maker. For 30 years he has been engaged in activist politics, slowly acquiring the experience, knowledge and respect on which his leadership depends. In 1999, he shot to fame for his role in the McDonald's dismantling and came to be seen as a leader of the French social movement. Although he later moved on to other things, including work with international peasant movement Via Campesina, he was, during the period of my field work, an official spokesperson for the Confédération Paysanne. As Conf spokesperson he became a more or less full-time activist, abandoning his farming activities for the most part, spending a couple of days a week in Paris and travelling widely.

In addition to his willingness to engage in action and to lead from the front, José possesses other qualities considered those of a leader. He is 'factually competent' (Berglund 1998, 49), intellectually astute and a lucid communicator. Pierre characterized leaders as those special individuals who have 'a global vision of things'. But leaders must also be articulate and express their ideas clearly and in a manner which attracts and informs rather than alienates. The contrast is no more evident than in that between Bové and Jacques Nikonoff. The activists I knew often criticized Nikonoff, the elected president of Attac, for being too 'intellectual' (*intello*). He fails to communicate in a way that people understand and thus struggles to fulfil Attac's self-declared aim of popular education. Bové, on the other hand, is an unelected leader of the social movement and his communication skills are seen to be one of his strengths. People listen to him because he speaks clearly and somehow expresses ideas they feel could be their own and in terms that could be theirs. On numerous occasions I have seen him, surrounded by the people who know him well, sharing his knowledge and explaining the complexities of neoliberal globalization, GM agriculture or the Israeli occupation of Palestine.

Outside the Larzac, it is the media who bring José's voice to the world. Through the media, José is often considered to speak for the movement as a whole, as though, indeed, he were the movement's voice. He is *of* the movement, in contrast to Nikonoff who, as overly intellectual, somehow stands above it. His authority stems from his perceived ability to contribute to the authority of the movement by articulating its concerns. It is not uncommon to hear people say that José is 'emblematic' of the movement or that he 'incarnates' it. He is the movement personified. While José was in prison in the summer of 2003, there were calls for the authorities to 'Free José': '*Libérez José*' was the slogan painted on walls, bridges, buildings and erected in fields throughout the region. Soon the slogan was transformed. It became 'Let's free José' ('*Libérons José*'). Finally, in jest, someone inverted it: 'José you set us free' ('*José tu nous libère*'). But the inversion is somehow serious. It points to the authority that José is thought to bring to the movement by 'incarnating' it, giving it voice, arguing its case. His own authority as a leader derives, in part, from this ability to 'channel the ideas of others', Jeanine explained to me.

There is another side to the way José gives voice to the movement. Since the McDonald's dismantling, José has become something of a media superstar. As Robert Albro writes of a Bolivian peasant activist who entered the arena of global media activism, his 'role [is] potentially at odds with his organic involvement in the [movement] itself' (2005, 260). Some on the Larzac dislike what they call José's *'mediatisation'*. They consider it excessive, part of a personal aggrandisement and search for stardom. People talk of his ego and desire for fame, of 'bovémania' and refer to his admirers as 'groupies'. José is sometimes considered to have been created by the media in their own image or 'assimilated to the media system'. A Parisian journalist spoke to me of how the media 'machine' had raised José up, made him into an icon, and would eventually take him down again. When I first started my fieldwork, I heard people on the Larzac worrying that the media had turned on José after having previously presented him in a favourable light. For some, José has become a media 'commodity' (*marchandise*), though the phrase for which he is best known, and the title of one of his books, is 'the world is not a commodity'. Some see a profound contradiction between his roles as media idol and movement leader. They are sceptical of whether someone who is a media 'icon', a 'hypersymbol', a 'star', the subject of a 'personality cult', and who has a 'market value', to use their terms, is ultimately beneficial to the movement as a whole. Bové undoubtedly attracts people to events such as Larzac 2003, but do they come as groupies or as activists, do they mobilize for the man or for the cause?[4]

Such reservations are normally expressed in private, however, and often emerged only after a little prompting on my part. Many consider José's mediatization to be an essential aspect of extending the struggle, educating people and increasing the strength of the social movement. They admit his 'charismatic' qualities and desire for media attention as integral to his success, but consider his media status to serve the interests of the social movement. When I suggested to Gilles, himself a journalist, that José was a media commodity, he replied: 'José ... has nothing to sell. ... For me the important thing is that ... the media aspect permits one to speak ... If it's only to touch people who are already convinced, I don't see the point ... You have to get the message across'. Through José, Gilles was arguing, the media bring the movement's vision of the world to a mass audience. Political reality, even for those who are critical of José's mediatization, requires such pragmatism.

It is in large part due to the mass media that José has become such a widely respected authority on globalization and a leader of the alterglobalization movement. Publication, however, also provides a source of authority that helps to define a person as a leader. Activists are much concerned with producing written versions of their world view for a wider public. José has, with the assistance of others, written several popular books in which he outlines his thinking on globalization, agriculture, civil disobedience and other issues. Occasionally, when I asked people about productivism or neoliberalism, I was referred to José's *Le monde n'est pas une marchandise*. 'Have you not read this book?' one man asked me, though he himself was an official Conf spokesperson. He seemed to consider José's book to possess a greater authority than himself on such issues, but no doubt suspected as well that I had already read it. Writing is seen as an expression of José's authority as a leader, just as it contributes to this authority. The same is true of other figures within the movement. Many of the keynote speakers at Larzac 2003 were published authors. In planning meetings, they were referred to as 'experts' whose writing was considered evidence of their expertise. From the books and articles such experts and

---

4 See Martin (2000) on the role of the media in Bové's rise to fame.

other 'ordinary' activists write, activists gain knowledge of the world. The Larzac's bi-monthly activist newspaper provides its readers with a view from 'the Larzac'. During Larzac 2003, the bookstall sold 70 percent of the books it stocked. Email lists disseminate information on Palestine. Leaflets outline the issues surrounding GMOs. The CUMS website www.monde-solidaire.org provides a store of written information on the 'fundamental questions' (*questions de fond*) of globalization. All are authoritative sources of information for activists, written by people themselves considered authorities.

A further aspect to the authority of leaders is the way they are seen to mediate between the local, the national and the global. José, again, is exemplary in this respect. For Larzac 2003, he played a coordinating role with respect to the integration of organizations operating at a 'local' level in Millau and a 'national' one in Paris. Through his involvement in both local and national organizations, he ensured that local and national acted in concert, shared a purpose and language of analysis, and contributed to a united social movement. For Larzac and Millau activists, José was a sort of go-between, taking the concerns of local activists to Paris and bringing information from Paris to Millau. He serves a similar role in mediating between the 'local' and the 'international' or 'global', the relationship between which, he told me, were of great importance. He regularly travels to conferences, protests, counter-summits and Social Forums which bring together activists from around the world. Through his participation in such events, he shares his knowledge and experience of the effects of globalization on the Larzac and on France, contributes to a global debate on globalization, and helps to create an activist movement capable of confronting the neoliberal global forces which are considered, however, to have diverse local effects.

In a sense, José embodies in his person both the local and the global. His highly mobile existence and his frequent media appearances mark him out as special. As a global actor, he operates on a different plane to grassroots activists. While everyone recognizes this, his friends simultaneously consider him 'one of our own', a local, a *Larzac* activist, someone who is far from exceptional. One woman expressed exasperation at the way people treated José as though he were different from other activists. Though he may have certain skills and find himself in the media spotlight, she affirmed his ordinariness and insisted that he was just the same as everyone else. People often insist that José participates in meetings as an equal, is accorded no privileges and has no greater authority or prestige than others. He may be articulate and charismatic, he may provide the movement with ideas, but to 'us', he is just another farmer, another member of the social movement among many.

José is the only person I knew regularly referred to (as I have been doing) by either his first name or surname. On a local stage and as a friend he is José; as a leader, public personality and global actor he is Bové. He is considered simultaneously special – a leader, authority, star or commodity – and an activist like any other. Indeed, he is somewhat anomalous (Douglas 1966). Anomaly, perhaps, is an important characteristic of 'leadership' within an activist world imagined to be organized along horizontal and non-hierarchical lines. The position of elected representatives as leaders, linked as it is to an office, is entirely clear, their place within a hierarchy unquestionable. It is the clarity of their power and authority which alienates them from their support base. The fact of being higher in the hierarchy threatens always to undermine the legitimacy of their authority over those they supposedly 'represent'. This is partly why activists tend to oppose the 'delegation of power'. But it is an essential characteristic of activist 'leaders' that they hold no place in a hierarchy because, formally at least, there is no hierarchy in which to hold a place. Leaders have no 'power', in the hierarchical sense activists give to the term, because they are considered just ordinary people, though their authority may be considerable due to their knowledge, communication skills, experience and other qualities considered to inhere in their person. Their ordinariness can be affirmed, despite evidence to the contrary, because they remain mere individuals and because of the absence of hierarchical structures to institutionalize their authority in a formally defined social role and thus to turn it into power. José is sometimes criticized for exceeding the bounds of democratic authority, for acting in the name of the social movement without the approval of others, but this is considered the action of an individual, not the consequence of a system which is hierarchical (Riles 2001, 61). Whatever 'leaders' do, it is clearly and irrevocably distinct from the exercise of power that is the right of those in office. A leader's authority is unstable and must constantly be proved (M. Weber 1991, 248–9; cf. Sennett 2002, 273).

José's authority stems from his personal qualities, his leadership in the realm of ideas and of action. Indeed, there is what people call a 'coherence' between the way he speaks and the way he acts. José backs up his words with actions. This coherence, a notion I discuss in the following chapter, is an important source of his authority. Any perceived lack of coherence, on the other hand, opens him up to criticism. José's mediatization is not always considered coherent because it does not quite accord with the non-commercialized vision of the world he espouses. But many see no problem and argue that the media provide an essential vehicle for political struggle. Ideally, however, a leader should never become more important that the movement itself, never divorced from the grassroots, and always concerned with the political cause and aspirations of others. Leaders must serve the movement and not themselves, and really it is this that is at question as far as José's mediatization is concerned. The point, here, is that leadership, because it is derived from an individual's actions in relation to a set of norms and ideals, is never clear cut. Leadership, like the horizontal organization of the movement, is not 'a given' but is rather 'a question', to cite Paul Rabinow's discussion of Foucault's notion of problematization (2005, 44). Both imply contingency rather than certainty, debate and critical reflection rather than agreement or acquiescence.

This problematization of leadership and horizontal organization, where actions are compared to ideals, also applies to the place of an activist in the world. A particular concept of the person, of activist-as-individual, is bound up with ideas of the network and a horizontally organized, egalitarian movement. Activists, in my experience, never use *vous*, the polite form of 'you', to address each other individually, as is standard in France. Irrespective of age or reputation, and even on meeting each other for the first time, they prefer the informal *tu*, along with terms such as 'comrade' or 'friend' when addressing someone at a debate whose name is unknown. Such terms emphasize individuality and equality. People participate in General Meetings as *themselves*, not as representatives or office holders which are features of a political organization considered to be vertical. Due to their open and inclusive character – whereby choice, not office, ensures participation and organizational efficacy – meetings contribute to the production of autonomous, responsible, politically active individuals.

Chapter 4

Being and Becoming an Activist

Throughout this book I have been using the term 'activist'. In French, people identify themselves as *militants*. In general, the term *militant* refers to anyone who actively works, by whatever means, for a political cause they consider just. *Militants* campaign for political parties, they protest in the streets, they can be right-wing as much as left. What different *militants* have in common is a desire to address proactively the issues that concern them, a commitment to act. But the term *militant* lacks the confrontational connotations of 'militant' in English and for this reason I do not use the English term. It does not imply extremism, violence or aggression (qualities more characteristic of *activistes* in French). The *militants* I knew saw themselves as part of a nonviolent movement of protest against neoliberal globalization. Within the English speaking world, this movement is considered a movement of 'activists' not of 'militants'. José, indeed, gave me 'activist' as the appropriate translation of *militant*.

This chapter is about what it means to be an activist on the Larzac and the moral dilemmas and creative process of self-reflection this entails. For activists, the relation of self to world is not something to be taken for granted. Anthropologists of social movements have seldom explored ideas about what it means for a person to be an activist, perhaps because their focus has generally been collective political action. Julie Pagis (2005, 9ff.) identifies various activist ideal-types within the French anti-GM movement, and Alland (2001, 133ff.), writing of the Larzac activists of the 1980s, distinguishes the 'affectives', who see problems in terms of human relationships, from the 'politicals', who place issues in a larger political framework. However, I am less concerned to categorize activists into different types according to their political preferences or cultural background than with the problem people face of what is means to be an activist in the first place. My interest is the category 'activist' itself and the relation between a person and the world in which they live. The category 'activist' designates, in the context I studied, a particular kind of person – a citizen-individual – critically engaged in a politics of protest. I shall argue that the category 'activist' is a normative one. It is a moral-political notion. By engaging in the moral activity of 'becoming aware' and acting 'coherently', people produce themselves as activists and as 'individuals'. Achieving a coherence between thought and action, private and public, is an imperative for many but also greatly problematic. The principle of coherence provides the cornerstone of an activist politics. It is a moral-political problem concerning an individual's conduct in everyday life, and it provides a foundation for creating a good society.

The imperative of action and the responsible individual

The thing that Larzac-Millau activists consider to be really important about political activism is 'action'. Action is key to the social movement and is the central point that unifies its disparate tendencies. The language of action is evocative. An activist, people agree, is essentially someone who 'acts', or who should act, by engaging in forms of protest, generally referred to as *actions*. Attac's educational role is one that is 'oriented towards action'. A citizen is considered by activists to be someone who actively participates in political life, who affirms the right to act. And action, for activists, begins at home. 'One begins by doing', Gilles affirmed, '... at the local level we do, we organize, we build alternatives'. An anarchist slogan similarly exhorts people to 'act rather than elect' ('*agir plutôt qu'élire*'), a position with which Gilles agreed. Explaining why he did not vote, he told me, 'Je ne mets pas ma voix dans une urne, je la garde dans ma gorge [I don't put my vote (lit. voice) in a ballot box, I keep it in my throat]'. Although he did not class himself as an anarchist, he considered that his 'duty' as a citizen was not fulfilled by casting his vote, thus delegating speaking rights to an elected representative, but by regularly taking to the streets, participating in protest actions and this way making his voice heard. This, for him, was an aspect of true democratic practice.

More than political opinions or ideas, action is the mark of an activist. Attac is often reproached by activists, including members of Attac itself, for being too intellectual and for not engaging enough in action. Driving from Geneva back to our camp site during the G8 counter-summit, we picked up two young men who turned out to be members of Attac. When we dropped them off, our driver, Jean-Marie, said to one of them that Attac needed to act more. The man said little in reply and went off to tell his friend, who was a few metres from the car at that point, what Jean-Marie had said. The friend then ran back to the car and said he agreed entirely about Attac's lack of action. Though its explicit vocation is 'people's education oriented towards action', he thought, like others, that Attac gets bogged down in heavy intellectual analysis that ordinary people find hard to understand.

Plenty of intellectuals with sophisticated theories of globalization and power participate in the alterglobalization movement. Bové is the Larzac's best known example. But those who fail to act 'on the ground' (*sur le terrain*), as Suzanne put it to me, come in for criticism. Suzanne distinguished positive and negative senses of 'intellectual': *intellectuel* and *intello*. An *intello* was unable to bridge the gap between abstract thought and real life action (see Barthes 1957). *Intellos* merely think or talk about things and develop complex ideas about the world without ever acting upon them. Action marks out an activist intellectual from an *intello*. Action is concrete, local, specific, collectively embodied and publicly visible, in contrast to the abstract, global, general and private theorizing of the intellectual. Activists often have very pragmatic aims which can be fulfilled in quite simple ways. In a sense, they aim less to change the world (an abstract intellectual idea if ever there was one) than to protest, for example, against GM food at Millau's Géant supermarket on Saturday morning by distributing leaflets and putting bright orange 'Warning GMO Danger!!!' stickers on GM products. Actions such as this were undertaken fairly regularly during my fieldwork. What really concerned Suzanne and others was to inform non-activists, to have some sort of concrete and visible political effect.

Often the issues do not need further intellectual analysis as the justness of the cause is already known. Numerous arguments can thus be made against Israel's occupation of Palestine, but, for most in Palestine 12, the important thing was the 'fact' that Israel is the oppressor and the Palestinians the oppressed. The aim of protest actions is ultimately to get Israel out of Palestine by educating the public and, with the aid of public opinion, influencing the French government and the international community to pressure Israel into change. Activists are always concerned to bring about concrete change, while *intellos* are imagined to spend their time working out ways of defending a political position that does not need defending. During a discussion at Le Cun, which accompanied a slide show about a civilian mission to Palestine on which numerous local activists had participated, one person said that our ultimate objective is the liberation of the Palestinian people. 'Understanding' is not necessarily useful, he said. What we really need is a 'citizens lever' (*levier citoyen*), an activist 'force' by which to bring about change. The main question is a 'technical' one, as Pierre suggested to me, commenting on the predominant focus of Larzac-Millau activists.

Activists try to encourage non-activists to act against oppression and there is a suggestion that so doing is a moral duty or responsibility (see Clarke 2003, 123ff.). Ideas of responsibility are common. Activists are sometimes described as 'responsible citizens' (*citoyens responsables*[1]), political action being an expression of their responsibility to work for the greater good of society. In public discourse, the notions of responsibility and duty are often affirmed. On his release from prison in August 2002, José declared that, in the face of injustice, civil disobedience was a duty (*devoir*). On the Larzac, there is a certain pressure for the plateau's residents to participate in political action. Jeanine, my 82 year old neighbour, was openly critical of some *purs porcs*, who greatly benefited from the help of outsiders during the military camp struggle, for not engaging their 'responsibility' to continue their political activities, thus 'returning the solidarity' they had received from others. Several newcomers to the plateau confided in me the difficulties they experienced in gaining acceptance by Larzac activists. One must 'prove oneself' by going to meetings and participating in the activist network, one told me.

Activists tend to think, however, that the responsibility to engage in political action must be self-imposed. A sense of responsibility can be encouraged in others, but, given a person's knowledge of injustice, they must decide for themselves what action, if any, to take. Thus, at his prison release, José immediately qualified his description of civil disobedience as a duty. It is the responsibility of each individual, the duty of each citizen, he said, to *choose* whether or not to participate in actions of civil disobedience. When I later asked José if there is not indeed a responsibility to engage in political activity, his reply was clear:

---

1 The word '*responsable*' has, in French, connotations of leadership. *Le responsable* is the person in charge.

It's more something individual, something profound (*de profond*). ... The necessity [or duty to act] is not an argument that, in my opinion, is sufficient in the long run, that is, if you don't feel a certain pleasure in action and in reflection. ... Political engagement must be a pleasure. It can't be lived as something forced, that you force yourself to do. The day you do that, you stop. And this is a little bit the problem with those [*purs porcs*] on whom the Larzac struggle was imposed. They did not choose to get involved in that struggle. Me, I chose to.

José is a *néo* in the Larzac system of classification, someone who lives on the plateau by choice. Many *néos* came to the Larzac because of its activist reputation and for the struggles in which its inhabitants were and are engaged.

An activist, in José's conception, not only chooses to engage politically but does so, ideally, on the basis of some personal motivation, enjoyment or pleasure. The emphasis on pleasure is not uncommon. Pierre had this to say:

What motivates me, profoundly and personally, is pleasure. If I participated in the Larzac struggle, ... if I have continued my activism, ... it's because personally I find pleasure in it ... People are motivated to do things because deep down they seek a situation they have lived through already and which ... satisfied them, which gave them pleasure. ... One must fight the conception [of the entirely altruistic activist]. It's false. People hide behind words saying 'if I did that, it's for others, it's for liberating the planet ... etc.' Yes, but it's not just that, it's because they find personal pleasure in their activity.

Another person, arguing along similar lines, said to me that activists, like people in general, do pretty much everything for selfish reasons. Their actions are founded on a sort of egoism. This he thought entirely compatible with acting for the common good and in solidarity with others. Selfishness can be channelled in good and altruistic ways. We need to stop associating the egoistic with something negative, he suggested.

The emphasis on the individual and on choice has a particular history. Choice was a key notion in the politics of liberation from structures of power which burst into French public life with May '68 and which played an important role in the Larzac struggle. On the Larzac today, it is perhaps anarchism which represents this tendency most strongly. Important to much anarchist thought is the idea of the morally responsible individual who is guided by his or her own understanding (Marshall 1992, 544). 'Anarchism', various activists told me, meant there was no 'delegation of power', no 'domination', no 'external structures' of authority, and that everyone was free to participate in decision making. Importantly, however, it did imply 'internal rules', as one woman put it, internal structures so that there was no need for external controls (cf. Humphrey 1997). Due to these internal rules, each individual acts in a 'responsible' way, a way coherent with the social good. For Barbara, who had participated in the German anarchist movement before coming to the Larzac, 'anarchy ... means making each individual responsible' (*responsabiliser chaque individu*). Afterwards they can choose how to live and whether or not to participate in decision-making processes. The anarchist notion of the person is thus one of a choosing and responsible individual. It is a notion broadly shared by the activists I knew, although only some call themselves anarchists. 'Activists' are people who choose to act in ways that are responsible and because, as autonomous individuals, they themselves *are* responsible, not because of externally imposed responsibilities or constraints (cf. Bellah et al. 1996, 167; Jacobson-Widding 1997).

The idea of a responsible individual is also linked to the notion of the citizen and the idea that the origins of the French Republic are founded in a social contract symbolized by the Revolution (Gildea 1996, 110). For the French revolutionaries, the category of 'active citizenship' was restricted to propertied men. For activists, however, citizens become active by choice based on their political awareness. Choice, as an expression of an individual sense of responsibility, today distinguishes 'active' and 'passive' forms of citizenship, not social status (see Bellah et al. 1985, 181). The activist agenda, as I explore in Chapter 6, involves converting passive into active citizens, or, to put it differently, making 'citizens' out of 'consumers', the politically passive and self-interested individuals of what activists call 'consumer society' (*la société de consommation*). Through a process of educating and informing, activists aim to have people choose to engage in political action. They want to convert citizenship as an abstract status into one that is enacted through protest (Lazar 2004a).

Choosing to become an activist is further dependant upon the modern division between work and leisure, public and private life, necessity and freedom (Prost 1987). Ongoing activism on the Larzac has, to an extent, been permitted by the modernization of agriculture and the rise, along with the neorural population, of a middle-class 'urban lifestyle' (Mendras and Cole 1991, 21). The GAEC,[2] a type of farming partnership in which several farmers pool resources and cooperate with agricultural tasks, plays an important role in freeing people's time for political activism (Martin 2000). GAECs were introduced and given legal status in the second half of the twentieth century throughout France. They became considerably more common on the Larzac than in other areas of the country, going against the grain of an agricultural 'individualism' – a desire for autonomous farm management – that elsewhere hindered the development of agricultural cooperatives (Ulin 1996, 109–10; Rogers 1991, 108). Forty two percent of farms on the Larzac are GAECs compared to just 6 percent nationally, a consequence, according to Oyharçabal (2001, 90–91), of difficult farming conditions and the 'taste for collectivity' that developed during the struggle. The GAEC is seen, by Larzac farmers, as part of a somewhat alternative approach to agriculture.

Cooperation, however, is also considered to make rational economic sense, and, in many ways, the GAEC is constrained to function as a business. Farming on the Larzac is, for some, part of a more general political activism, enacted through an emphasis on the small-scale, sustainable and organic. Activism may certainly find expression in agriculture as people attempt to live out their beliefs in the way they farm. But farming is not considered a political (*militant*) activity to the extent that farmers must work within the very capitalist system that, as activists, they tend to reject. Activism as a process of actively engaging in 'public' life – of going to meetings, taking to the streets, protesting, occupying, uprooting, informing, dismantling – is not a matter of production or work.

---

2 Groupement Agricole d'Exploitation en Commun.

With the exception of José, who is effectively a professional activist, activism is consigned to one's own, personal time. It is for this reason that the most active activists within CUMS are people with time to spare: those who are retired, on benefits, who work part-time, are self-employed, have flexible jobs, or who are supported by a spouse. It is also the reason that, while the GAEC allows farmers to free up time for protests considered important, such as crop destructions and 'Free José' demonstrations, members of the Confédération Paysanne are often not present (or are under-represented) at small protests such as anti-GM actions at supermarkets, even though other activists consider the presence of 'the Conf' at an anti-GM protest to be essential. Farmers find it hard to take time off work. For many, political activity is just one aspect of their lives amongst others. Jean-Emile, National Secretary of the Confédération Paysanne at the time of my fieldwork, stressed to me that while activism was very important to him, he did not wish it to take over his life and become a burden. It had to remain a choice in order to remain a pleasure, something he wanted but was not obliged to do, except by some inner sense of responsibility.

If activism tends to belong to the domain beyond work, there is also a belief that it ought to be fun, that protest and partying should be combined. 'Since neoliberal globalization excludes all human values', begins an article in GLL, 'resistance must involve festivities' as an expression of such values (Mainguy 2005, 6). Both small demonstrations in Millau, and large ones in Paris or Florence, are often accompanied by music, costumes and forms of street theatre (cf. McDonald 1989, 143ff.). People smile and enjoy themselves. Larzac 2003, with its two nights of free music with big name acts, was explicitly designed to combine festivities with politics. The value activists in the alterglobalization movement place on fun distinguishes them from what Graeber calls 'the old breed of grim, determined, self-sacrificing revolutionary' (2004, 74). On occasion, however, some consider a festive atmosphere to be inappropriate. When José was in prison, some of his closest friends affirmed, on numerous occasions, that they were not going to party until he was released. Christine was reluctant to celebrate her own birthday. One person thought the situation in Palestine to be so serious that it was not justifiable for activists in France to have fun (cf. Jean-Klein 2001, 96). But for most, activism does not mean bearing the world's anguish on your shoulders. They believe that it is both possible and desirable to strike a balance between the festive and the political. While in planning meetings many commented on the need for the activist side of Larzac 2003 not to be submerged by the festivities – a danger given that the presence of rock stars was one means of attracting people to the gathering – most were satisfied at the balance eventually achieved.

It is the festive side of protest activity that is the public counterpart of a perceived individual need to find pleasure in protest. Pleasure is seen to reinforce individual commitment and thus to add to the strength of the movement. Pierre, for whom pleasure was so important, claimed that 'if the Larzac struggle was won, ... it's because people managed to maintain a certain pleasure, living together, fighting together, doing things together' against a 'situation of injustice'. 'On the Larzac', he said, 'there is much collective pleasure', a 'liberating' and 'convivial pleasure', and it is this that contributes to the strength of political activism on the plateau. On the Larzac today, the collective pleasure of activism finds expression in the food, drink and experiences shared at the Montredon market, film screenings and gatherings at Le Cun, or Larzac 2003. Pleasure arises from the merging of individual and collective. Individual pleasure is found in the 'collective', through 'solidarity', through festivities.

Significant, here, is the double emphasis on the 'activist-as-individual' and on the 'collective'. Such notions are normative ones as much as they point to perceived facts about the world. Activists both ought to be choosing individuals and ought to engage in political action, people believe, but as autonomous individuals they cannot be compelled to act. They can only impose upon themselves this ethic of political engagement in conformity with an activist norm against which they judge their own actions. Individuals must make themselves into activists. Ideally, the social collectivity is something for free, choosing individuals to create and in which to engage. This is how the Larzac community of the last two decades is perceived to have come into being – through individuals choosing to come to the plateau because of its reputation for activism and solidarity. The Larzac and the social movement more generally provide normative models for a social collectivity which, in principle, always allows for individual autonomy and expression, one which, unlike 'capitalist society', is not hierarchical. The question here involves how, as an individual activist, one can help transform the current hierarchical society into a future horizontally-organized collectivity. How, to borrow terms from Norbert Elias (1991), to build a 'society of individuals'? The problem is an old one, grappled with by French Revolutionaries, by the anarchists and utopians of the nineteenth century, and by Marx whose central revolutionary problem, Louis Dumont holds (1977, 111ff.), was to bring about a social order based on the emancipation of the free, autonomous individual (see Marx 1967).

Becoming aware

The 'individual', as Foucault argues (1977, 1990), is a subject created rather than emancipated, however. Certain activist practices reproduce 'individual' and 'self' as conscious categories. The social movement and meetings of the previous chapter are arenas for individual expression, contexts in which people participate as individuals. This section discusses the process of 'becoming aware', a self-reflective endeavour that contributes to the creation of activist-individuals, subjects who act politically upon themselves and society in particular ways.

Becoming aware involves what people call a *prise de conscience*,[3] a 'becoming conscious' of structures of power and domination. Consciousness raising, of course, has long been the concern of feminists and Marxist intellectuals, the latter aiming to make the workers conscious of their historical position as part of the process of transforming a class-in-itself into a class-for-itself and thereby creating a truly revolutionary force (Pratt 2003, 14; Eley 2002, 371). The 1970s are often cast as the period during which the Larzac peasants became conscious of the reality of their social position. 'Seen in their own terms', Alland writes,

---

3 The term '*conscience*' evokes both conscience and consciousness in English.

the history of the Larzac protest is the history of the lifting of the veil of false consciousness from the ideology of a group. Up until the announcement of the camp extension the farmers of the Larzac had been sincere believers in law and order and followed the secular and religious authorities of their conservative region (2001, xxxv).

The struggle taught them, however, that the 'authorities' were not always right and that the claims of the latter to knowledge and truth often served their own elite interests.

An awareness of domination and injustice is partly what makes ordinary people into activists. Activists hope that once people know what is 'really' going on in Palestine they will want to change things, for the facts of Israeli occupation and brutality – the numbers of Palestinians killed and homes destroyed – speak for themselves, hard evidence of Israeli oppression. For Christine, as for others, her awareness of injustice created in her an obligation to act.

[Once] I have become aware of an injustice, I can no longer do anything but fight against that injustice. And certainly, for me, one way [of fighting] is also to bear witness to my becoming aware and to to make others want to lead a similar fight in their own way. ... One thing I want is to show that there are things to change in this society and to encourage others to do the same. For me, that's political activism (*c'est ça militer*). It's carried out in my daily life and through my work in associations. You don't transform the world alone. And, in addition, it's enriching at a social level to meet people from different associations, different unions, who have thought about a whole heap of problems. It opens your mind to problems in areas of which I previously knew little ... and it gives me a desire to continue in the same direction.

As this passage indicates, participation in the social movement is considered to play an important role in further developing awareness. Consciousness raising is a collective endeavour and educational project whereby activists organize to increase awareness in themselves and others, as I discuss further in Chapter 6, in the hope that it will create or cement a desire to engage in social struggle.

But becoming aware is also part of a personal journey. Christine described activism as something you 'mature' into as part of a developmental process. She was brought up a Catholic in Belgium and in the mid 1970s, at the age of 23, set out on a pilgrimage to Santiago de Compostela in Spain with her future husband, a friend and a donkey. They were 'friends of the Arche' and on route visited the Arche community at Les Truels on the Larzac. Christine's encounter with the Larzac was the beginning of an awareness of injustice that would develop over the next 25 years. She was not an activist when she first came to the Larzac, she said, and her involvement in the Arche had initially been a matter of 'faith' not of 'activism', as it has been for some inhabitants of Les Truels. But now she was 'against religion' and the 'hypocrisy' and hierarchy of the Church. She had awakened to 'injustice', an awakening which is the first step to engaging in the social movement.

The process of acquiring an awareness of injustice is an ongoing one and activists often speak of an '*évolution*' in their thinking on various issues. Concern for the plight of the Palestinians is relatively recent, Christine told me on one occasion. Before the second intifada she and others did Israeli folk dances. It never occurred to them at the time that they were dancing the dances of those who oppress the Palestinians. 'We never thought about it', she said, speaking of a lack of political consciousness of the situation in Palestine that now seemed strange to her.

Becoming aware is also considered a moral task faced by individual activists (cf. Berglund 1998, 11; Humphrey 1997). One woman expressed to me the moral imperative of awareness when she affirmed that 'it is up to each individual to become aware' and only then could society improve. In part, this is a question of actively 'informing oneself' (*s'informer*). While eating kebabs between two meetings for the organization of Larzac 2003, Gilles and I had a conversation about the need to inform oneself. Gilles had come to the Larzac from Paris five years before, attracted by the emphasis on action that he found in contrast to the intellectualizing of Parisian activists. We had been talking about how the next meeting, a General Meeting, would be full of rarely-seen people who wanted to find out about the gathering. Gilles criticized these people for coming to inform themselves but for never getting involved in smaller organizing committees. But he also expressed his frustration with those who did not inform themselves actively. People complain all the time that they are not informed, he said, and expect those in the know to inform them. In his opinion, however, they needed to get out there and inform themselves.

The idea that one must actively inform oneself is not uncommon. Becoming informed more generally – about Palestinian oppression or the dangers of GMOs – is thought to require work. It is not a matter of passively receiving information from the press. The mainstream press is much criticized for its 'biased' representation of the 'facts' and for misinforming the public. Given this situation, it becomes imperative that activists inform themselves by recourse to alternative information sources within the activist network and beyond – websites, journals, newspapers, debates, Social Forums, political associations or weekend workshops.

The other significant aspect to the moral task of becoming aware is that activists ought to seek out injustice even in their own lives. 'How does injustice touch me and what can I do about it?' is a question many find themselves asking. Such a question is key to developing awareness and it is one that is very practical.

> The transformation of society begins with raising our own awareness (*une conscientisation de nous-même*). We have to become aware of what's not right and that inequalities exist and start by changing things in our own lives. ... Personally, I have a lot of things still to change ... but the first thing is to become aware.

Christine is talking here of making changes in her own daily existence, such as choosing to 'consume differently', as she put it, by buying fair-trade, organic or locally-made produce, avoiding goods made by multinationals or in Asian sweatshops, buying for need and not in support of what she described as 'that infernal economic machine' of global capitalism. Many believe that changing the world begins at home. The problem is that all participate in the same 'system'. 'Sure, I'm thoroughly implicated in this system too', Christine said. 'There's an interior struggle (*lutte intérieur*) needed to try to change things'.

For some, particularly those who are more 'spiritually' minded, this 'internal struggle' requires grappling with the way domination dwells within your own person.

Everyone, they believe, has an aggressive side that it is imperative to manage or control if one is serious about creating a better world. Jean-Luc from Les Truels, speaking of members of the Arche, told me that 'we are not "nonviolent" ... but people who try to ... manage our own violence. ... Violence is inherent to all and needs to be managed ... First recognize it ... and then get rid of it little by little'. In order to change the world, a person must continually engage in 'work on the self' (*travail sur soi*), as Arche members call it. As part of a more general goal of 'self-realization', an activist faces the moral obligation of dealing with what is problematic within themselves and with the way their own behaviour participates in reproducing forms of domination, conflict or inequality. The aim is to change the way you engage with the world by bringing an awareness of self to all social situations in order to live by your nonviolent beliefs and help to create a nonviolent world.

This focus on self leads some to criticize the way other activists are quick to condemn domination elsewhere – in Palestine, in international affairs, in consumer society – but blind to the way they themselves help to reproduce forms of domination, albeit on a minor scale, in their attitudes and behaviours. For Hervé, founder of Le Cun centre for nonviolence, they fail to face the relation of self to the problem or conflict with which they are concerned. They fail to deal with the problem within themselves. He thought that the things to which people object, such as domination, are frequently indications of tendencies in themselves they do not like. To externalize the problem of domination, to treat it as someone else's problem, was, at least in part, to ignore it.

Others are a little sceptical of this concern with the self, perhaps, one person suggested to me, because of its association in the minds of many with 'spirituality'. The activist world is largely a secular one (cf. Berglund 1998, 41–2). When, at a GM debate, someone asked what role the Church had to play in the fight against GMOs, the response of the person chairing the debate served to distance the secular majority from the view expressed that 'God made nature and it was not man's place to modify it'. People are against GMOs for different reasons, he intimated, and individuals must involve themselves as they see fit. Activists often look down on the Church as a tradition-bound, conservative and hierarchical organization. One newcomer to the Larzac wanted to 'depaptise' himself, to formally leave a Church whose real interest, he said, was power. Of those who participated in the struggle in the 1970s, the *purs porcs* were certainly practising Catholics. The struggle introduced them to atheist outsiders, who one *pur porc* characterized as having another faith, 'a faith in the human'. Influenced by their experiences during the struggle, many of the older Larzac activists have moved away from the Church. One woman who settled on the plateau with her husband in the 1960s, told me that the Church had initially helped them gain acceptance from local peasants. But shortly after the struggle was won she stopped attending mass. The Church, she said, supported the traditional hierarchies that so many had come to question during the struggle, and she felt that Catholics were intolerant the more they were integrated into the Church. Now, she is not even sure that she is a believer. Léon, another veteran of the struggle, told me he may still believe in God, but whether it was a Christian or Buddhist god mattered little. He had developed an interest in religion more broadly, and faith, for him, required a personal quest more than institutionalized practice. Many *néos* would similarly want to affirm that religion – or, rather, spirituality – is a personal thing, a choice, and as such is not an affair of the Church but of self.

For the majority of activists, however, the self is not quite where the real struggle is located. Most are more 'political' in orientation and concerned with protest in the public domain (cf. Alland 2001, 133ff.). But despite this, the self does, in a sense, remain an important focus of thought and action for many activists. Through the work of becoming aware and seeking out injustice in their own lives and elsewhere, people construct themselves as activist-individuals with respect to an activist norm (Foucault 1977,182–4). They consciously attend to their understanding of and action in the world, and conceive of both self and world as things upon which work may be done in order to bring about some sort of evolution and progress. Political (*militant*) action may, therefore, be carried out through explicit forms of protest in the public domain, the realm to which most commentators confine political activism, but one may also act politically by endeavouring to become aware and in one's own 'private' existence. The political sphere of activism is not merely the association and the street (Alvarez et al. 1998, 11–12). Amongst activists on the Larzac, some tend to focus more on the side of publicly visible protest and participate regularly in associations such as CUMS, while others consider the best focus of political (*militant*) activity to be the way you live your own life, something you really have the power to change.

Perhaps the most interesting example of this on the Larzac is the farm of Mas Razal. The farm, which is unconnected to either water or electricity supplies, was abandoned for 150 years until an ex-sailor, airline steward and TV cameraman called François was granted the lease on the land by the SCTL, the society responsible for collectively managing the land once purchased by the army for the military camp extension (see Alland 2001, 81ff.). By the summer of 2003, four or five others had joined him at Mas Razal, although the farm had seen various people come and go over the years. Their collective project was to abandon the hierarchies and injustices of capitalism and to build a micro-society that was organized in a horizontal and egalitarian manner. The aim was to create a more or less 'autonomous' community, one in which they constructed their own housing, grew their own food and relied on what was locally available for the majority of their needs. 'We're against "the system" ... For us the aim is to get out of it. By getting out, we stop feeding it', one person explained. Thinking of the many demonstrations I had been on with Larzac activists, I asked why the aim was to get out of the system rather than actively changing it. The reply was unequivocal: 'getting out is changing. If you're against nuclear power, you don't light up with Electricité de France. Period'.[4] Their aim was thus to live out in everyday life the ideals to which they aspired, to ensure that their 'everyday life is compatible with a global choice' or vision, to be 'radically anticapitalist'. Because they rejected capitalist society, they withdrew from it and tried to create an autonomous alternative from the ground up. This they intended explicitly as a constructive 'political' act. It was also 'radical' in that it was a return to 'roots', radical in its etymological sense. 'It's at the most radical level of social organization (the individual) that the most radical action is possible: abandoning the wheels of the system', one Mas Razal member wrote in a GLL article (ismaël 2003, 5).

---

4 Three-quarters of France's electricity is nuclear.

Coherence

The Mas Razal project was motivated by a desire for 'coherence' (*cohérence*) in daily life. To live coherently means to live in accordance with your principles, to ensure an agreement between ideas and practice, between the way you think about the world and the way you act in it. Coherence is both a political and moral notion. It serves to distinguish an *intellectuel* such as José from an *intello* who fails to act on their ideas. Neither action nor ideas are thought to be enough on their own. 'Just as action without reflection is doomed to failure, reflection without action serves no purpose', Gilles told me. This concern with the coherence of action and ideas was evident in Communication Committee discussions on the design of the CUMS website. The site, one member of the committee insisted at a meeting, both had to explain the fundamental ideas of alterglobalist thinking, with the aim of 'transforming people's consciousness', and it needed to outline how people were acting, and how they might act, to create 'other worlds'. Others agreed. In the final design of the site, topics such as globalization, the WTO and GMOs were classified under a double heading: 'Understand, Act'.

The coherence of action and thought is integral to what an activist is or should be. In reply to my question about what makes an activist, José puzzled a moment and wondered if it wasn't 'someone who lives out their ideas'. 'I think I would define it like that', he said. 'It's someone who tries to have a coherence between their life, as lived everyday, and the ideas in which they believe and wish to develop'. The Larzac, for José, is a place where one can live out this desire for coherence.

> Here activism involves all at once how we manage the land, the earth, how we organize work and production, how we insert ourselves into economic circuits, what global reflection we have on the economy, what international relations. ... The whole of daily life is involved. There's no break [between activism and daily life], if you like. ... Here we are lucky to be able to have a coherence between the everyday and our [activist] ideas.

As an 'activist place' and 'symbol of resistance', the Larzac is partly defined by the coherent practices of its inhabitants. Since the end of the military camp struggle, many farmers have diversified their agricultural practices so that they accord somewhat more closely with their ideals of a non-intensive and non-productivist agriculture. Some produce their own cheeses rather than supplying the Roquefort firms with ewes' milk. Others sell direct to the consumer in an effort to distance themselves from the commercial retail trade. Many have converted to organic agriculture. And people in general tend to be sceptical of consumer society and attempt to reduce their dependence on the market economy.

If coherence is much valued, a lack of coherence is much criticized by activists themselves (and, indeed, by non-activists who see it as a major contradiction of the alterglobalization movement). Examples of the small everyday ways activists don't quite manage to live in accord with their convictions are numerous. Many activists shop in supermarkets while agreeing with a CUMS email that described supermarkets as 'tools of imperialism'. Some from outside the area have holiday houses on the Larzac, which remain empty for much of the year, and yet they support rights of use over rights in property. Barbara pointed out to me that activists tend to consider oil a symbol of neoliberal globalization and yet they also tend to drive to protests and meetings alone in their cars. On one of the monthly hikes I used to go on with Larzac activists, one woman at one point pulled out a can of Coke. Somewhat amused, I asked her where she had left her principles. She agreed, a little sheepishly, that she shouldn't really be drinking Coke given her opposition to multinational capitalism, but she needed a good shot of caffeine. She said she was going to convert to fair-trade coke.

The notion of coherence is generally used with reference to everyday life, but it can refer to the world of public political action. Those who criticize Bové for becoming a star or for having a market value are essentially pointing to the 'incoherence' of a media-oriented politics. Bové's status as media commodity does not rest easily with his claim, made on behalf of an entire movement, that 'the world is not a commodity'.

Larzac 2003 was similarly subject to criticism for a certain lack of coherence. Although many were proud of the way they managed to bring so many together to demonstrate their opposition to neoliberalism and to exchange ideas, I often heard examples of how the gathering failed to live up to its slogan 'other worlds are possible'. After the gathering I spent several days helping sift through tonnes of rubbish, sorting out the glass from the plastic from the cans which had all been mixed in together. The sorting had been improvized by a few people who expressed amazement at the lack of an organized recycling system. Others I met commented on how the food was often 'fast' and poor although the Confédération Paysanne had insisted on 'quality'. Some saw the whole gathering as large-scale and expensive, relying on sales, at a good margin, of beer and tee-shirts to break even. Essentially, it reproduced the relations of capitalism rather than enacting alternatives. During the clean-up, one of those helping said to me that the volunteers were little more than 'workers' whose labour was exploited to ensure the gathering was a financial success.

For some, a certain incoherence is structured into the Larzac's agricultural economy. Several people spoke to me of the contradictions inherent in organic agriculture. One man, a non-organic farmer, told me that organic farmers often adhere to fairly conventional farming practices, only they replace everything that is not approved by organic labelling authorities with that which is. Most importantly, he said, the sheepfold remains at the centre of farms producing organic milk. Farmers who convert to organics continue to raise their sheep indoors for a considerable part of the year. The fact that they receive a subsidy linked to flock size ensures that the concentration of ewes in the sheepfold remains high, which in turn requires farmers to buy in feed that they are unable to produce themselves. They also continue to confront problems of disease, a product of the cramped, warm and damp conditions inside the sheepfold. Antibiotics therefore become necessary, indeed a certain number of treatments per year are allowed by organic regulations. For some, this whole style of agricultural production exemplifies a lack of coherence because it goes against the ideals of organic farming. Organic farmers continue in the same intensive vein as non-organic producers. Farms continue to depend on subsidies, which may provide up to 50 percent of their income (although in the context of international trade, the Conf opposes subsidies because they are disastrous for Third-World farmers).

Growth rates, milk quantity and profitability remain the measures of a good farm. Many organic farmers thus fail to abandon the intensive, productivist methods to which they object. Their thinking doesn't go far enough, one person told me.

But economic reality means that things are not straightforward. Subsidies may not be ideal, one man commented, but no farmer in France could survive without them. Like others, he told me bluntly that he converted to organics because it meant he got higher subsidies, while another farmer said he converted because there was increased market demand for organic produce. Others deplore such cold economic reasoning. There is, however, a growing tendency to assert that activism and the 'commercial' are not opposed. This idea was made explicit at APAL meetings on the renovation of La Jasse, an old sheepfold that APAL owned. In summer, La Jasse became the site of a restaurant, run by a team of three, and a shop for local artisans and craftspeople. APAL's aim was never to make money by leasing the building but to provide a space for the Larzac's activist inhabitants to meet and to sell their wares. But by 2003, La Jasse was in need of restoration, and the imminent completion of the Millau viaduct would see the re-routing of the main highway on which La Jasse stood and the consequent loss of holiday traffic on which restaurant and shop depended. APAL, assisted by a grant from the regional council, decided to employ an outside consultant to do a feasibility study on the future of La Jasse. The consultant came up with a proposal to restore and redevelop the building at considerable expense. He envisaged a place that would continue to serve as restaurant, bar and concert venue, but that would become a themed 'place of destination' for activist customers (*un lieu de destination*), rather than a holiday stop-off point. Significantly, he proposed that La Jasse be run independently of APAL. The new managers would pay a market rent – in place of the nominal one that APAL had previously charged – in order to cover the costs of renovation. La Jasse would thus need to be run as a professional and commercially viable business.

Finally, APAL announced its desire 'to put the site at the disposition of a third party to develop it as a place for festive activity, entertainment (*animation*) and exchange ... while maintaining its very particular spirit' in which the 'memory' of the Larzac struggle and a concern with contemporary movements of resistance continued to be central. But the proposal did not meet with universal approval. Young people – those not old enough to have participated in the struggle of the 1970s – especially had reservations. At a public meeting on the matter, a number of people questioned the commercial feasibility of the project and whether a commercial venture was compatible with the continued use of La Jasse by local activists and associations. Some worried that La Jasse would enter into direct competition with Le Cun and undermine the cooperative spirit of the Larzac. Others thought the commercial imperative would put La Jasse beyond the reach of the young and of those unable to pay for the services it was bound to offer at a price. Questions were raised about what renovations were essential and about the possibility of restoring and running La Jasse with voluntary activist labour. Those who had devoted their time to the redevelopment project were sceptical, however. There was no energy on the plateau, one insisted, and the age when everything was done on a voluntary basis lay in the past. Some seemed annoyed and frustrated with those who questioned the wisdom of the proposal they had devised.

APAL, it must be said, was dominated by older activists, most of whom had settled on the Larzac in the 1970s or in the years following the military camp struggle. During APAL committee meetings, from which young people were absent, they sometimes commented on the reluctance of young people to get involved. The young were scared of the need for some sort of professionalization, one said. But young people – both recent arrivals on the plateau and those who had grown up there – felt there was no place for them in an association dominated by the veterans of the Larzac struggle. Indeed, the older generation prevented them from taking the initiative. APAL's insistence on a commercial project was just one example of this.

At APAL committee meetings on La Jasse, people often asserted, in defence of the redevelopment, that one could quite legitimately run a business *and* be an activist. In part, this idea is a reaction to the notion, subscribed to by both young and old, that activism involves a rejection of the commercial. Those who run successful businesses on the plateau sometimes feel marginalized due to their success or the fact that their energy has gone into the business and not political activism. One person said to me that activists are distrustful of commerce. Many, in my experience, assume that business is what neoliberals do and oppose their own morally motivated activism to an immoral commercial sphere. They tend to be suspicious of the neoliberal idea that the market has, to cite Dumont, a 'special moral character of its own' or that it makes for any sort of 'public good' (1977, 61, emphasis removed). Indeed, their political actions are aimed at countering the market's perceived immorality: its production of inequality and injustice (see Dilley 1992, 3ff.). The idea that activism and business are nonetheless compatible is also linked to the development of a sort of activist tourism as the 'activist' part of the Larzac (including La Jasse) has, in the past two decades, been increasingly 'commercialized' and 'developed' in order to provide people with a good income and a comfortable, critics would say 'bourgeois', existence. But this is reality, the defenders of development say. It is not incompatible with changing the world. No one produces for production's sake. Businesses, like farms, remain small-scale and respect their clients, their employees, local traditions, the environment. They are not, unlike multinational capitalism, exercises in exploitation. Nobody ever intended that La Jasse cease being an activist place, and the proposed project would further the activist cause rather than undermine it. No one, as someone put it at an APAL meeting, had 'commercial obsessions'.

Common to discussions of coherence is a concern with the way activists insert themselves into neoliberal capitalist relations of production, consumption, exchange and power. Because the capitalist reality in which all participate is so far removed from activist ideals, coherence is simply not a straightforward thing. Whether mediatization, Larzac 2003, coke drinking, supermarket shopping, organic farming practices, the consumption of nuclear energy, the redevelopment of La Jasse, or the organization of the social movement, which I discuss in the previous chapter, are coherent with political ideals is a question that has no easy answer. The coherence or otherwise of particular practices is always debatable, always open to different interpretations and perspectives. While some are much concerned with coherent living, others focus more on the pragmatics of public political action. To withdraw from capitalist society, like those at Mas Razal, means, for others, not accepting the obligation of public protest. Refusing the media as a tool undermines the possibility of having a political effect on a wide scale. Opposing activism to the commercial ignores the way business offers a means to put food on the table before it becomes an exercise in domination. For most, idealism must be tempered with pragmatism.

But the ideal of coherence remains. Coherence is necessary to an ethical life and to an everyday politics of resistance. It provides a normative model for action, a moral starting point. It is problematic for activists given that it is both an ideal so hard to attain and that it implies more than just following externally imposed moral rules. Because it requires an accord between your own beliefs and the way you live, coherence is never given according to a proscriptive moral logic ('thou shalt not...'). The notion of coherence exemplifies a sort of moral problematization whereby action in the world becomes an 'object of thought', in Rabinow's terms (2005, 43). As an 'activist' you ought to achieve a certain coherence in your life, and the only way to ensure this is to make your everyday action the subject of conscious and ongoing reflection. This is a moral-political task and is part of the developmental process of becoming aware. The process is considered a gradual one – 'evolutionary' not 'revolutionary' – of producing, in your own life, relations of coherence. By attempting to live coherently and by reflecting on the coherence of your actions, you create yourself as an 'ethical' and 'political' being. In the contradiction between ideal and reality there is a creative tension.

To act coherently is to affirm, through everyday action, the way the world ought to be. But in this, coherence has a promise that extends well beyond the confines of the activist world. Acting coherently offers a means for building a new global society based, as the activist ideal would have it, on universal principles and a respect for fundamental rights, as I further explore in Chapter 7. The idea of coherence opens the world to choice, in a sense. It makes 'society' imaginable as something that can be chosen and created on the basis of an ideal. A coherent society is one which conforms to the prior idea activists have of it. This idea is one in which the values of democracy, freedom and rights – which are commonly given voice in the political discourse of elected representatives, in international agreements and human rights declarations – are also inscribed in social practice. One of the great troubles with today's world, as activists see it, is that it fails to live up to the principles and ideals espoused in some form by pretty much everyone, even powerful elites. There is a lack of coherence between ideals and social practices. The liberalization of the global economy, they will argue, is frequently promoted by the powerful in the name of the greater good, poverty reduction, human rights and freedom, but in reality economic liberalization benefits a small minority, increases forms of inequality and injustice, and denies people their autonomy, their livelihoods and their rights. The powerful may claim to act in the name of freedom and the public good, but cynically act to further their domination over others in their own private interest. The 'shameless lies' they tell, in the words of Gilles, serve to mystify their power. The strategy of developing awareness is concerned with revealing the 'true' beliefs and aims of the powerful, rendering incoherence and domination visible. Activists are thus involved in a struggle for coherence, a struggle for an alternative, egalitarian social order and an alternative globalization.

Coherence, then, is both a moral-political problem concerning conduct in everyday life, and it provides a principle for the creation of a new society. Unlike the Mongolian 'morality of exemplars' discussed by Caroline Humphrey (1997), one in which notions of self are also central, a morality of coherence requires that the individual and the social, or individual and social moralities, be brought into what activists consider a proper and just relation. 'Moral exemplars' in Mongolia – stories, precepts, teachers – are chosen by individuals in order to judge the virtue of their own actions as part of their construction of self. Different exemplars, however, need not be consistent with one another, Humphrey argues, nor coherent with society in general (1997, 38; cf. MacIntyre 1984, 27ff.). In contrast, individual moral action, as Larzac activists understand it, must cohere with a moral social order founded on codes of rights and ideals of autonomy. For the social to be organized coherently, the individual must retain their autonomy and their rights. For the individual to act coherently, their private understanding of things must be given social expression. In creating 'other worlds', activists hope to bring about a coherence between realms considered distinct: society and the individual, action and thought, public and private, external and internal, is and ought. They must be made to cohere, for their separation is deemed problematic: a sign of moral imbalance, corruption, dissimulation, of secret and invisible realms which allow the uncontrolled reign of power.

Chapter 5

Power and Domination

When I arrived on the Larzac, José Bové was in prison. I often came across people wearing tee-shirts in support of him – farmers in their fields, tourists, those working at Le Cun where I was staying, people taking care of the stalls at the Montredon weekly market. 'The world is not a commodity ... nor a prison!', affirmed one tee-shirt. A similar poster adorned the walls of Le Cun. At La Jasse a banner declared 'No to the repression of the social movement', a repression José's imprisonment was thought to signify. In a GLL article I read at the time, the author writes that by throwing José in prison 'the justice [system] and political power have decided to treat the social movement [and its] participation in democratic debate with disrespect' (Castelbou 2002b). These were my first experiences of activists' conceptions of power. The power that activists oppose, however, is much more than just the repressive state apparatus. José was in prison for destroying GM grain as a way of acting against the power of multinationals, and Larzac 2003 was organized against the power of the WTO. Power in its various guises was much talked about by those who considered themselves to participate in a movement often described as a counterpower.

Activist discourse often portrays power as both the condition and the result of neoliberal globalization, imperialism, capitalism, government and other forms of hierarchy. Much that is bad about power seems to stem from the way it is seen to depend on or create social hierarchies. This hierarchical power is embodied in specific mechanisms and institutions through which the dominant accumulate power and exercise it over others: the police and the judiciary, the media and the school, electoral democracy and party politics, multinational corporations and capitalism, the WTO and the General Agreement on Trade in Services. Through such political vehicles power emerges as a capacity, an ability to impose one's will, to act autonomously and to rule (Lukes 2005, 69). There are four modes by which activists consider power to operate that I shall consider here: the power of repression; the power to infect; the power of party politics; and the power of globalization and money. All are considered to depend on some sort of accumulation, appropriation or denial of a positive power inherent in the individual.

Repressive power

In speeches, banners, articles and conversation, the social movement is very often cast as subject to the state's power of 'repression' (*répression*). Repression, in activist discourse, is exemplified by the power of the state to deny the democratic right of citizens to freely engage in protest as a form of political activity. Above all, it is thought to involve the power to 'criminalize'. In part, 'repressive power' is police power, something with which activists are confronted every time they demonstrate. It is a power activists can 'see'. At large demonstrations – those involving tens or hundreds of thousands of protesters – people often remarked on the riot police and their 'robocop' appearance, on their numbers and regimented lines visible down side streets, on their batons and the possibility of a police beating or of arrest. They talked of tear gas and the way lemon juice served to neutralize its effect. Batons, gas and police numbers are seen as the physical tools of repressive power. The police are frequently perceived as troublemakers and their tactic of provoking trouble is considered one of the marks of their repressive capacity. On a march in Geneva at which there were groups of protesters in black dress and with masked faces – known as the Black Blocs and often portrayed in the press as violent – Georges spoke to me of how the police were adept at exploiting the supposedly violent tendencies of this minority of protesters in order to discredit the movement as a whole. Through the creation of confrontation, the police, he said, are able to cast activists as violent and 'criminal'. On criminals the repressive power of the police may be wielded legally as well as legitimately in the public eye. Repressive tactics, as many see it, thus involve turning a 'political' demonstration into a series of 'criminal' acts.[1]

More importantly, criminalization is seen to depend on the laws and judicial apparatus of the state. Through the formation of laws, the state classes particular activities as 'criminal', activists argue, and it is by means of the judicial application of this category to particular acts that forms of political resistance may be repressed. The security law (*Loi sur la sécurité quotidienne*) introduced by then Interior Minister Nicolas Sarkozy in the aftermath of September 11 is considered by many to threaten the very freedoms that allow political association and which make resistance and the social movement possible. An anarchist newspaper, distributed at an anti-repression demonstration, expresses the widely held view that 'the occupation of the public spaces (*espaces communs*) of a building' becomes reason to call the police under the new laws, and a section stipulating the illegality of 'the illicit capture of state or government facilities, of means of transport, infrastructure, public spaces and goods' can be applied to 'any strike of the public service, any demonstration' in public space (Gandini et al. 2002, II–III). In their book on civil disobedience, Bové and Luneau note that the concept of a *bande organisée*, defined as a group of three or more people, can be used to repress any 'organized group' thought by the police to be, for whatever reason, a threat to public order and security. '[W]e are all criminalizable', they write (2004, 278).

It is José's imprisonment, however, that epitomizes state repression for Larzac activists. 'With the incarceration of José Bové, the whole world of unions and political associations, which guarantees freedom of expression, is threatened', affirms a GLL article (Castelbou 2002b). Following the prosecution in 1999 of José

---

1 See Graeber's (n.d.) discussion of the police in the United States whose tactics for dealing with political activists tend to be more savagely repressive than in France. Graeber also discusses the US Black Blocs at length. They are often 'aggressively nonviolent' and engage in direct confrontation (nonviolent warfare) with the police. Their nonviolent tactics imply not causing harm to another living being, while private (not personal) property may be considered a legitimate target.

and nine others for their part in the McDonald's affair, the Support Committee for the Millau Accused was established to fight the 'repression of the social movement'. In 2003, its duties were assumed by CUMS. Many meetings were held by CUMS to decide on forms of resistance to repression and to José's incarceration that year for his anti-GM activities.

The protest actions of José and other activists are consciously 'political'. The category of the political (*le politique*) was explicitly discussed at a meeting about whether or not to financially support a couple facing prosecution for renovating an old sheepfold without a permit. The renovation was part of an effort to establish themselves as farmers on unused land. For some at the meeting, it was not clear in what sense the couple's actions were political. One woman said she agreed with giving money to assist in fighting repression, but only in the case of supporting those who fight on behalf of the 'collectivity'. The couple's project appeared to her to be a private matter. Others argued, however, that the two concerned were participating in the 'reinvigoration of the countryside', making their actions part of the 'collective struggle' of the Confédération Paysanne, which has a policy of 'no land without a farmer'. 'The collective character [of an action must be understood] in relation to its finality', to its aims, José said. The political 'concerns the society we want', someone else added. What makes something political was thus cast in terms of a concern with the good of the 'collectivity' and the future of society. At other times, activists define as political those actions carried out in the interests of the 'common' or 'public good', in support of the 'general interest', 'society', or the largest possible number.

José's destruction of GM grain was conducted for the collective good and in support of the rights of citizens everywhere to healthy food, a safe environment and freedom from the power of multinationals. It is viewed as an attempt to 'create debate', as people often put it, about a matter of public concern. Many activists from the Larzac and Millau find it intolerable that José was sent to prison as a criminal for 'defending rights and the public good'. This criminalization of the political activity of unionists such as José is considered to threaten the social movement and society itself. 'Unionists in prison, society in danger', proclaims the slogan painted on a huge placard on the main road near José's home. Danger, because prison, or the threat of it, is part of an attempt to quash democratic debate and impose political 'silence' on those concerned with the public good, a view often symbolized by the wearing of gags in protests against repression.

Activists thus describe José's sentence as 'illegitimate'. It is seen as a case of a judicial double standard, of what Confédération Paysanne spokespeople often call 'two-speed justice' (*justice à deux vitesses*). Not all unionists who break the law end up in prison. The commonly cited example of this is the case of unionists from the right-wing farmers' union, the FNSEA,[2] who caused damage to the value of €10 million at a refrigerated warehouse without prosecution. Moreover, Larzac activists consider them to have acted in their own interests and not for the common good. This is evidence, for many, of the negative 'political' character of the justice system

---

2 Fédération nationale des syndicats d'exploitants agricoles.

and of its repressive nature, although politicians claim its political neutrality. The repressive power of the state silences only those who pose a political threat.

Viral power

The notion that activists must 'become aware' is suggestive of another form of power which is not considered to be repressive. In Foucault's terms, one might call it a productive power, but, for activists, it is the power of 'infection' or 'contamination', to adopt the biomedical metaphors used by Attac (see Cassen 2003). This power is likened to a 'virus' that gets inside its victims and captures their minds. It is the power of 'ideology' and it is the ideology of neoliberalism that activists are much concerned to combat. As Attac's national president Jacques Nikonoff said in a public forum in Millau in June 2003, Attac aims 'to deconstruct neoliberal ideology' and 'decontaminate minds infected by the neoliberal virus'.

In this ideological form, power is disguised. It is considered to manifest itself as the will of the person it infects and to express itself in their opinions and actions. Viral power thus becomes indistinguishable from the person that is its vehicle. But what makes it power and what makes it recognizable, for people such as Nikonoff, is its foreign origin and the interests it serves. It does not come from within the person, but invades them from without. And although people infected with the neoliberal virus may think they are acting as free and autonomous agents, in fact they act in the interests of global capitalism and 'consumer society'.

Activists often talk disparagingly about 'consumer society' and the way 'we are pushed to buy ... to change our appliances as often as possible just to maintain that infernal economic machine', in Christine's words. Consumer society functions by creating a 'desire to consume', as the sociologist Guy Roustang said at a talk at Le Cun on the subject. It turns people into 'consumers' who reflect little on the course of their lives or the social consequences of their actions. 'Consumer', unlike 'citizen', tends to be viewed as an apolitical category. However, even citizen-activists are unable to escape the ubiquitous pressures of consumer society, as Marie-Jo, a member of the Arche at Les Truels, told me over lunch in her relatively comfortable family home. Members of the Arche pledge themselves to a life of simplicity, and until recently, Marie-Jo told me, those at Les Truels had lived without electricity, TV, washing machine, flush toilet and other modern conveniences. But you are surrounded by a world in which everyone has these things, and the influence of this world is substantial, she said. Her kids, for example, rarely used to invite friends from Millau because they were embarrassed about their lack of a proper toilet. Along with others at Les Truels, she and her family decided to move from living as 'simply' as possible towards a more 'comfortable' existence, seeking, apparently, some sort of middle ground between an ideal simplicity and consumer society. Now, she told me, all at Les Truels had electricity, telephone, a car per household, and her family had a computer and Internet connection. But this did not mean abandoning a critical approach to material goods. The influence of consumer society continued to be a worry for Marie-Jo, especially in relation to children. She considered her young ones to be too impressionable for them to consider getting a television because it was a window onto a consumerist world.

For others, television and the mass media more broadly provide a platform for so-called serious journalists to pass off neoliberal ideology as fact. Rather than being critical and objective, many journalists are considered to be biased, selective and manipulative in the interests of powerful elites. They frequently misrepresent the issues that concern activists and descend into sensationalist reporting. Some accuse journalists of merely repeating the lies of politicians and business leaders, rather than attempting to get at the truth, as I further discuss below.

The school may also be considered to allow an ideological power to take hold, as I discovered while returning from a meeting with Hervé and Christine. Heading to the primary school for the *ramassage scolaire* (to collect the pupils and drive them home), Christine remarked that the school is a place where discipline and a sense of hierarchy are instilled in children. Hervé added that it created economic units and people who would be obedient to those in authority. Christine said she was frequently amazed at the attitude of many adults who just accepted the word of authority figures without question. She found it terrible. An 'adult', for her, was not someone who did that. Adults made up their own mind about things. They were 'responsible'. But the aim of the French education system, in Christine's eyes, was not to encourage the autonomy and freedom of thought that she associated with adulthood and citizenship, but to create obedient drones, workers and consumers who would serve the interests of capital and government.

Political power

Such obedience is demanded by political elites seeking to impose their will. The idea of 'imposition' is basic to activists' conceptions of power in its various forms. Christine:

> If we don't want a society of increasing injustice, inequality, poverty, misery to be imposed upon us, then we have to be vigilant, we have to fight, we have to refuse certain laws ... that the government wants to impose on us. ... The problem is that once they're in power they have the impression that they've got everything, that they have acquired everything, and that they have all the rights and we have only to bend ourselves to their decisions.

Power here involves relations of authority and hierarchy: the right to command and the obligation to obey.

Power and hierarchy are closely related for many activists. Power concentrates in the upper reaches of social hierarchies and is all but absent at the very bottom. Power, on this view, has a 'vertical' nature (cf. Ferguson and Gupta 2002). Only those higher up in the hierarchy are considered truly able to act autonomously and their so doing is seen to deny the autonomy of others. Hierarchy is what permits the dominant to rule in their own interests, for their own private benefit, but it is also seen to result from the exercise of power. Hierarchy is viewed both as a consequence of power and as its prerequisite.

One of the principal means by which hierarchy is created and power accumulated, many activists affirm, is through 'politics' (*la politique*), the political sphere of parties and electoral democracy. Parties and elections, conventionally seen today as definitive of democratic politics, are phenomena made possible by the Revolutionary idea that citizens have a right to electoral participation. Before 1848, however, with the introduction in France of universal male suffrage,[3] elections were limited. In 1849, national elections were fought by parties from two opposed camps with clear and distinct political programmes, representing the (republican, radical) 'red' and the (pro-clerical, conservative) 'white'. The distinction between 'left' and 'right', which stems from the spatial arrangement, according to political persuasion, of members of the National Assembly of 1789, did not gain hold of the popular imagination before 1900, the terms remaining a specialized political idiom linked to parliamentary life (Gauchet 1992; Ormières 1992, 237; Rosanvallon 1992, 284, 293). Broadly speaking, activists in the alterglobalization movement today consider the right to be the champion of 'economic' rights and the left of 'social' rights. But as the Socialist Party is perceived to have moved increasingly to the right, many now see little difference between mainstream left and right.[4] Invariably, they place themselves on the 'far left' (*extrême gauche*). Many, however, have become disillusioned with far-left parties, although a few from Millau and the Larzac are active within the Parti Communiste, the Ligue Communiste Révolutionnaire and the Greens, with others having in the past supported the Lutte Ouvrière (Workers' Struggle). The extreme-left parties are tainted by the very fact of their participation in hierarchical party politics.

I discussed the nature of party politics with several activists in the car on the way to the G8 counter-summit. The conversation was sparked off by a woman who said she was a member of the young Greens. Christine and Gilles expressed their scepticism that party politics could lead to anything positive. The aim of political parties, they emphasized, is to get 'into power'. Although parties of the left may profess the fight for social equality, justice, the environment or human rights to be central to their political agenda, such matters become secondary to their quest for power. Consequently, they are 'not effective', as Christine put it, in addressing the injustices and inequalities which ostensibly concern them. The system of electoral politics constrains parties to place their own interests above those of the people in whose name they claim to speak. The notion of 'appropriation' (*récupération*) is here important. Activists often speak of political leaders' attempts to appropriate the ideas and discourse of the social movement for their own political, self-interested ends.

Scepticism about party politics is often tempered by a certain political realism. While many activists do not vote, a vote may be used strategically to reduce the chances of a right-wing government, even if it means voting for the Socialist Party in whom few have confidence. The most ironic example of this tactic came during the 2002 presidential elections when many of those I knew voted for Chirac in his

---

3 Women only acquired the vote in 1944 (Rosanvallon 1992, 393).

4 See E. Weber (1991[1959]) for a discussion on the vagueness of the categories 'left' and 'right'.

run off with Le Pen, the leader of the far-right National Front. No one supported Chirac, considered a corrupt conservative, but preventing the xenophobic Le Pen from getting into power became the priority.

Some see voting as complementary to action in the streets, but never enough on its own. An editorial in GLL expresses the common sentiment that 'yes, voting is useful ... but not sufficient'. '[I]n electing representatives who defend our ideals ... we can still change things ... [but] if electing is acting, sometimes acting [through protest] seems more effective than electing' (Letort 2004, 1). Elections, for many, offer no more than the pretence of democracy and are, rather, one of the principal mechanisms whereby people are excluded from participation in power and thereby denied their rights as active citizens. Democracy, Gilles insisted on our way to Geneva, does not mean casting your vote in a ballot box every five years and forgetting about things in the interim. It requires an ongoing political participation. Gilles had not voted for over 20 years. To vote, for him, was to delegate power to elected representatives who are then within their legal (but not legitimate) rights to exercise that power over ordinary citizens. Between elections, decisions may be imposed by politicians without demanding the opinion of the people. The vote he thus conceived of as the mechanism whereby power is appropriated from the people and concentrated in the party-political domain.

Elections, in this view, represent one of the ways in which power is made hierarchical. Through the institution of the 'democratic election' and the occasional participation of citizens in political life, a few acquire political power and many are deprived of it, some become rulers and others the ruled, some gain the right to make laws and others the duty merely to obey them. The nation is thereby divided into a 'representative' 'political' class and the 'represented' of 'civil society' (see Spencer 1997, 9–13). José told me that in such a 'vertical' electoral system 90 percent of people were alienated from decision-making. Electoral politics is thus hierarchical politics. It is not considered truly democratic but is seen as the formal political means by which people are silenced and power wielded over them.

Economic power

What most concerns activists, however, is the power that operates in the 'economic' sphere. The institutions of corporate capitalism, neoliberal globalization and the WTO allow for power to be accumulated and for the powerful to impose their will on the powerless. For most, it is the power associated with globalization which is the target of their protest.

Activists often distinguish (in French) between *globalisation* and *mondialisation*. The term *globalisation* is taken from English and denotes a certain kind of neoliberal domination. Sometimes it is identified with Westernisation or, more commonly, with US or 'Anglo-Saxon' (US and English) hegemony.[5] But the term *mondialisation* may

---

5 McDonald writes that the term 'Anglo-Saxon' took 'moral shape' in the nineteenth century in opposition to a 'morally privileged' Celt and came to signify, in the twentieth, what was most un-French and 'morally repugnant' about the English and Americans (2000, 128–9).

also be used in a similar sense. It is a term some find problematic. At a meeting of the Communication Committee on the design of the CUMS website, Gilles said he envisaged an introductory text on *mondialisation*, which for him meant, essentially, the WTO. But then he said, to nods of approval, that he didn't like the term for a variety of reasons. First, it was unsatisfactory because it was overused and had become vague and meaningless. Secondly, he was not against *mondialisation* as an 'historical force', the inevitable process of interaction between peoples across the globe which began millennia ago and continues today. He cited, as an example, the ruined Graufesenque potteries outside present-day Millau whose wares were exported all over the Roman Empire almost two thousand years ago. Thirdly, he said that the term *'antimondialisation'* had first been used by the extreme right and had then been taken up by left-wing activists because it suited their cause. But the origin of the notion was objectionable and we didn't want to be associated with the extreme right. Fourth, 'anti' was negative. We need, he said, to find a positive, constructive term and attempt to develop new conceptions of the world and its organization, a concern expressed by many during the organization of Larzac 2003.

No one could come up with a satisfactory alternative to *'mondialisation'*. The discussion does highlight, however, that *mondialisation* is only really considered a bad thing when it takes on a particular neoliberal form, at which point it may be referred to as *globalisation* or given the qualifier *libérale* or sometimes *ultralibérale*.[6] Most activists have no objection in principle to mobile phones, the Internet, international trade or cultural exchange. The question concerns in whose interests such things function. In principle, also, globalization is considered to be negotiable and not inevitable. It is a process whose direction should not be determined by the powerful and over which activists aim to have their say. Ideally, it should be carried out through truly democratic and participative means.

Multinationals, for activists, epitomize neoliberal globalization and countering them is the ultimate goal of much political activism. Of particular concern to CUMS activists are multinational biotechnology firms involved in agricultural and GM research, just five of which control 100 percent of the global agricultural GM industry (Pons 2001, 114). During my fieldwork, I attended numerous gatherings, information evenings and public forums on genetic modification, multinationals and agriculture, both in the Millau region (organized by the Collectif OGM Danger or the Confédération Paysanne) and other parts of France. Books and leaflets explaining the issues were often available to complement the speakers at forums, who generally formed part of a panel of 'experts' and addressed their audience with the aid of a microphone.

Biotechnology multinationals are perceived to be bent on the accumulation of profit and power. The same companies engaged in GM research also produce seed and pesticides, a fact they are considered to exploit to make farmers dependent upon them and their products. Key here, for activists, is the use of patents, which,

---

6 I shall translate *libérale* (and *ultralibérale*) as neoliberal. 'Liberal', in English does not, to me, convey ideas of free trade or privatization to which activists are opposed and which they connote by the term *libérale*. See Marshall on the history and varied meanings of the terms 'liberal', 'liberalism' and 'libertarian' in French and English (1992, 39–42).

as explained at a public talk on agriculture and genetic modification, permit 'the privatization of the living'. The talk was organized by the Confédération Paysanne and held, on a cold night, in a hall in a small town outside Millau. The Conf had invited 900 local-body representatives in the hope of persuading them of the need to pass by-laws banning GMOs from their *communes*. But few turned up, due to the fact, according to Georges, that most were right wing and supported the business interests behind the development of GMOs. Georges, an activist I knew well from Palestine 12, often had his tongue in his cheek. He was highly active and visible within the Larzac-Millau movement, but often boasted (self-deprecatingly) about being a former businessman and a castle-owner (he had purchased a ruin in the 1980s which he had done up himself). He claimed to be acquainted with the well-heeled and those on the right of the political spectrum, something making him more than qualified to comment on the motives and interests of local politicians. They were absent for a reason, he assured me.

We sat down amongst the audience of about fifty, many of whom were activists, facing the three Conf members sitting at a table on the stage. While one speaker said he hoped for a debate and not an 'evening of preaching' (*soirée de messe*), events were dominated by those up front. As the speakers explained, there are no GMOs without patents. Patents allow for the control of industrial commodities of which GMOs are one. Seed companies become the indirect owners of the fields in which 'their' patented seed is planted and can force farmers to constantly repurchase the seed they sow. Farmers who resow seed they have reaped in the previous year's harvest are in breach of contract because that genetically modified seed belongs to the patent owner. Patents are thus conceived to allow multinationals to control for their own private good what should, for activists, be the common property of all. One speaker said that a grain of wheat is part of the natural 'heritage of the world' (*patrimoine mondiale*). Patents allow the privatization of that heritage, the transformation of living things into commodities (see Purdue 2000, 15ff.).[7]

The speakers highlighted other problems with GMOs beyond those associated with questions of property and privatization. GM crops are pesticide dependent: '*plantes à pesticide*'. They are designed to be grown in conjunction with a pesticide to which they are resistant, Monsanto's Round-up being the classic example. Apart from the harmful environmental consequences and the dangers of consuming plants with high pesticide residues, planting GM crops entails, for the farmer, the use of a specific pesticide, one produced by the same company that owns the patent on the seed. A farmer who purchases a company's seed is thus bound into purchasing its pesticide as well. GM crops were also said to make alternative forms of agriculture, such as organics, impossible. Because of the natural and uncontrollable process of cross-pollination, non-GM plants cannot be kept free from the manipulated genes of GM crops. Organic crops are by definition GM-free, but when grown in proximity to GM crops, genetic 'contamination' becomes a possibility.[8] The potential consequences

---

7 These notions of common property and heritage echo ideas of a biological commons that elsewhere have emerged in debates over biodiversity and intellectual property rights (see Brush 1999; Goldman 1998).

8 See Levidow (2000) on pollution metaphors.

of contamination are not considered to be simply environmental. Contamination is said to be irreversible, denying farmers the choice to go organic. And, because of patents, it can lead to serious legal repercussions. In an oft-cited case, a Canadian farmer was sued by Monsanto 'for having used its genetically modified rape without having bought it, though ... [his] field had simply been contaminated by the GM rape of his neighbours' (Confédération Paysanne 2003b). Genetic contamination is thus much more than an environmental problem. GM seed and GM genes are thoroughly neoliberal in nature. They move, at the behest of corporate capital, in networks of ownership that are global in extent.

Much of the discourse on GMOs, then, is not so much one of 'risk', which has become an important analytical category in the social sciences,[9] as one of domination, subservience and moral transgression (Heller 2001, 2004; Levidow 2000, 328, 347). In a 'risk society', the problem is how to control and manage the risk of some possible or probable future harm. Science has a privileged role to play, according to Ulrich Beck, creating risks in the first place, defining them and eventually producing solutions to them (1992). Science is also central to the political movements to which risk societies supposedly give rise. Eeva Berglund, who draws extensively on Beck in her ethnography of environmental activism in Germany, argues that protest is based on scientific knowledge. Objective, disinterested science becomes, in activists' hands, a 'mouthpiece for nature' and provides a tool for influencing political decision making and countering the 'interested' scientific claims of the military/ industrial complex (1998, 155, 162). This is undoubtedly true in the case of French alterglobalization activists, but science does not play quite the same crucial role. Science is certainly enlisted in activists' struggles, as I discuss below, but somehow the problem is not essentially a scientific one, nor one located in an unknown future. GMOs are a current and pressing reality irrespective of anything science might have to say about them.

Patents, seeds and pesticides are considered the technical and economic means by which power is exercised and farmers forced into dependence on biotechnology multinationals. Once they partake of GM technologies, farmers cannot choose to sow the seed they reap, nor to abandon pesticides. Nor can they choose to convert to non-GM agriculture. Their autonomy is denied as a matter of fact. Their use of GM crops transforms farmers into 'technoserfs' bound forever to their industrial master, as put by Jean-Pierre Berlan, biologist and anti-GM activist, to an audience of a couple of hundred activists at a forum at the G8 counter-summit. As Christine later told me, the farmer, rather than being a guardian of nature and a producer of food, becomes 'no more than a worker for those big multinationals or those big seed enterprises that impose their way of seeing, impose prices, impose trade, impose everything. They impose an agricultural system that will impoverish farmers ... and that will not at all allow [them] ... to live'. Berlan elsewhere describes GM multinationals as having 'a political project for social control'. Their aim is 'to create new sources of profit at the expense of the collectivity' (2001, 6–7). While biotechnology companies often promote genetic technologies as being for the social good (solving the problem of

---

9 Risk is generally presented as something negative. Cf. Zaloom (2004) on the 'productive life of risk' in the Chicago futures exchange.

world hunger) or for the good of the environment (reducing the need for pesticides), the true interest of these firms, for Berlan and others, is private. Profit and power are what they seek (cf. Stone 2002). For José, also speaking at the G8 counter-summit, GM crops are one of the means by which biotechnology companies further their 'will to dominate' and bind farmers into a 'totalitarian system', a 'system that kills freedom' (*système liberticide*). Their 'single objective' is to control world agriculture.

Activists thus clearly place the issue of GM agriculture in a global political-economic context and see the dangers of genetic modification as a reality not just a possibility. The domination of biotechnology firms is permitted, as most see it, by the liberalization of the global economy, a process driven by the WTO and its vigorous promotion of 'free trade' as the path to prosperity for all. Any introduction of GM crops should be a 'political' decision, for activists, one that results from democratic debate between citizens over the public good, but it is instead presented as an 'economic' concern. The WTO is thought to play a major role in the domination of the economic realm and in the marginalization of politics from social life. It greases the wheels of what people often call the 'economic steamroller' of globalization.

The WTO was created in 1995, the successor to the General Agreement on Tariffs and Trade established after World War II. Its website describes it as

> the only global international organization dealing with the rules of trade between nations. At its heart are the WTO agreements, negotiated and signed by the bulk of the world's trading nations and ratified in their parliaments. The goal is to help producers of goods and services, exporters, and importers conduct their business (WTO n.d.).

When I asked Gilles about the WTO, he characterized it as 'the only international institution to dispose of legal, though illegitimate, means for imposing its decisions'. The WTO seemed to embody neoliberal globalization for Gilles. He considered it the principal tool for the imposition of a neoliberal regime on everyone and for the privatization of everything. He described the neoliberal globalization promoted by the WTO as the 'single and unique cause' of much injustice in today's world – the growing gap between rich and poor, social exclusion and repression, environmental degradation, the domination of multinationals, the denial of people's rights. Many would agree. As the organization responsible for liberalizing world trade through the abolition of restrictions on capital, the WTO had much to answer for.

Larzac 2003 was designed as a way organizing 'against the WTO', in the words of the slogan which appeared on advertising for the gathering. One of the gathering's key aims, frequently expressed in meetings and public discourse, was to mobilize opposition to the upcoming WTO negotiations in Cancun, Mexico, to turn Cancun into a 'second Seattle', after the protests in 1999 which brought about the 'failure' of WTO meetings in the city. Of particular interest to many in the lead-up to Larzac 2003 was the WTO's General Agreement on Trade in Services (GATS). The purpose of the GATS is to open to competition services that had previously been assured by the state such as healthcare, education, transport and water.

As explained in leaflets, on the CUMS website and at forums, the GATS requires member states to list the services they wish to see privatized in other member states and also to offer to open a number of their own services to privatization and competition. The process is irreversible. Any agreement to liberalize services cannot be broken without financial compensation being paid to governments whose 'service providers' are adversely affected. Governments lose their freedom to regulate unless they adopt regulations in line with the GATS. 'Any law or by-law at national, regional or even local level', states an article on the CUMS website, 'can be contested and its suppression demanded if it "compromises the advantages" that foreign companies can gain from the Agreement' (Auteurs divers 2004). The GATS is thus seen to strike at the heart of existing democratic practice – the making of laws through agreed political process – and at national sovereignty, as the following excerpt from the CUMS website makes clear.

> The GATS presents a serious threat to all public services, throws into question the social model developed over 150 years in European countries and threatens the democratic rights of citizens everywhere in the world. It calls, no more and no less, for the dismantling of national laws protecting the environment, social and cultural life, laws which it considers obstacles to free international trade. Moreover, negotiations unfold ... without any public and democratic debate. The GATS obliges member-states of the WTO to open their public services to the voracity of private firms whose only objective is profit, to the detriment of the collective interest and well-being. It constrains them to consider their engagement to be irreversible, thus placing unconsulted parliaments and local administrations in front of a fait accompli. Everything must bow before the interests of transnational firms, even the law. The European Commission (... the driving force behind the WTO in Europe ... [and] unelected), had the amazing cynicism to recognize this: 'The GATS is more than an agreement between governments, it is an instrument in the service of the business world' (Gesson 2003a).

By subscribing to the GATS, member-states are seen, ultimately, to abandon their sovereignty and to submit to the will of multinational firms. Ordinary people have no choice over their entry into global networks because they are denied access to the negotiation process that is the preserve of national and transnational elites (see Fraser 2005, 78ff.).

In the process of 'liberalizing' the economy, the political sphere is thus undermined as decision-making passes from the hands of elected representatives and 'citizens' to economic elites and 'consumers'. 'The economy has become autonomous of the political', José said to me. 'The economy has become autonomous of all control. ... It functions completely on its own without constraint and ... even political debate no longer makes much sense because, in fact, politics no longer really decides on the functioning of the economy'. The 'economy', the sphere in which things are bought and sold for private gain, acquires, in a neoliberal world, a precedence over all other spheres of activity as the public good is subordinated to that of private companies. In practice, activists argue, liberalization means that the provision of quality services to all citizens will be replaced by the provision of profitable services to those consumers who can pay. Public services – 'the least that we can provide so that people can live in this society' – will be 'swept away so as to allow space for business', Christine told me. 'There will no longer be any notion of public service. We will have ... a society where everyone will just have to manage'.

Regular marches and other protests – often gatherings in the middle of the street or other public spaces – were held in Millau during the spring and summer of 2003 against the liberalization of the public service. Slogans adorning leaflets and banners declared such things as 'The commodification of services is unacceptable' and 'The school is not a business. Education is not a commodity' ('*L'école n'est pas une entreprise. L'éducation n'est pas une marchandise*') (Sud éducation 2001). Of special concern to local activists was the health system with hospitals in Millau and nearby St-Affrique threatened with closure. The provision of services by the state, one retired couple told me, had been hard won over the course of the twentieth century by unions and the social movement struggling for social equality, rights and the well-being of all. Through struggle, the welfare state had emerged as a provider of public services. But all that had been gained, they claimed, had come under fire in the last decade of neoliberal madness. What Bourdieu calls the 'left hand' of the state, 'the trace within the state of the social struggles of the past', was being attacked by the right (1998, 1).[10]

Neoliberal globalization is conceived of as a process in which all are forced, via the mechanisms of the WTO, to compete on a global scale. The 'local', as activists tend to think of it, ceases to exist as an autonomous unit, in control of political and economic decision-making, by the fact of its integration into a global trade regime dominated by corporate capital and WTO bureaucrats. There is, according to activist experts on such matters, just one market as far as the WTO and multinationals are concerned and it is a global one. People everywhere must compete against the cheapest producer on the planet who determines what José, in an address on the liberalization of agriculture at the 2002 European Social Forum in Florence, called the 'world price' (*prix mondial*). Neoliberal globalization transforms everything into commodities, hence activists' insistence – in banners and tee-shirts, books and leaflets – that 'the world is not a commodity'. The commodification of the world is generally assumed to entail its standardization and the effacement of local diversity as the same consumer goods are sold everywhere. McDonald's epitomizes this standardization. 'You can't have the logic of the global market without the logic of industrialization and without the logic of the standardization of production', José told me. Even thought, people claim, becomes standardized as the ideology of neoliberalism takes hold. Only neoliberal ideas are admissible: a neoliberal *pensée unique*.

Many see the process of liberalization as an Americanization, the extension of US culture and hegemony into Europe. In a discussion with two activists, Georges and Gérard, just before Larzac 2003, both affirmed that it was American firms who dominated the world economy and who would most benefit from the liberalization of trade in services under the GATS. Neither mentioned European multinationals, and the WTO they took to work predominantly in the interests of US companies. While they and many others would admit, when pressed, that European multinationals, are equally a problem, and while activists generally refuse the accusation that they are anti-American, the tendency to distance France and Europe from neoliberal

---

10 On the idea and emergence of the public service and welfare state see Donzelot (1991), Habermas (1989, 224ff.), Sainsaulieu (1998, 138).

globalization is common. Neoliberalism is often seen as the consequence of an external American power imposing its will on what activists call 'social Europe' using the WTO as a front to do so. Jean-Claude from Les Truels suggested to me that the US still operated according to a logic of war and imperialist expansion, in contrast to Europe, which for the last half-century had been fighting for peace and diplomacy. This opposition between the US and Europe often came up in discussions on the American invasion of Iraq. Christine told me on the way to an anti-war demonstration that the Americans had no way of understanding what war could destroy, not just things and people, but history. She felt that the US, unlike Europe and Iraq, lacked history and culture. Often this opposition is cast as one of 'values'. The US is said to value the neoliberal virtues of money and competition, while European values extend to the public good, human rights, history, culture, tradition and regional diversity. On the way to a local market to help Jean-Claude sell his handmade cheeses, he told me that this difference of values finds expression in food. American food – standardized, processed and 'fast' – is a consequence of the emphasis on competition. The food he and others sold at the market – 'noble cheeses', as he put it, fresh produce, bread, unpasteurized milk, free-range meat – reflected values of diversity, locality and tradition. He recognized that processed and standardized food was increasingly available in France, but this was due to a certain US cultural and economic imperialism. McDonald's symbolized this and a society that was the antithesis of the one he favoured.

Neoliberal globalization, promoted by the WTO and the GATS, thus tends to represent, for alterglobalization activists, the victory of American over European values, of the global over the local, of the consumer over the citizen, of standardization over diversity, just as it signifies the triumph of the private over the public and the economic over the political and the social. The WTO, in one person's terms, does 'economic violence' to the social sphere. This is often perceived as a destruction of 'social bonds' (*liens sociaux*) and, as Christine put it, a 'breaking of the system of solidarity between people' (see Donzelot 1991, 173–7). 'And after', she continued,

> we're surprised that there is no longer any social conscience (*conscience citoyenne*)! ... If we are not capable of educating people with the idea that one should be solidary (*solidaire*) with others ... then it's normal that there are problems and that we arrive at an individualistic society where everyone tries to profit and gain to the maximum by whatever means they can.

This notion of the social as something distinct from and threatened by the economic domain is not new in the history of left-wing thought. With the birth of socialism across Europe in the nineteenth century, the 'social' came to imply a contrast to the capitalist world. It was the sphere of mutual cooperation and solidarity, based in the shared experience of working-class life from which socialist parties grew, in opposition to the individualism, competition, private ownership, wage labour and liberalism of emerging capitalist society (Eley 2002, 21).[11] For activists today,

---

11 The social also came to be associated with the state as provider of social services and manager of society (Rose 1999, 98ff.). Like the economic and the political, the social domain was thought to have its own logic and properties, an idea which began to emerge,

the economic policies of the WTO have seen a return to the unfettered economic liberalism of the nineteenth century. The central problem is that the economic sphere assumes a pre-eminence over the social – the realm of human beings and citizens, their needs and rights – and over the political, which ought to be the domain of collective decision making about the social and the economic. The social consequences of economic actions (inequality, unemployment, exclusion, deprivation, poverty) are often neglected, political 'choice' is abandoned to the 'necessity' of the market and of trade 'free' from political concerns. Neoliberalism is thus perceived to deny political and social autonomy in favour of economic autonomy. People are free to act as producers or consumers – 'economic man' is given free reign (Dumont 1977) – but people have no right to interfere politically as 'citizens' in the economic sphere. Human beings, as activists often remark in discussions about neoliberalism, thus find themselves subordinated to the demands of the economy, inverting what they consider to be the proper order of things – expressed in the English slogan 'people before profits'. The highest, some would say unique, values become economic ones: money, profit and growth. Neoliberalism reduces the full range of possible 'human values' to the single value of money. 'The individual no longer counts', Claudine, one of the leaders of CUMS, said to me, echoing a common sentiment, 'only money and the economy count'.

Capitalism and domination

The primary actors in a neoliberal world order are multinationals corporations. The power of multinationals is seen to derive from their massive accumulation of capital which enables a series of economic strategies of which I often heard activists talk at forums. In addition to patents and other monopolistic mechanisms that create relations of dependency, multinationals can relocate to exploit cheap Third-World labour, undercut their competition, dump excess production on 'local' markets (those not oriented to production for export), and impose on producers everywhere a price regime out of all proportion to local costs of production. Their autonomy is thereby increased and so is their power to deny the autonomy of others. Multinationals, aided by the WTO, work to create hierarchy, which in turn allows the further accumulation of capital and power. Neoliberal globalization is thus, by its very essence, an exercise in power and domination, as activists imagine it.

Multinationals are often thought to exemplify 'capitalism'. But while all Larzac-Millau activists are opposed to neoliberal globalization and more or less agree on what it is and how it functions, not all are opposed to capitalism. Some would certainly pronounce themselves against capitalism on occasion, and anticapitalist rhetoric is evident within the movement more broadly. 'Let's tear down capitalism' (*abattons le capitalisme*) is a slogan you often see at protests. What activists understand by capitalism varies, however.

---

governmentality theorists argue, in the seventeenth century (Foucault 1991; Barry et al. 1996, 9).

Some consider the emphasis on globalization to hide the real source of inequality and oppression which is capitalism. They criticize the alterglobalization movement for being reformist rather than radical and distinguish capitalism from neoliberal globalization. Following a film screening at Le Cun called *Davos, Porto Alegre et autres batailles* (Glenn 2002), presented to around thirty people from the Larzac by the director Vincent, there was a spontaneous debate about whether we should be antiglobalization (*antimondialisation*) or anticapitalism. Do we seek to destroy or reform capitalism? One man thought it wasn't good enough to be antiglobalization or to fight for 'another world'. He suggested the antiglobalization movement ignored the capitalist basis of exploitation. Christian, a farmer who came to the Larzac during the struggle in the 1970s, responded that globalization (*mondialisation*) was inevitable. You can't be for or against it, he said, but you can try to make sure it takes place as fairly and as equitably as possible. Vincent proposed that we could create a plurality of noncapitalist worlds, not just a single alternative to capitalism. He suggested the debate we were having and the World Social Forum in Porto Alegre were examples of noncapitalist worlds. Christian, however, was sceptical. We are always subject to capitalist relations, he protested. Even the film we had to pay to see. Vincent replied that capitalism reduces everything to money, but, he insisted, we needn't do the same. Porto Alegre and the Larzac were places where other values, human values, were proposed and lived. He thus cast capitalism as something you could escape or ignore to an extent. The point, as it is for many, is to create alternatives as much as to fight.

For many Larzac and Millau activists, the terms 'capitalism' and 'globalization' seem to be used almost interchangeably. When activists talk about capitalism they often mean *neoliberal* globalization. It is the neoliberal dimension they oppose, the lack of constraints on capital that enables it to grow, to convert all things into commodities, to exploit, profit and accumulate an oppressive and frightening power. Capital itself is thus less the problem than its regulation and control (see Latouche 2002; Mestrum 2004, 199). Rather than locating the source of inequality in the relations of production or appropriation of surplus value, many seem to find it in the absence of constraint.

Some alterglobalization activists would leave capitalist relations of production and exchange in place, but restrict capital by political means, have it serve 'social' ends and ensure that 'economic values' do not predominate over 'human values'. One day shortly after Larzac 2003, as we sat in Millau's market square, Jérôme told me that he was opposed to capitalist power-seekers but wasn't entirely anticapitalist. He worked for a local photocopying business, run by his mother, which produced many of the leaflets and posters for CUMS. He said he sought something between capitalism, which gave too much importance to the individual, and communism, which denied the individual and emphasized the collective. He proposed rugby as a model for a good society, a sport, he said, in which individuals play for the team and for their team-mates. Like many, he wanted to subordinate capital to the democratic power of the people, to make business socially responsible, to have it respect human beings. The social movement, as a counterpower, he considered a movement of control on power and capital.

The reason globalization and capitalism can almost be used as synonyms is that both point to what is considered a more profound problem: 'domination'. Domination in all its forms was what concerned many of the activists I knew, including Catherine who, in the months prior to Larzac 2003, acted as the main secretary at the CUMS office in Millau. On board a train for Paris for a meeting about Larzac 2003, she had been telling me about growing up with a strong class consciousness and about her previous involvement in Marxist organizations. When I asked if she considered the notion of globalization to hide the more fundamental problem of class, she replied 'no'. The problems, for her, were the same. Globalization occurs through the exercise of domination by the powerful over the subordinate. Domination is what class is, she said, and the domination of the WTO is just a form of class domination. It dominates in the interests of a minority, those of the ruling class (see Hardt and Negri 2005, 103ff.).

What is interesting here is that at the centre of everything is a generic sort of domination. Class domination as Marx would understand it – something dependent on capital and wage-labour – merges, for many, into domination more generally (E. Weber 1991[1974], 324). Capitalism and globalization thus become virtually the same thing. To fight against the WTO *is* to fight against capitalism. This generalized understanding of domination is reflected in the inclusive nature of the alterglobalization movement and is part of the reason one can speak of *a* global movement, one into which diverse and independent movements are able to merge. The activists I met included anarchists, libertarians, communists, socialists, unionists, humanists, ecologists, Christians and the range of political opinions represented at events such as Larzac 2003 is always broad. All, including Marxists who see domination primarily in the capital-labour relation, find a place within the movement (see Riles 2001, 182). In the meetings I attended, ideological differences were rarely to the fore. People sought what they had in common and were united in directing their energies in practical ways against concrete incarnations of domination: McDonald's, GM multinationals, the WTO, Israel, the state. Most abhorred domination in all its forms and seldom reduced it to the relation between labour and capital. Whether the 'real' problem was capitalism or neoliberalism was not the issue, nor was deciding just what these terms might refer to or how best to understand them. According to context, the opposing forces of today's world varied. The powerful versus the '*sans*' (those 'without'), multinationals versus the social movement, the prophets of neoliberalism versus the people, the state versus French citizens, the WTO versus global citizens, or the private versus the public were some of the oppositional pairs activists invoked. Most importantly, the focus was always on action.

This diversity and inclusiveness, the refusal to focus on matters of theory or ideology, and the emphasis on commonality and action are characteristic of other contemporary political movements (see Hardt and Negri 2005). Graeber, in his study of anarchism and direct action in the United States (n.d.), insists that the direct action movement emerges not from theory but from practice. The point is not to arrive at some sort of correct theoretical understanding of the world, but to act. Anarchists thus spend their time organizing and debating ways to confront illegitimate structures of authority and ruling elites. In practice, it is the police – the 'bureaucrats with guns' who patrol city streets and defend political and economic summits – against whom anarchists act. Rarely do they come into contact with corporate and government leaders but with those who keep order at their behest. The police, in Graeber's account, are 'the exterior face of power', the visible and violent arm of the state. But the police protect all institutionalized forms of authority and rule. Like Larzac activists, it is this American anarchists oppose.

The origin of power

Power, Graeber suggests, is based on violence. This politics of violence, which allows the police to 'define the situation' and to reduce a complex world to one of 'simplicity' and 'stupidity', US anarchists meet with a 'politics of the imagination' based on various forms of subversion: innovative nonviolent confrontation, pleasure, costumes, giant puppets, self-mockery and the proposal of endless alternative frameworks. Power here becomes something negative or destructive, in contrast to the imaginative and creative 'political ontology' of anarchists. The destructive simplicity of violence, however, does not entail that there are not more subtle political mechanisms at work that violence or the threat of violence serve to protect. And Graeber's contrast between two different political ontologies suggests both negative and positive conceptions of power.

Activists in the Larzac-Millau movement often seemed to understand power and domination as the ability to impose one's will. This is precisely what violence, authority structures, electoral politics and the mechanisms of globalization allow. This notion of power as an expression of will is akin to Enlightenment conceptions of power as sovereignty, which I discuss in the introduction. For Hobbes, power resides in the person of the *Soveraigne*, to whose will all are subject, and, for Rousseau, in the general will. For both Hobbes and Rousseau, to exercise or participate in power is to exercise one's will. The stress on will is also evident in twentieth-century theories of power. For Bertrand Russell, power is 'the production of *intended* effects' (my emphasis), and, for Max Weber, it is the capacity 'of a man or number of men to realize their own will even against the resistance of others' (quoted in Lukes 1986, 1–2). Power, in this view, depends on agency, freedom and autonomy (cf. Mageo and Knauft 2002, 3ff.). To have power is to have the capacity to act autonomously. Power resides not in action, but in the potential for action (Lukes 2005, 68ff.; cf. Aron 1986, 256–7). To be subject to power is to have one's will, agency, sovereignty and autonomy denied in some form. It is to be dominated and controlled.

This logic of power in which activists I think share entails a sense in which power is legitimate and positive: the power that is innate to all individuals in the form of their autonomy of will and action. This power, what John Holloway calls 'power-to' (2005), is the origin of power-as-domination. It is this positive power that, by political or economic means, is thought to be alienated, appropriated, accumulated, concentrated, taken from the many and given to the few, and thereby converted into hierarchical power. Hierarchical power creates a lack, a power that is missing (violence, perhaps, does this most absolutely). Activists often refer to the powerless as the '*sans*'. The *sans domicile, sans emploi, sans papiers* are those homeless, unemployed, or alien non-citizens without rights and without power.

But everyone has their power appropriated to some degree in a hierarchical world. In the realm of electoral politics this is seen to be achieved, as I have described above, by means of the vote. The power of ordinary individuals is delegated and amplified by being condensed into political office. In the economic sphere, the free flow of corporate capital is also considered to permit an accumulation of power which permits exploitation, domination, the creation of dependencies and the further acquisition of capital and power.

Hierarchy, in this logic, must therefore be created and recreated by political and economic means. It is considered neither natural nor moral. Activist thinking denaturalizes hierarchical power. Activists refuse the 'idea of natural inequality' (A. Béteille 1983) whereby competition supposedly reveals the natural ordering of individuals. Although autonomy may be the mark of both positive and negative forms of power, hierarchical power is viewed as 'illegitimate', as people often put it, because produced through institutionalized means of domination. The power of the individual self, in contrast, only flourishes when domination is absent and is considered a good and, in some sense, natural form of power.

The social movement also constitutes a form of power, one capable, in activists' eyes, of taking on the power of governments and multinationals. People speak of it, however, as a 'counterpower', indicating their refusal to seek any form of institutionalized power or to deny others' autonomy. The counterpower of the social movement ideally preserves the power and autonomy of individuals. Activists aim to constitute a movement by adding the power of individuals together to yield a collective and legitimate counterpower in which all may participate as they desire. The legitimacy of such a counterpower is based on the addition, rather than the denial, of the power that resides in the self. Legitimacy implies that individuals do not cede their power and autonomy to a greater sovereign.

Chapter 6

Resistance

My fieldwork was constantly punctuated by political actions of various sorts. They ranged from the relatively humble Hour of Silence for Palestine, often consisting of fewer than twenty people, to Larzac 2003 and huge marches in Florence and Paris against the US invasion of Iraq. One of my most enduring memories of demonstrations is the repetition, on banners, in leaflets and in chants, of the word 'resistance'. One chant goes like this:

> To those who want
> to dominate the world,
> the world responds
> RE-SIS-TANCE.

Enthusiastic emphasis is placed on each syllable in 'resistance', as though to underline the power and autonomy of the movement. Resist is what activists perceive themselves to do. To resist is to engage in a particular kind of politics, one whose logic is expressed in a slogan from the 1970s, related to me by Léon, a veteran of the Larzac military camp struggle: 'Don't delegate power, exercise it'.

This chapter is about how the 'political' (*le politique*) is constituted through protest. In a sense, activists are anti-politics (see Holloway 2005, 36–7). This is the premise of what, in another sense, is their political engagement. In contrast to political parties and capitalist corporations, as I have said, the social movement does not seek power. Activists are concerned with what they call 'the social good', while parties are commonly assumed to be concerned with their own good within the narrow domain of 'politics' (*la politique*). Politics and society are here opposed, an opposition which allows activists to speak of the institutionalized 'political left' (*gauche politique*) and the 'social left' (*gauche sociale*), the 'autonomous' left that takes to the streets. The social movement emerges out of 'civil society' and aims to give voice to ordinary people. 'Civil society', a term activists use often (see Bové and Luneau 2004, 226ff.), is the realm in which citizens individually and collectively exercise their power of decision and action.

As a 'counterpower', the social movement is often considered to be a movement of 'control'. If capitalist forms of power operate in today's global world by a tactic of liberalization that allows capital to move freely and to turn everything into commodities, resistance is a matter of preventing this free movement. Resistance comes in many forms and activists often talk of 'levels of struggle'. Power can be fought by organizing both locally and globally, through education or action in the streets, through legal and illegal means, through official and unofficial channels, through both talking to elected representatives and harassing them. But on the streets and in the media the counterpower of the movement is considered to be most visible and effective. Such 'public' spaces offer the movement a stage where it can effectively engage in a politics of resistance and where it can reassert the democratic power of the 'social' sphere.

Solidarity and the collective political force of the movement

Activists self-consciously resist and declare their 'resistance' to the world. There are many ways in which resistance and opposition are clearly articulated. 'We do not accept ... (the privatization of the world, GMOs, US hegemony, neoliberal regimes of domination, the repression of the social movement)' was an oft-repeated cry in speeches at Larzac 2003. An Aarrg poster states simply: 'Refuse the unacceptable'. And a poster calling for people to protest José's incarceration proclaims that 'to resist is to cultivate freedom'. Other chants and slogans explicitly oppose the movement and the forces of power, us and them. 'Everything is *ours*; nothing is *theirs*; everything they have, they stole ...' was sung, with variations, at protests against the G8, the WTO and the Iraq war. 'Our lives, our rights, are worth more than your profits', stated a poster at a demonstration against repression. Through such slogans, the political agency of the movement is publicly asserted. The movement is affirmed as a collective force of resistance to power.

This collective force is something constantly referred to in the discourse on numbers, as I discuss in Chapter 3, and it is based, in part, on what activists call 'solidarity'. Solidarity – a term which appears in the name of the principal activist association in Millau, Construire un Monde *Solidaire* – is an important part of the way activists imagine themselves and their movement, as it was for earlier generations of communists, socialists, unionists and others. Following the Larzac struggle, the activists of the plateau decided on the need for a 'return of solidarity', as they put it, a return of the help and support they had received from outsiders during the struggle. They established the Fondation Larzac, later to become Larzac Solidarités, in order to support struggles elsewhere. The Larzac itself is considered a place where relations of solidarity, of mutual support, are strong. The notion of support is integral to that of solidarity. Activists demonstrate solidarity and support through protest. Those who participated in the Hour of Silence for Palestine described it as an expression of solidarity with the Palestinians. Others viewed the daily 'tam tam' outside the prison where José was incarcerated as an exercise in solidarity. For twenty minutes or more, anything from a handful to a thousand activists would bang repeatedly on the steel roadside barrier with stones, creating a deafening blare that could be heard inside the prison.

Acting in solidarity with others is often considered the political act of a 'citizen'. Solidarity is 'an aspect of citizenship' ('*la solidarité fait partie de la citoyenneté*'), as put by Jean-Claude Amara, leader of the Paris-based association Droits Devant (Rights First), at a meeting in preparation for Larzac 2003. Somewhat off topic, we had been discussing the case of three activists facing prosecution for 'hindering the circulation of an aeroplane'. Just before take-off on a flight to Mali, they had objected to the forced repatriation of illegal immigrants, *sans papiers*, on the plane, their intervention leading to a flight delay of thirteen hours. The activists involved considered themselves to be acting in solidarity with those subject to the government's 'politics of expulsion' by force. Their legal defence, said Patrick, one of the accused, would be 'focused on citizenship'. In legitimately responding to a situation of violence, they had intervened as citizens. One woman later said that they had committed 'offences of solidarity', 'offences of citizenship'. They had, in other words, exercised their 'right to express themselves' in relation to a perceived injustice. Such, in her view, was the political role of the active citizen.

The social movement is often called a 'citizens' movement' (*mouvement citoyen*). It is seen as a movement of citizens linked by bonds of solidarity and who extend that solidarity to others in need. The notion of citizenship implies membership of a common society, although the terms 'society' and 'citizen' need not refer to the nation state, nor does citizenship need to be understood in terms of legal rights. Alterglobalization activists often speak of global society and global citizenship (*citoyenneté mondiale*) in the face of 'common challenges' that surpass the nation state. At an activist conference on leadership and citizenship I attended, the construction of a 'global citizenship' – based on what one man called a 'consciousness of a spontaneous human affinity' – was offered as one way of combating a shared regime of domination. Participants stressed the need to extend notions of citizenship and citizens' rights beyond the nation state because all human beings were confronted with the same global political order. They pointed towards what Evelina Dagnino, writing of social movements in Latin America, calls the struggle 'to secure a citizenship "from below"', the struggle of the excluded for a 'new citizenship' focused on 'the right to have rights' (1998, 50–51). For those present at the conference, the idea of a global citizenship was a step towards the creation of global solidarities in the struggle against globalization.

Solidarity is here 'imaginary' in a sense akin to Benedict Anderson's (1983). It exists as a political relation between people who have never met, by virtue of what is considered a common humanity and a common subjection to a neoliberal global regime (cf. Holmes 2000, 94ff.). As such, solidarity differs somewhat both from that which marked socialist movements in the past and from that which Durkheim argued was central to the organization of modern society (Stjernø 2004). European socialist and labour movements of the nineteenth and much of the twentieth centuries emerged out of a common experience and common culture. Local communities and workers' associations tended to be integral to their formation (Eley 2002, 25). They were based in a solidarity of the working class, which, even to the intellectual vanguard, was crucial. Class thus defined solidarity in a way that today it does not. For alterglobalization activists, solidarity has none of its earlier working class limitations. Alterglobalization movements incorporate solidarities between the global South and the global North, and between landless peasants and Western elites. The anarchists that Graeber discusses are as likely to be privileged rich kids as working class, indeed he characterizes the movement as a meeting place of the downwardly and upwardly mobile, the alienated and the oppressed (n.d.). Larzac activists include the sons and daughters of generals, teachers, preachers, university researchers, railway workers, farmers, sailors and others fighting for the rights of Palestinians, public servants and Third-World peasants. Class is not quite the point and solidarity cannot be conceived in such terms. Solidarity is, however, extended to anyone based on their humanity and subjection to domination.

The solidarities of old class-based movements were overseen, moreover, by a party or union elite. They were bound up with social hierarchies. Hierarchy was also a feature of Durkheim's thinking on solidarity. Durkheim's notion of organic solidarity was very influential on political life in France in the twentieth century. Donzelot claims that it underlies the idea of the public service and of state intervention in social life (1991, 172–3). For Durkheim, organic solidarity refers to the interdependence that is characteristic of the division of labour. While Durkheim associates organic solidarity with the rise of individuality and affirms that each part of society has its own autonomy within the social whole (1933, 131, 172), solidarity, in his conception, must be understood within the context of social hierarchy. It is a functional solidarity that enables society to produce and reproduce itself. The stress on individual difference is a consequence of being differently situated within the hierarchy. Durkheim, himself, drew on late nineteenth-century ideas of society as a *sui generis* reality prior to and greater than the sum of its individual members. In the doctrine of solidarism, society had prior rights over individuals who, following a notion of social debt, had pre-existing obligations (Rabinow 1989, 185). For Larzac-Millau activists, however, solidarity is voluntary and egalitarian. It is enacted willingly out of a concern for others and points to what is shared in common. In this, it resembles Durkheim's mechanical solidarity, one which 'comes from likenesses' (1933, 130). The activist notion of solidarity is based on ideas of symmetry in social relationships, of a sort of partnership between equals whose differences are ignored or irrelevant. As Žižek says of Solidarnosc in Poland, this form of solidarity designates 'the "simple" and "fundamental" unity of human beings which should link them beyond all political differences' (1999, 178).

Relations of solidarity, as activists understand them, must be actively created and recreated. They are never simply given. Unlike relations of kinship, relations of production or hierarchical social relations, relations of solidarity do not pre-exist their cultivation on the part of citizens or activists. In this sense, solidarity partakes of the logic of friendship[1] – an ideally egalitarian relationship between individuals or human beings – in contrast to the idiom of kinship on which the French Revolutionary notion of fraternity draws (see Ozouf 1998, 87–90, 109–14; E. Weber 1991[1974], 311). Solidarity here points to a particular notion of the social, one which designates the sphere that emerges from autonomous individuals acting in concert. The model for this form of the social is an idea of local, everyday, face-to-face interaction between individuals participating voluntarily in associations, collectives, committees or communities. Activists aim to build such a 'solidary world' based on respect for the needs and rights of all and on a coherence between the social good and the individual good.

When enacted via the organizational strategies I discuss in Chapter 3, however, solidarity is also what allows the movement to hold together as a collective force capable of resisting power. Solidarity practices link individuals together within an

---

1 See Polletta (2002, 149ff.) on how friendship provides an organizational model for political activism.

association, they link associations together into a movement and movements together into one 'social movement' within civil society. The counterpower of the movement is brought to life when activists collectively take to the streets. It is the street where solidarity and activists' demands for a solidary world are expressed through protest. The street is viewed as the sphere in which all participate equally in the political life of society. It is a public sphere for collective political action, for the 'plurality' which, in the words of Arendt, is '*the* condition ... of all political life' (1959, 10).

The street

The street emerges as a site of political struggle because electoral politics is perceived to deny what activists consider their right to participate in the political life of society. If politics as suffrage is the formal means by which people are silenced, activist politics seeks to give voice to ordinary citizens, as Christine explains:

> Why do people take to the streets [to protest]? Because the system does not respect the voice of the street (*la parole de la rue*). Once someone gets into power there is no longer any means today for [ordinary people] to make themselves heard.

The street and activist associations become the only domains in which political participation can be ensured. This engagement in the social movement is considered 'grassroots' or 'bottom-up' politics: *la politique de la base*.

This history of social movements and mass demonstrations in the street coincides roughly with the emergence of capitalism and the nation state (Tilly 1986). The French Revolution provides street-based politics today with its greatest myth of origin and May '68 with its most recent. May '68, Ross suggests, saw a 'dislocation in the very idea of politics' as it was moved out of 'its proper place' in the party-political realm and, at least in part, into the street (2002, 25). The 'street' today provides alterglobalization activists with a political stage on which to give visible public expression to their concerns. It is where they insist on conducting a politics of protest against the politics of elected representatives and capitalist elites. By shifting politics to the street, activists constitute a sphere for 'autonomous' political action, one untainted by the realm of party politics and threatened only by the repressive power of the state. The street is part of the social or civic sphere for resistance to the tyranny of power and symbolizes a refusal to be silenced. Activists reject completely the idea that the political sphere can be enclosed within the walls of parliament. Politics, they believe, is a public concern and must be carried out in public space. The voice of the street must be heard.

The street, then, is a metaphor designating both the 'public' site of struggle and those who engage in struggle: the public, the people, civil society, citizens. The term refers to the public spaces, normally of towns and cities, to which all citizens have free access and upon which acts of political resistance unfold. The street is the site of demonstrations in public, as opposed to private, space.[2] The epitome of

---

2 See Habermas (1989, 1ff.), Weintraub (1997) and Sennett (2002, 16) on the varied historically informed meanings of 'public' and 'private'.

public protest is the march. Marches are generally organized and publicized around a particular cause. One publicity leaflet called for participation in a 'big international march in Marseilles' for 'the protection of the Palestinian people, against the occupation, colonization and apartheid in Palestine'. Others state simply such things as 'No to the war in Iraq' or 'Let's free José Bové. Stop the repression of the social movement ... 2pm Demonstration in Millau'. For many participants, the purpose of marches is quite straightforward. Marches are an expression of discontent at the actions of political or economic elites, aimed both at those elites and at the general and non-participating public. Although they may be undertaken in solidarity with the victims of power, marches, like other forms of protest, occur within a framework of opposition and are frequently conceived to be 'against' something: war, repression, the WTO, the occupation of Palestine, GMOs.

The social movement, the voice of the street, is most concretely embodied in the march. During my fieldwork, I participated in marches in Marseilles and Florence, a couple in Geneva, and many in Millau and Paris. Those in Millau sometimes involved barely a hundred people while the anti-Iraq war march in Florence was reputedly graced by a million concerned citizens. Participation was always diverse. In Florence there were all sorts of individuals, movements, unions, organizations and parties present – communists, socialists, anarchists, activists, ordinary people, factory workers, civil servants, farmers, teachers, Christians, alterglobalists, liberals, libertarians, punks, environmentalists, revolutionaries, pacifists, young and old alike. As on other large marches, the members of each organization marched together, dividing the procession into blocks of colour, each block clearly identifiable by its own flags and banners, chants and songs. Some were accompanied by cars or trucks adorned with loudspeakers from which music blared or from which a voice initiated a new chant, taken up immediately by those in earshot. Each group had its own interpretation of the war to which all were, however, opposed. Representatives of parties, unions and associations handed out leaflets explaining their position on things. Wandering through the crowd and sometimes perched on top of bus stops and walls were TV crews, photographers and journalists. There were pram wielding parents, musicians with gleaming instruments, street theatre troupes with props, people draped in peace flags, some in eccentric costumes, but most in their everyday attire. On the sides of the river of people that moved down the street were many onlookers, often clapping and obviously supportive of the march. From the windows of some apartments people had suspended banners with anti-war slogans. You could easily feel that everyone was against the war. Although at some marches there are hecklers or counter-demonstrations by those opposed to the marchers' cause, in Florence the war's supporters were invisible.

For those who participate in it, the march generates a concrete solidarity (Kertzer 1988, 57ff.). Although marshals ensure order amongst the marchers and union leaders may direct their own rank and file, the march is a liminal time of what Victor Turner calls 'communitas' where equality and humanness are stressed, not social position and hierarchy (1969, 96ff.). The march produces commonality (Hardt and Negri 2005, xiii, 100). Difference remains clearly evident, but everyone within the crowd of marchers is, in some sense, equal, their differences of status and opinion cast aside, 'discharged', in Elias Canetti's terms (2000, 17). People feel united, solidary.

It is the public act of marching together for a common cause or against a common foe that creates this equality and solidarity.

Marches take over public space. The march in Florence was due to start at 3pm but it actually began hours before. Many completed the three hour route before others began. At midday, the four lane street the march was to follow was overflowing. As far as the eye could see, people were standing, waiting for those in front to move. In place of cars, throngs of people filled the streets, taking them over completely, endowing them with a colour and life they normally lacked. The march involved an occupation of public space, one that had been agreed in advance with public authorities. Roads had been closed and shops boarded up. The city stopped functioning as it normally did because of the political display activists brought to the streets. This sort of cessation of activity does not always have official approval. In Millau, gatherings outside the courthouse or prefecture often spilled into the road, disrupting traffic. Authorized marches, which for the police should have entailed constant movement, sometimes came to a halt as the marchers demonstrated the perceived legitimacy of the occupation of public space, and of the public's participation in politics, by sitting in the middle of the street.

At other times, a specific public space becomes the target of occupation. On another march I joined against the G8, we left our tent village in Annemasse at 4am and set out for Geneva to try to occupy one of the bridges in the central city as part of a larger coordinated effort. We first had to cross the border into Switzerland. Many people thought the police would try to stop us, and as we approached the border, everyone linked arms and put scarves round their faces in case the police used tear gas to make us disperse. But there were no police at the border. Near the river in Geneva, however, police were everywhere, standing in tight lines with riot shields and batons. Although they blocked the entrance to certain streets, our access to the bridge was easy. The police stood back and watched and we joined others and sat in the road. A public announcement insisted that all bridges were to be blocked as a way of 'symbolically saying that it's we who decide on what we are going to do', we who determine the future of the world, not the G8 elites.

The street signifies the public and common good in opposition to the private. The street can be metaphorically extended into what is viewed as private or non-public space. Occupations of places considered by activists to symbolize power – those of the state, such as the prefecture, or of capital, such as Nestlé's head office – take the public and the street into spaces from which the public is normally excluded. During José's incarceration, there had been elaborate plans (never implemented) to occupy the sub-prefecture in Millau in protest against state repression of the social movement and the violation of a unionist's rights to raise questions of public interest for political debate. The attempt to occupy Nestlé was partly aimed at demonstrating that the company had no right to dump milk products on countries of the Third World and no mandate to genetically modify its products. The goal was to expose the ostensibly private and self-interested as matters of utmost public concern and to ensure that the political ramifications of the private were made public.

Taking protest into the domain of power is considered a necessary and legitimate political act, but it is also one that may mean infringing the law. Activists distinguish the 'legal' from the 'legitimate'. The destruction of GM crops and the dismantling of a McDonald's may be illegal and yet retain their quality as legitimate political actions. Their legitimacy is seen to reside, partly, in the assumed right of all citizens to engage in politics, to participate in public discussion and decision-making concerning the social good. Activists consider illegitimate the government's decision to allow GM field trials precisely because it was taken without sufficient public debate, in flagrant opposition of the will of the people (70 percent of whom are said to oppose GM food), and for the private and not common good. Legitimate but illegal actions must always be conducted with the public interest and the common good in mind. They are always considered to go beyond personal, private or 'corporatist' concerns and are acted out in the interests of society as a whole. Corporatism (see Sainsaulieu 1998, 123) is considered to involve a furthering of 'private' interests – the interests of a few – over the general interest. I sometimes heard criticism of the Confédération Paysanne for its corporatism, given that it is a union and bound to defend the interests of its members. But the discourse of spokespeople such as Bové very much casts the Conf as defending the public interest. One activist insisted to me that the Conf fought for the interests of the 'majority' and that its discourse was 'not at all corporatist'. It fights against subsidies that materially benefit its members, he said, because they 'strangle' farmers in the countries of the South. Bové's discourse was a 'global' one which 'posed true questions of society'. The public and private interest are thus perceived to coincide in the Conf's discourse. Making them do so is part of its political strategy, as is making publicly expressed ideals cohere with the practice of political action. When the Conf organizes a GM crop neutralization, it does so in the name of the general public interest. The interests of its members are subsumed within this general interest as a condition of its 'political' legitimacy (see Gledhill 2003, 211; Berglund 1998, 81).[3]

The pairing of legitimacy and illegality thus belongs to the public, political sphere. Illegal actions are only considered truly political and legitimate because they are also public (see Weintraub 1997, 2). Although they may involve an invasion and destruction of private property, all acts of civil disobedience are, in a sense, carried out in public space. They aim to bring the illegitimacy of the private to public attention, to create public debate, to reveal in public a private agenda. Through acts of civil disobedience, the actions of the powerful are laid open to public scrutiny as though they occurred in the street. 'Political' actions, Larzac-Millau activists believe, must have a public face, they must take on the quality of the street – open, accessible, visible, direct. Thus the publicness of a GM crop destruction is considered a condition of its performance, just as it is a condition of a march that it occurs in the streets. Although they risk trial and eventual imprisonment, activists participate openly, unveiled, in the light of day, in the public eye, in the media spotlight. As a metaphor, the street connotes visibility and responsibility.

CUMS activists were often disparaging of people who participate in mass demonstrations with their faces concealed in order to avoid the legal consequences

---

3 Cf. Pagis (2005, 6–7) who identifies opposing notions of legitimacy amongst Conf anti-GM activists in different parts of France: one based, as for those I studied, on ideas of citizenship, participation and the common good; and a legitimacy conferred by being the party directly affected by GM crops.

of illegal action. Of masked protesters who, on a march in Geneva against the WTO, were tearing down advertising hoardings and spray-painting anticapitalist slogans on buildings, Christine asked, somewhat mystified, 'why don't they do it unmasked, show who they are?' While José was in prison, there were heated discussions about the need to continue the work for which he had been incarcerated and to neutralize GM crops. 'Who is willing to participate, openly, in broad daylight, and with face uncovered?', Jean-Emile asked repeatedly at one meeting. Finally, most raised a hand, though some later admitted to me that the threat of prosecution was a worry. Following GM crop neutralizations, large numbers of participants often voluntarily submit their names to the police inviting prosecution (see Gesson 2005). 'The logic', Bové writes, 'is clear: ridicule the rules of the judicial system in order to stigmatize the absence of democratic debate on GMOs' (Bové and Luneau 2004, 14). To activists' dismay, legal proceedings are only ever conducted against a small number people who the authorities consider leaders, a couple of whom have faced periods of imprisonment. But acting openly in such ways is part of assuming responsibility for one's actions, and prison is the ultimate expression of this. Acting openly is considered the mark of the 'political' act of engaging with the idea of the public good, as opposed to the 'criminal' act of harming private property.

Acting openly, politically and assuming responsibility for your actions are also related to the notion of coherence. An 'activist', as I have argued in Chapter 4, must act in accordance with their privately held convictions, ideals and vision of the way the world is and ought to be. Not to do so is to refuse the political and moral responsibility of coherence. It is to refuse the political and public consequences of one's otherwise private existence in the world and to close one's eyes to the public and social nature of one's being. To act openly and coherently, however, is to bring the private into the public domain.[4] This is the mark of all legitimate political action. One must show on the outside what one believes on the inside, give public expression to private belief, act in concert with other individuals, take the private into the street, often with the aim of publicly exposing illegitimate private agendas.

The street, as the space where the private is made public or where the private and public meet, is thus the space in which legality and legitimacy confront one another, where power meets counterpower. Through acts of protest, activists make the street a thoroughly political public space. But its meaning is contested. Like the political life of the university in Kerala discussed by Ritty Lukose, politics involves a struggle over the meaning of space. Student leaders in Kerala politicize the college, Lukose writes, by turning it into an 'empty space where no formal learning happens' as 'part of a mobilization against the privatization of higher education and the liberalization of the Indian economy' (2005, 515). This 'politics of emptiness', however, is resisted by 'antipolitical' 'student-citizens' in their attempts to build a garden as a 'place of youth', a public space of 'civic virtue' where they can freely congregate. But the garden is always destroyed by politicized students, only to be rebuilt the following year as part of an ongoing struggle (517). 'The struggle about what constitutes politics', Lukose concludes, 'happens through a struggle over literal spaces' (523). Something similar can be said of the politics of the street in France. The repressive

---

4 Cf. Sennett's discussion of the modern 'confusion' of private and public (2002).

tactics of the state are aimed at denying the street the political quality with which activists attempt to invest it. Police arrests, the control they wield, and their legal right to act against 'trouble-makers' serve to affirm the street as the sphere of law and order. As such, it becomes a sphere of 'strangers' whose paths never quite touch as they go about their private lives (Sennett 2002, 47ff.). The street, in the dominant vision of things, should be the domain of legal but not political activity, a space to pass through rather than a space for political gatherings (Ross 2002, 22–3). The state's concern is to impart the message that, as ironically cited in a pamphlet during the political upheaval of 1968, 'Each citizen must learn that the street no longer belongs to him, but to power alone, which wishes to impose muteness, produce asphyxia'.[5]

The case should not be overstated. Street demonstrations are permitted by public authorities. The New York police, in contrast, 'never give up the streets', Graeber says (n.d.). In New York, the street truly belongs to power alone and police meet activists with violence and 'systematic brutality'. Beatings and the use of tear gas at demonstrations and the infliction of pain and humiliation in detention are the norm. In France, such repression is more the exception than the rule. The state reserves the right to maintain order by means of force but local administrations, like those in most of Europe and America, also allow the social movement the right of protest in the street. Political leaders refuse, however, any obligation to listen and any notion that politics ought to be oriented around the publicly expressed demands of the social movement. Prime Minister Raffarin's claim that 'it's not the street that governs' is an affirmation of the right of government to ignore 'the voice of the street'. Politics is thereby cast as a matter of delegation and representation, not open participation. But activists resist the attempts of political elites to control the street and to define the political. They affirm the street – as a metaphor for the public – as the sphere of politics par excellence, as *the* domain of political struggle.

Showing, seeing, participating

The street is a space that is open to everyone. This is what makes it somehow the epitome of 'public' space. As a political domain, the street is the site where activists 'demonstrate' in both the political and technical senses discussed by Andrew Barry. Since the revolutions of 1848, the terms 'demonstrator' and 'demonstration' came to be associated with political protest and 'the emergence of the masses as a political subject' (Barry 1999, 76). But in the middle ages, the demonstrator in an anatomy lecture was the person who pointed out various features of the body to the audience. 'The truth of the lecturer's knowledge was established through observing a demonstration' (1999, 77). Activists both protest, on the one hand, and make manifest a political truth that can be witnessed by the public, on the other.[6] To demonstrate is to make public. Indeed, the term 'public', in one of the historical senses mentioned by Sennett, referred to that which is 'manifest and open to general observation' or

---

5 Comité d'action Étudiants-Écrivains, 'La rue', tract dated July 17, 1968, quoted in Ross (2002, 64).

6 MacIntyre (1984, 71) writes that 'to protest was once to bear witness *to* something'.

'open to the scrutiny of anyone' (2002, 16). When activists demonstrate, they make manifest and attempt to open to scrutiny political issues they consider to be of public concern. The French term for demonstrate is *manifester*. Like its English counterpart, it means to show.

One of the things activists intend to display is the numerical strength of the movement. This was one aim of Larzac 2003 and the march in Florence. They were demonstrations of the movement as a collective political force. But activists also aim to demonstrate a truth, to communicate a political message, to put power and injustice on display (see Clarke 2003, 122). Carrying a message to a wider public is perhaps the most important aspect of political activity because only by so doing can public opinion be influenced, participation encouraged, support for the movement cultivated and its strength increased. In this, the media are key (see Castells 1997, 106). The media bring the street and the political activity that occurs there to the private domestic sphere. Through their use of the media, activists aim to reach out to strangers, to constitute an activist 'counter-public' out of the broader public mass (Warner 2002).

The media provide both a direct and indirect vehicle for diffusing information to the public. Meetings often involve discussion of who will write a small opinion piece – on the situation in Palestine, for example – for the local newspaper in the hope that it will be published. Activists can in this way speak directly to the public and not via an intermediary. In general, however, activists depend on journalists to pass on their arguments to the public via the mainstream press and consider them an ally in the fight against neoliberal globalization. In order to ensure that the activist viewpoint is presented in a fair light, journalists' sympathies are cultivated. Educating the public thus first depends on educating journalists. 'We know how to use the media on the Larzac', Léon told me with a dry smile. You speak with journalists, explain, make them understand your point of view, he said. Then they explain in their articles what you have explained to them.[7] Protest thus involves developing personal relationships and the practice of a sort of 'pedagogy' with journalists. Indeed, nonviolent protest actions are described by some as 'pedagogical actions'.

Ensuring a media presence at political actions is an essential principle of activist politics. To small protests, journalists are pretty much always invited in advance, although sometimes at the last moment to avoid leaks to the authorities. Some, of course, are activists themselves, their professional lives wedded to the cause of the social movement. One photographer, Georges Bartoli, often accompanies José to places such as Nestlé, Palestine and Porto Alegre. His photographs grace the pages of many alterglobalist publications, offering visual evidence of police repression, Palestinian oppression, the resistance of the social movement or the everyday lives of activists. On our way to Switzerland to occupy Nestlé we picked Georges up so he could record the events. When José and six others were finally allowed into the building for discussions with management, Georges tried to follow but was unceremoniously dumped on his backside and shoved, through shards of glass,

---

7 The process depends on the existence in France of a relatively 'free press'. In some parts of the world, journalists who oppose the ruling regime face the possibility of being arrested or even murdered.

back out the door. Afterwards, Georges sat outside uploading photos from his digital camera into his laptop in order to email them off to a newspaper. While the seven were inside, a number of activists sprayed the windows of the building with slogans, and Christine called out to Georges to come photograph it. Media coverage and documenting our actions were clearly in the back of her mind throughout the protest.

Occasionally, activists forget to organize some sort of media presence, leading to expressions of exasperation. At one anti-GM action at a Millau supermarket, involving the handing out of leaflets and a few banners, the media were conspicuous by their absence and afterwards people kept grumbling that no one had phoned the press and wondering whose responsibility it had been to do so. This neglect, however, tends to be exceptional, and, in general, the media are well catered for. For major political events, they are very well catered for. In preparation for Larzac 2003, the Communication Committee was established to ensure media involvement in the gathering, both that of the mainstream and the activist press. It sent out press releases and established a web page with information specifically for the media, including a downloadable fourteen page *dossier de presse* containing a programme of events and outlining the Larzac's history of struggle, the gatherings' purpose, the major objections to the WTO, and how this particular historical moment – marked by ongoing protests over the future of the public service and just before the WTO was to meet in Cancun – provided an opportunity to bring about change. The committee also arranged for a quite elaborate temporary infrastructure to be set up in the middle of what had, a few days earlier, been a dry and dusty paddock. There was a place for press conferences with activist leaders, a radio station transmitting from the site, an Indymedia space, ten Internet connections, computers, computer technicians to ensure everything kept functioning, and a marquee where journalists could sit and relax in the shade.

Gaining media coverage often appears to be the principal aim of political actions. Many actions are planned in order to have maximum media impact and the measure of their success is often considered the degree to which they make the news and the extent to which the coverage is deemed 'correct', a fair presentation of the 'activist' point of view. Larzac 2003 represents merely the most coordinated and extravagant effort in this regard. Activists aimed to make the gathering newsworthy by organizing an event of unprecedented scale. But there are other means of gaining media attention. Numbers are not always considered necessary. Even small actions are designed to 'target' the media and to be, by their very nature, 'mediatizable'. Frequently they are described as *actions médiatiques*. The dismantling of the Millau McDonald's in 1999 retains pride of place in the activist imagination as the most significant of all recent protest actions, although the number of participants amounted to only a few hundred.

At weekly meetings in the summer of 2003 to organize resistance to state repression of the social movement and José's incarceration, participants often said that even twenty or thirty people could have a huge media impact, given the right conditions. One of these conditions is that actions must have what activists, like certain scholars, call a 'spectacular' element (Castells 1997, 106). At 5.30 in the morning of 14 July, a bus-load of Larzac-Millau activists set out for Paris to make a self-consciously spectacular call for José's liberation. At about 1.30pm we were met by a Parisian activist outside the Château de Vincennes. She outlined the plans for the day and at 2.05 everyone took the metro in the direction of the Louvre. Our intention was to launch a surprise invasion through the Louvre's exit, occupy the café located on the balcony overlooking the central courtyard with its glass pyramid, erect banners, shout 'free Bové' and generally attract as much attention as possible. At Reuilly-Diderot metro station we were joined by more activists from Droits Devant and by a television camerawoman, before continuing on to the Louvre stop. There were fewer than a hundred of us. Once off the train, someone called for ten 'pushers' to lead the way. The big guys went forward and packed in tightly behind Jean-Claude who headed off immediately towards the museum's exit. The pace was really fast – you almost had to run to keep up – and Suzanne, who had a walking stick, and some of the older activists were quickly left behind. The role of the pushers was to clear a path, first through the crowd of tourists and general public, then through any security guards who might block our entry. Some resistance was anticipated but there was almost none. Two employees were swept aside and everyone, even the stragglers, entered with ease.

Most managed to make their way past marble statues up three flights of stairs to the balcony café overlooking the courtyard, but ten of the slower ones were trapped on a lower floor as the galleries were quickly closed off by security. Inside, people donned political tee-shirts of some sort (against repression or GM crops or the WTO – anything you have in your wardrobe tends to be fine for such an occasion) and a couple put on mock prisoners uniforms, one draping himself in chains. Stickers – bearing slogans such as 'Free José', 'Not a single unionist in prison' and 'No to the repression of the social movement' – were passed around on the balcony and stuck liberally on people, café tables and whatever was at hand. Many protesters wore symbolic gags – torn strips of white sheet – with '*liberté*' written on in red marker pen. '*Libérez José*' was chanted rhythmically, while the same slogan adorned the canvas banner I helped string up between two statues on the wall of the balcony. Leaflets in both French and English, entitled 'Union leader in prison = democracy in danger', were then thrown down into the court below and handed out to the bemused clientèle of the café. Jean-Claude made some sort of speech, though it was very hard to hear in all the curfuffle, and someone put on a CD before turning it off again because the music was not loud enough to hear either. Security guards arrived pretty quickly and tried to keep people off the wall. Otherwise they did little and seemed mildly amused. The waiter claimed we didn't bother him a bit. 'All in a good cause', he said. We had planned to stay on the balcony for an hour but we left after just half that, politely saying goodbye to café staff, customers and security, because no one below really seemed to be able to see or hear very much.

It wasn't the end, however. We made our way outside and assembled in front of the glass pyramid where scores of tourists were queuing to gain entrance to the Louvre. We displayed banners and launched into another round of chants: 'Enough repression, let José go home', 'Danger GMOs, Free Bové'. By this time, at least three camera crews, plus press photographers and journalists had joined the camerawoman who had been with us throughout. The riot police also turned up as expected and formed their habitual lines, but they did no more than look on. People said that the whole thing about an action in a public space like this was that, surrounded by tourists and watched by journalists, the authorities were limited in what they could do to stop it. Anything more that politely requesting that we leave would make for very bad publicity. A couple of people handed out leaflets to onlookers, and others laid out one of the banners in front of the police. After an hour or so the riot police left, possibly with more urgent demonstrations to contend with elsewhere in the city (casual workers in the entertainment industry – *les intermittants du spectacle* – had been protesting angrily all over France throughout the summer). Shortly afterwards, two guys who had been hiding from the gaze of the still-present security guards, suddenly emerged in climbing gear and attempted to scale the glass pyramid with the aid of ropes and suction cups in order to unfurl a banner – '*Libérons Bové*' (Let's free Bové) – from the apex. The climb and unfurling were supposed to provide the day with its most spectacular and memorable moment. The climbers, however, found the glass hot and slippery and didn't manage to get very high. People tried to prevent them sliding back down by standing on each other's shoulders and helping to stick the banner in place with tape.

While technically the attempt was a failure, the whole affair was quite amusing and certainly provided a talking point and a few good images. Many were therefore pleased with the day. The media had been there to witness the incongruous spectacle of a hundred odd protesters chanting, some gagged, a couple dressed as prisoners, two climbing a piece of industrial glass, and all mixed in with tourists, art works, security guards and riot police in a well-known public location on France's national day. With luck, Georges said, the events would result in good coverage, otherwise we would have wasted our time and money (the bus for the 8 hour drive from Millau cost €2,200, though expenses were subsidized by CUMS). But while no one can determine the editorial policy of national television networks and newspapers, activists seldom leave it to luck. They ensure some sort of media presence, they choose their time and place carefully (July 14 and national institutions like the Louvre or Versailles – the venue for a similar protest the year before – always provide occasion for protest), and they ensure that the spectacle is sufficiently eccentric to attract attention.

This spectacular form of politics is inspired by Greenpeace, one man told me, although similarly spectacular actions, such as the 1972 grazing of sheep under the Eiffel tower, formed part of the repertoire of protest during the Larzac struggle, before Greenpeace was established in Europe.[8] In attracting media attention, it is the form of such actions that counts, the way they unfold, the physical events they embody. Getting a political message across depends on first securing access to the media, and this is ensured by the use of spectacle (cf. Clarke 2003, 134; Levidow 2000, 335). Daring, unusual, attention grabbing actions are designed to be attractive to the media in spite of their political content.

A second and related condition of the effectiveness of *actions médiatiques* is that they be what activists describe as 'symbolic' (see Bourdieu 2003, 40). The symbolic

---

8 Greenpeace was founded in 1971 when activists in a boat by the same name undertook 'non-violent direct action against US nuclear weapons testing on Amchitka Island, Alaska' (Greenpeace n.d.). Greenpeace's first European offices, including one in Paris, opened in 1977.

dimension is the counterpart of the spectacular; in the symbols the message is seen to reside. In anthropology, common wisdom has it that symbols are what Victor Turner called multivocal (1967, 50). They admit of numerous and often opposed interpretations and meanings. This ambiguity can be used strategically for political ends, as Jane Cowan makes clear in her study of the struggle of Macedonian minority rights activists for some sort of autonomy (2003). As a way of appealing to diverse audiences – neighbours, governments, rights groups, international and local media – Macedonian activists adopted the tactic of strategically using ambiguity in their symbolic action. 'They selected symbols [Albanian flags, Cyrillic signs] which could be read as "merely cultural" and non-political, on the one hand, and on the other as "national" and aggressively political, indeed, as signalling ... a challenge to state legitimacy' (2003, 143).

I do not want to argue against the multivocality of symbols, but it is their solidity rather than their ambiguity that is useful to alterglobalization activists. Ideally, for activists, 'symbols' – and this is a political category which they commonly invoke – should not be overly multivocal for that would undermine their suitability as political symbols. Activists at least attempt to subvert any ambiguity by making the meaning and the message explicit, thereby educating the public about the significance and 'symbolic' nature of their action. The gags worn at the Louvre action and other protests during José's imprisonment were thus said 'to symbolize state repression and the manner in which the justice system attempts to silence unionists'. 'Unionists', in one person's words, 'no longer have the right to speak in this country'. Protests against repression also often consciously target the 'symbols of the state': *gendarmeries*, court-houses, prefectures, prisons. These become the focus of protest because of the power they are imagined to symbolize. Spectacular actions thus tend to be limited to such appropriate symbolic targets. While the new viaduct being built near Millau, the highest in the world and the pride of city officials, offered great potential for something spectacular, the fact that it was not considered clearly symbolic of the state meant that many activists were reluctant to use it to protest state repression and José's incarceration. When, in a meeting, one man suggested targeting the viaduct, another objected that the public would not understand, while someone else asked what the connection was between José and a big bridge. Protest actions must always be transparent to the wider public because influencing the public and incorporating the public into the movement is their aim.

The 'prison' often appears in protests in some form as a metaphor for an inverse social order. On one occasion we attempted, unsuccessfully, to appropriate a manager's desk from a company engaged in GM research in order to take it to the nearby prison in Rodez, capital of Aveyron. The protest, described as a 'symbolic action' by one of the Conf organizers, was explicitly designed to demonstrate that the current order, in which José was incarcerated for defending the public good, was the inverse of a just one, in which those who further their own private interests to the detriment of the collectivity would have their freedoms restricted. 'GMOs in prison, not unionists' was the order of the day, announced before we began our march to the company's buildings. The action was intended as a symbolic 'parody, an inversion and a subversion of "ordinary" perspectives' (Butler 1996, 341). Elsewhere, the prison plays a similar symbolic role. One slogan affirms that Jacques Chirac – widely suspected of political corruption but, as president, exempt from prosecution – should trade places with José: 'Chirac in prison, José at home'. On the big march through Millau during José's incarceration, a symbolic prison, built on the back of a trailer, enclosed a can of coke, a GM corn cob and an effigy of Chirac.

The McDonald's dismantling remains the epitome of the symbolic action. It was something 'everyone understood', in Bové's words, '[because] the symbolism was so strong' (2001, 93). Everyone understood the *affaire McDo*, however, because Bové explained it – most thoroughly in his best-selling book *Le monde n'est pas une marchandise*, which begins with a chapter on McDonald's and a section entitled *McDo, un symbole*. Bové emphasizes that the dismantling was not a populist exercise in nationalism or anti-Americanism, although for some it symbolizes both, but one directed against a productivist economic system. McDonald's is a 'symbol of industrial food and agriculture' and of 'economic imperialism' (Bové and Dufour 2000, 18, 29). Referring to the WTO condemnation of the EU's refusal to import American hormone-raised beef, which led to US import tariffs on Roquefort to which activists responded in turn with the dismantling, he writes of activists' 'denunciation of the dictatorship of international exchange' (25). He coins the term *malbouffe* (bad food) to describe the 'tasteless' and 'standardized food ... that McDonald's symbolizes' (96) and, in the lines which follow, explicitly links it to questions of health, hormones, GMOs, pesticides, chain production, centralization, productivism and the profit motive. 'McDonald's symbolizes anonymous globalization, in which food is emptied of all sense', he states (98). In opposition to this, Roquefort symbolizes taste, quality, diversity, cultural identity, tradition, locality. It is 'the most local product possible and the most symbolic of local products', José told me, one that is the product of a small-scale, autonomous peasant agriculture, a long-standing *savoir faire* and an intimate link to the land (238). It is precisely this uniqueness, autonomy, diversity and quality that neoliberal globalization and standardized techniques of production threaten. Faced with a 'loss of cultural identity' and the immanent imposition of a standardized neoliberal world on all (41), the peasant, symbol of a diverse and authentic France, must resist (see Heller 2004, Lebovics 1992, Rogers 1987).

Notions of homogeneity and diversity, economic imperialism and resistance, draw on a vision of the nation in which 'diversity [is] as ineradicable as bindweed', in Fernand Braudel's colourful phrase – ineradicable despite, or rather because of, active opposition to the 'tendency toward unity' advanced by a highly centralized French state (Braudel 1989, 125). Today, activists' attention is often focused beyond French borders, but the symbolic opposition between McDonald's and Roquefort, between a neoliberal economy and one rooted in land and tradition, draws some of its force from older oppositions between Paris and the provinces, centre and periphery, sameness and difference, often seen as part of the very 'identity of France', to cite the title of Braudel's book quoted above (1989; see Agulhon 1992; Corbin 1992; E. Weber 1976). This might help explain why the McDonald's symbolism was 'so strong'. But the symbolism is also made explicit by people like Bové in the books he writes and the things he says for the press. Bové helps to link categories such as 'McDonald's', 'multinational, '*malbouffe*', 'globalization' and 'standardization', in opposition to another set of categories: 'Roquefort', 'peasant agriculture', 'quality food', 'locality', 'diversity'. The strength of the McDonald's symbolism, the apparently self-evident and obvious connection between McDonald's and neoliberal globalization, stems in part from its place in an argument.

None of this is to say that the symbols are not contested. McDonald's may well symbolize innovation, success, rationalization, efficiency and so on, and political activism may symbolize illegality and disorder. What activists describe as a 'dismantling', the mainstream press portrayed as a violent 'ransacking' (*saccage*), much to the ire of activists. Even activists may be divided on the fine line between the violent and the nonviolent when the destruction of property is concerned. But, in general, those who would contest the symbolic associations of activists are considered to be subject to neoliberal ideology or to be defending the private and not the public good. The 'symbolic' world is thus divided in two. Its logic mirrors that which separates power and counterpower. The symbols of the powerful confront the symbols of resistance, and the media is where this confrontation takes place, witnessed by the non-activist public which activists hope to influence.

Sometimes the symbolic realm is not so clear cut, but at this point we stray out of the domain of the political and into 'culture'. At a meeting of Palestine 12 following the screening of a film by Elia Suleiman, *Divine Intervention*, there was much discussion about the film's symbolism. The film, which activists had eagerly awaited, was about daily life in occupied Palestine and Israel. But the story it told was not one of domination and oppression, power and resistance. It was strange and baffling. Arafat's image appears on a balloon floating above the city, angry youths stab Santa Claus, a neighbour throws rubbish into the property next door and has it thrown back, soldiers sing and dance and wipe their boots. There were 'too many symbols', one person said, and their meaning was not at all clear. Another suggested that we had needed a commentator to explain the film's message to us, while others thought the message didn't need making explicit, it wasn't that kind of film. People disagreed about whether or not it was a political (*militant*) film and whether or not it ought to have been. Most were clearly expecting it to be political, and although some thought it was (just not explicitly so), others were annoyed that it wasn't. In response to this, one woman said that film-makers, even activist film-makers, 'have a right to a cultural life'.

What was so interesting about this discussion was just how much puzzlement the symbolic realm, to which activists refer all the time, could provoke. The film and its symbols slipped between the clear categories of activist analysis. Many seemed to be looking not for complex cultural symbols but for unambiguous ones. At least it was symbols of the latter kind that they were used to dealing with, symbols that were politically useful, that could be presented to the media as part of an argument. Giving to symbols a fairly clear meaning was central to their political strategy of 'mediatization'.

Activists' use of the media for political ends is premised on a distinction between medium and message (cf. McLuhan 1964). This distinction is implicit in the contrast between the spectacular and the symbolic. The message and the symbols that help to convey it are thought to have effects independently of the media that carry them to the public, while the spectacular serves to attract the media in the first place. But not everyone is quite so confident of this separation between medium and message, or of the virtues of mediatization, although the issues are rarely debated and I seldom heard direct criticism of *actions médiatiques*. After the Louvre action, Jean-Marie was less enthusiastic about what we had accomplished. 'All we did was get ourselves in the press', he said, continuing that he preferred actions that achieve something concrete. He gave the example of the way Droit au Logement, a housing-rights association, occupies unused buildings to lodge new tenants. During the organization of Larzac 2003, there was much concern that the gathering would be overly festive. Some worried that the mass media would miss the point of the gathering as they focused on the concerts and the spectacle. The event would be presented as just another festival rather than a political event, and its message would be lost due to the form it took. Something similar might be said about the Louvre invasion. The whole action risked becoming merely one television performance among many, one that was hard to take seriously.

Perhaps the issue here is the way mediatization involves a certain commodification of political action. The media, or at least the mass media, deal in commodities. Protest must be sold to the media in order to get the message to a wide audience, which means packaging it in some suitably spectacular form. The form, however, threatens to become part of the message or has effects beyond those intended (McLuhan 1964). It is criticism of Bové, who is so central to the whole media agenda, that points most clearly to this problem of commodification. Bové, as I discuss above, is sometimes thought to have become a media commodity while simultaneously affirming that the world is not a commodity. He is a symbol himself, as some people said to me, although 'Bové the symbol' is somewhat ambiguous and multivocal. For critics like René Riesel, he is a star concerned with his own image and popularity, a symbol of the neoliberal world of sound bites and media ratings. Along with Bové, Riesel had been sentenced to prison in 2003 for destroying GM rice plants at CIRAD, an agricultural research centre. An active member of the Confédération Paysanne until his resignation following the McDonald's dismantling, Riesel had also been a prominent *Enragé*, or pro-Situationist, during the mass demonstrations of May '68. The Situationists argued that capitalism and consumer society had reduced the world to a 'spectacle' based on the manufacture of 'false' needs (Seidman 2004, 79–80). Riesel today believed that 'blood and tears' were needed to change the world, not events staged for the media (Boucomont 2002). 'I participated in the organization of the intercontinental caravan that acted at CIRAD. I brought the Indians [activists who played an important role] while José Bové brought the journalists', he stated in a newspaper interview, before charging Bové and the Conf with a certain 'media cretinism' ('*crétinisme médiatique*') (FB 2002; Heller 2004, 91).

But if Bové symbolizes media stardom for people like Riesel, for many on the Larzac he is the voice of the alterglobalization movement, a highly effective symbol of resistance. For many who are sceptical of mediatization, the problem, I think, is actually one of efficacy. Mediatization, they worry, is not effective as a political strategy. The attention of the public and the press is diverted from the real issues, whatever they might be, and trained on the star or the spectacle. And the efforts of activists are directed towards getting in the press, with little regard for what doing so might achieve or what effect it has, rather than actually doing something more concrete to bring about change or to create viable social alternatives. Most of the activists I knew, however, even if they recognized its problems and contradictions, seemed more sure of the effectiveness of a media-oriented politics. Political reality requires that the battle be fought in this way. In a discussion I had with Catherine about Bové and Riesel, she insisted on the need for pragmatism. She appreciated Riesel's position but preferred Bové's media-focused methods. José successfully brings the struggle to others, to a wide audience, she said. Those, such as Riesel, who reject the media and aim to maintain a certain political purity fail in this. They remain on the margins and exclude others from their fight (cf. Clarke 2003, 132–3). Because the media reach into homes everywhere, they are a powerful political force.

The practical question of whether or not mediatization is an effective political strategy is a common one in the context of anti-neoliberal globalization more generally. If, in France, the media are a force activists can use, some American activists are highly sceptical, as Graeber makes clear in his ethnography of direct action (n.d.). The way the US corporate media frame things in terms of (police) order and (activist) violence, their bias and simplistic representation of events, and their unwillingness to investigate the issues behind the protests mean that anarchists opposed to corporate capitalism are very reluctant to have anything to do with them. Anarchists abhor the corporate media, Graeber states. Instead, they rely entirely on Indymedia, as use of the mainstream media is simply not effective.[9] Larzac activists also see an essential role for the alternative media, and even those most convinced of the wisdom of mediatization are sceptical of the mass media, as I outline below. But despite media bias, they have greater faith in their ability to educate journalists and that their message will be conveyed via conventional channels. Mediatization is always part of a broader political strategy. It is never merely about playing with symbols or engaging in spectacular actions. 'The important thing', as Bové writes, 'is the educational value of an action. The aim of action is not action for action's sake, it's ... to make people aware and to get them to participate' (Bové and Dufour 2000, 281). The point is always to create debate, to inform, to sway public opinion, and in this the media have their role to play. Symbolic protest and spectacular actions form part of a more general type of educational activism, what people call an activist 'pedagogy'.

Pedagogy and knowledge as tools of resistance

Activists are very much concerned to change the way people think, to deliver them from neoliberal ideology, as a prerequisite of changing the way they act. Pedagogy is seen as a process of demonstrating the truth about the world and is considered a means of resistance, as indicated by the title of a CUMS email advertising two lectures on Palestine ('Education as a means of resistance in Palestine'). From a practical point of view, pedagogy is a matter of informing, passing on the right

---

9 Graeber does, however, say that activists do inadvertently play a media game that has, in some ways, been extremely effective. Coverage of mass protests against the IMF and WTO has lead to the shattering of the previously unchallenged idea that neoliberal policies were necessary and inevitable.

information.[10] 'Information' is conceived of as something that circulates. Activists often talk of 'circulating' (*faire circuler*) information or of 'diffusing' it (*faire diffuser*). They thus participate in a more general discourse of circulation which, as Anna Tsing notes (2000, 335–8), is linked to notions of globalization. Things are often said to 'circulate' in today's 'global' world, in contrast to previous Marxist-inspired conceptions of the global which evoked ideas of capitalist 'penetration'. In the latter imagery, the domination of ideas and institutions is akin to 'rape'; it is forced and total. In the former, circulation implies that the dominant cannot completely control the flow of ideas. Ideas circulate underground or in alternative activist networks. Dominant ideas can be reinterpreted, appropriated or resisted. The metaphor of circulation makes the possibility of resistance and education more easily imaginable.

An important goal of activists' educational project is to inform those who are 'disinformed' (*désinformé*). In a draft charter of a proposed department-wide Palestine 12 (uniting the separate associations of the main towns of Aveyron), one of the aims of the association was listed as 'informing and fighting against disinformation'. Disinformation is considered to be rife, particularly in certain sections of the media. In a letter of complaint to a journalist at Radio France Inter on his coverage of the Palestine-Israel conflict, one member of Palestine 12 wrote: 'the ethics of your trade demand that you inform (and not that you disinform) your listeners on the nature of this colonization ... [otherwise] you transform yourself into a spokesperson for Israeli settlers' (*colons*). For some, the media are guilty of a little more than just disinformation. Gilles, who worked as a journalist, accused them of dealing in lies and counter-truths:

> When you read in the press, for example, on the question of GMOs, or ... when you see journalists on TV interviewing politicians or leaders of business and finance, [they] come out with aberrations, shameless lies. To see journalists content to repeat [such lies] and the media providing a platform [for elites] and not at all arguing with them and challenging them, I tell myself that effectively we can expect nothing of the media. ... Some astounding things [get reported], ... counter-truths that the media get away with.

Activists aim to combat media propaganda through a variety of educational initiatives. In forums, debates, leaflets, articles, Internet reports, books, films and educational protest actions they endeavour to inform the public of the truth. They realize the job is not an easy one, that they will fail to reach many whose minds are made up. 'But its worth trying', Gilles told me. 'If an action is understood by ten and misunderstood or condemned by fifty, it's worth doing just for those ten people you touch'.

---

10 One veteran of the Larzac struggle suggested a different view of the pedagogical process. The 'teacher', conceived of as mediator, seeks not to introduce new ideas but to act on what is already present within the person. They aim to direct an already-existing potential, rather than contributing something new. Pedagogy, he suggested, is analogous to acupuncture. While some would agree with this conception of pedagogy, it does not, in my view, describe the general form that educational activism takes.

The actions to which Gilles refers are partly the media actions I discuss above, whose aim is to point to the existence of a problem and to 'create debate', as people often put it. Neutralizations of GM field trials are performed for the media in an attempt to force the issue of GMOs onto the political agenda (cf. Pagis 2005, 5). But most protests also involve attempts at education that do not rely on the media. Informing the public via leaflets and displays is one of the key goals of small-scale and relatively unspectacular actions, such as the weekly Hour of Silence for Palestine or supermarket protests. Several of my Saturday mornings were spent handing out leaflets to shoppers as they entered Millau supermarkets. On one fairly typical occasion, two people stood at each entrance to ensure that everyone coming and going received a page of information on GM food. The leaflet's main thrust was to raise awareness of the presence of GM food on supermarket shelves – bright orange stickers were also placed on GM products throughout the supermarket – and to suggest that consumers had a right to choose not to buy GM. The better part of the leaflet was simply a list of 'products and manufacturers not guaranteeing the non-use of GMOs'. A thousand copies were distributed in one hour and the general opinion was that people appreciated having the GM issue brought to their attention. Similar actions were carried out on several occasions to inform people of the situation in Palestine. During José's incarceration, leaflets on repression were handed out weekly by a team of around twelve to all the holiday traffic that passed through the roundabout next to the Millau McDonald's. One outlined the injustice of José's incarceration when well-known 'criminals' such as Chirac walk free.

Attempts to inform often employ what are regarded as straight-forward and objective 'facts'. At each Friday's Hour of Silence, activists used pieces of hardboard pasted over with white paper to display the facts, hand-written in marker pen, of Israeli occupation. Most commonly they attempted to quantify the death and destruction wrought by the Israeli army, illustrating the occupation with numbers (cf. Riles 2001, 138):

In January: 70 Palestinians killed by Israeli armed forces ...

On the night of 12–13 May, 33 houses destroyed, 58 families cast into the street, 15 injured ...

This week ... in the Gaza strip, 200 hectares of agricultural land razed ...

19 May in Bethlehem, two cameramen violently attacked.

The numbers – always thoroughly precise to indicate that real people had been victimized at a particular time and place – tended to be accompanied by visual images. Most weeks in the summer of 2003, waist-high laminated photographs of terrified children, rubble and dead bodies graphically depicted what the captions described as 'suffering' and 'massacre', while similar small photographs, uncaptioned, were pinned to display boards.

The visual and numerical facts, however, were never quite enough on their own. They were normally supplemented by some sort of written commentary, handed out for passers-by to take home, and providing people with greater detail, argument and a language of interpretation for what was going on in Palestine. One leaflet, announcing an international march in Marseilles in September 2002, told, in terms that were common, of Palestinians' 'hunger' and 'humiliation', of their 'resistance', of Israel's 'crimes against humanity' and its Palestinian 'victims', of its 'brutal and murderous colonization', of its 'daily violation of ... human rights', of how it 'asphyxiates the Palestinian economy', of the 'apartheid in Palestine'. Such language was considered to refer to the basic facts – clearly demonstrated by numbers and images – of the 'domination of one people over another' in which Palestinians go hungry, are killed and have their lives disrupted. Illustrated by the facts, 'domination' itself acquires the objectivity of fact.

But even the basic facts are perhaps not quite so innocent and objective. Richard Clarke, in his discussion of Israeli activists opposed to the human rights abuses of their own government in occupied Palestine, argues that a key part of their strategy was not just to inform people with 'data', but to 'interpellate', 'to challenge Israelis and to shake them out of their (literal) ignorance about events taking place so close to their lives' (2003, 121). The activists in Palestine 12 are similarly concerned with 'knowledge which disrupts, renders uncomfortable, challenges and interrupts' and which provokes a subjective reaction (134). The facts of death and suffering that they display at the Hour of Silence are intended to be shocking. Activists aim to awaken people to injustice and to convince them of the need to act.

Educational actions such as the Hour of Silence are directly targeted at the non-activist public. But there are other pedagogical events to which members of the public are welcome, although the audience is almost always predominantly an activist one (see Chapter 3). Activists put much effort into organizing information evenings, workshops (*stages*) and forums to which they hope to attract as many non-activists as possible. Information evenings generally involve an invited speaker – a visiting Palestinian to talk about life in the Occupied Territories, a biologist or Conf farmer to discuss GM crops, a political scientist to explain the American agenda in Iraq – with questions and comments from the audience at the end. One-off events held in a small hall somewhere, they are always advertised in the newspaper and in posters pasted around town. Workshops are somewhat longer and more intensive than information evenings, taking place over a day or two and going into considerable depth on a given subject, while forums form part of activist events such as the European Social Forum or Larzac 2003 and may involve an audience of up to a thousand people.

Activists organize all these events with education in mind and attend them because they are sources of information. 'That's where you learn things', Jean-Marie said of the forums at the G8 counter-summit in order to convince a sceptical first-timer. Forums are run by experts in the 'mechanisms' of globalization and repression, he continued, people who are strong at a 'pedagogical level'. Most debates and forums take on a similar pedagogical form, with a clear educational hierarchy. They consist of a speaker or speakers who sit up front, sometimes on a stage, and address their audience via microphone. Audience participation tends to be limited to a question-and-answer session after speakers have had their say. People often take notes during forums and workshops, and it is not uncommon for someone to record proceedings, sometimes on video, to use later as a 'tool' of reflection and struggle, as part, perhaps, of another forum. Information acquired at forums is thus very frequently circulated to a broader audience. Even small forums and debates generally lead to an article in the activist press. During Larzac 2003, there was an intention to record all forums and to broadcast highlights over the radio, while 'web reporters' published summaries of forums on the Internet within the hour.

The speakers at forums and similar events provide their audience with an alternative expertise, one that contrasts with media disinformation and that collectively covers every domain from agriculture and genetics to economics and international relations (cf. Berglund 1998; Purdue 2000, 59ff.). This alternative expertise is often used to expose as 'shameless lies' the so-called knowledge of elites. At a forum on GMOs and agriculture at the G8 counter-summit, biologist Jean-Pierre Berlan distinguished two 'sciences': 'their science', or 'technoscience', which serves the interests of the powerful; and 'our science', a citizens' science, in the service of humanity and rights (cf. Berglund 1998, 116, 152). To think, he said, that the former will bring well-being to humanity, as its adherents claim, is completely mistaken. Technoscience is controlled by five firms who produce 'agrotoxics': the '-cides' (pesticides, herbicides, fungicides). These firms deal not in biotechnologies but in 'necrotechnologies'. They use the science of genetics for their own private gain.[11] Technoscience, as Berlan described it, is thus subordinated to profit. 'Our science', in contrast, still in its infancy, would promote a new agriculture based on biodiversity, not monoculture; respect for the environment, not its destruction; sharing and not individualism; the 'autonomy of producers and not their subservience'. It would work with farmers and not in spite of them. 'Our science' would be subordinated to life and the greater good of all.

The role of expert speakers at forums, then, is to explain the workings of power and to suggest the possibility of alternatives that can be achieved through collective action. By its very nature, however, expert knowledge can be abstract, complex and hard to understand, a far cry from the facts of oppression displayed at the Hour of Silence. Some thus regard experts with a little scepticism, as I discuss in Chapter 3, and demand that forums impart a concrete knowledge gleaned of experience. During a meeting in Paris on the organization of Larzac 2003, there was much concern that forums not be reduced to an 'affair of experts', as one person put it. People insisted that forums be as inclusive as possible and involve two types of speakers: experts and witnesses (*témoins*). Witnesses, who I shall discuss further in the next chapter, are people capable of testifying to their experience of struggle and oppression. They may be citizens fighting state repression, farmers battling GM multinationals, Palestinians from the occupied territories, the homeless and disadvantaged from the Paris suburbs, or landless Brazilian peasants. The knowledge of witnesses is often considered somehow more fundamental and authentic than that of experts. Witnesses are seen to deal in facts, information and experience rather than complex (and possibly deceptive) argument. As Donna Haraway writes, the witness is 'endowed with a remarkable power to establish the facts. ... His subjectivity is his objectivity'

---

11 Such knowledge may be used to induce fear in people (see I. Scott 2000). Neoliberalism and productivism have often been associated with mad cow disease, and a neoliberal system is also thought to have led to the blood contamination scandal that rocked France in the 1990s (see Bové and Dufour 2000, 169ff.). GMOs are seen as another product of this neoliberal system. Activists, however, tend to emphasize people's ability to change things through action. Thus there is nothing really to fear, although fear may encourage action.

(1997, 24). Witnesses, activists believe, provide down-to-earth accounts of what it is like to live under conditions of domination and demonstrate that oppression is about 'humans, not abstractions', as one woman put it at an information evening on Palestine (see J. Scott 1994, 371).

The knowledge of experts and the knowledge of experience, along with a knowledge of basic facts, are thus all integral to the educational agenda of activists. There is something strikingly egalitarian and democratic about this conception of different yet complementary kinds of knowledge, used together to oppose the knowledge of those atop the social hierarchy (*ceux d'en haut*). Everyone who participates in pedagogical events can share in this knowledge to some degree, even if they never themselves become scientists and never experience the horrors of Israeli occupation. It is a willingness to learn and to engage which is important. Knowledge is not cast merely as the preserve of elites. 'Who are we to concern ourselves with problems that are beyond us' and 'so complex', asks Thierry, ironically, in an editorial for GLL. 'Neither graduates, nor politicians, nor strategists, nor experts, by what right do we enter the court of the great to disturb their games?' His reply:

> It is, however, our right and our duty as citizens of the world to inform ourselves, to seek to understand. And it is our right and our duty not to leave exclusively to the 'specialists' the decisions that weigh on the world (Castelbou 2002c, 1).

Knowledge, he is saying, is something all can and should acquire as citizens as part of their participation in political life. Pedagogical events aim to interpellate and to produce knowledgeable individuals, alert to injustice and convinced of the importance of political action. Along with journals, books and Internet articles, such events contribute to a knowledge economy that forms part of the foundations of the social movement's struggle with power.

Chapter 7

Moral Foundations

One of the first things I read when I arrived on the Larzac was an editorial in the latest edition of the plateau's activist newspaper, GLL (Castelbou 2002a, 1). The editorial was about the farmer as defender of the general interest. The author, Thierry, who I later met at Les Truels, begins with a vision of rural decline: 30,000 farms disappear each year, while fewer than 6,000 new farmers establish themselves on the land. 'It is urgent', he writes, 'in order to maintain a certain rural vitality ... [and] to escape the industrial standardization of agriculture, to make the installation of new farmers a priority'. Why not, he says, 'offer them a contract defining their rights and duties as guardians of the earth?' Speaking of the case of a young farmer illegally occupying a privately owned but disused Larzac farm known as the Cisternette, Thierry asks: 'When will we desacralize the right of ownership of the earth so as to privilege the right of use?' Following a long legal battle, the farmer was threatened with immanent expulsion because the land he farmed was not his property. For Thierry and the hundreds who protested in solidarity at the Cisternette the following spring, rights of use take precedence over rights in property. '[T]he land ...', Thierry continues, 'constitutes a common good with multiple uses ... welcoming holiday-makers and hikers. ... Farmers, when they defend their tools of production, defend the general interest as well'. Importantly, farmers are thought to perform the essential task of maintaining the countryside for the good of all. The occupation of the Cisternette was supported by the Confédération Paysanne and its main slogan, which featured on posters and leaflets, was 'No farmer without land, no land without a farmer'. The slogan was considered a claim for rights of use in support of the common good.

The Cisternette provides one example among many in which the discourse of rights is much in evidence. Rights, and particularly human or fundamental rights (*droits fondamentaux*), are central to the political claims of alterglobalization activists, as they are to activists around the world (Nash 2005, 4). This rights activism is relatively recent. Universal rights have been firmly on the political agenda since the American Declaration of Independence and the French Declaration of the Rights of Man and Citizen of 1789. The revolutions of the eighteenth and nineteenth centuries, however, made the question of rights one for sovereign nation states, and within their borders states could do what they wanted. 'This presumption', as Kenneth Cmiel notes, 'does not appear to have been dramatically challenged until the 1940s, when international law against genocide was written and when it was proclaimed that the world community needed to monitor basic human rights' (2004, par. 30). The UN Universal Declaration of Human Rights gave international legitimacy to the making of rights claims across borders in 1948, and yet rights did not really become central to political movements for another couple of decades. There was an explosion of human rights NGOs in the 1970s as European and American activists, often supported by government officials (Cmiel 1999, 1239), developed ways of collecting accounts of 'some of the vilest behavior on earth' and 'mov[ing] this information to wherever activists had some chance to shame and pressure the perpetrators. Theirs was a politics of the global flow of key bits of fact', Cmiel states (1999, 1232). This new politics of human rights was thus linked to globalization and emerging transnational communication networks (Cmiel 2004, par. 41). But only in the late 1980s and early 1990s did Western human rights activists widen their focus to include health, economic justice and the rights of women and indigenous peoples, and only then do non-Western activists begin to frame their struggles in terms of rights (Cmiel 2004, par. 43–4). Anthropological work on rights also takes off around this time (Messer 1993, 223–5).[1]

Unsurprising, then, that the Larzac struggle of the 1970s was a struggle for land, a struggle against the state, but at the time was not really conceived of as a struggle for rights. Studies of the period at least give rights little mention (see Alland 2001, Martin 1987; Vuarin 2005). Larzac activists today, in contrast, are very much concerned with rights. Rights, they insist, are frequently denied by power, and a defence of rights justifies illegal protest tactics. Rights also offer a means of controlling power, and they provide part of a moral foundation on which to build 'other worlds'.

This chapter is about the way rights are fundamental to activists' struggles and, more broadly, about the moral foundations of political activism. I consider, in particular, the notion of 'fundamental rights', drawing much on the interviews I was asked to do for the Larzac 2003 radio project and on conversations, particularly with activist intellectuals, about a notion that is ubiquitous. I ask, in what consists the fundamentalness of rights, and how may they be considered basic to activists' political project? I shall argue that the notion of a fundamental right draws on both the categories of nature and society, and on ideas of morality and truth. Truth, while it is considered objective, is simultaneously imbued with a certain morality. The last section explores the processes by which activists on the Larzac produce this moral truth through evenings in which 'witnesses' testify to the truth of oppression and domination. This truth is one in which power and resistance are opposed.

Rights

Almost everything activists defend, they defend in the name of rights. Rights are absolutely central to activists' discourses and aims. In speeches at demonstrations or in the activist press, rights are frequently invoked, as they are in casual conversation over what activists hope to achieve. As José once told me, the goal of activism is 'to rebuild the world on the basis of rights'. Many of the activist battles I have discussed in this book involve a protest over rights denied or threatened. Palestine 12 leaflets and Larzac Solidarités newsletters often mention 'violations of Palestinian rights' and the struggle 'for the rights of the Palestinian people'. Larzac activists protest the

---

1 See Wilson (1997), Cowan et al. (2001), Wilson and Mitchell (2003), Goodale (2006) and the other contributions to the 'In Focus' special issue on rights of American Anthropologist (vol.108 no.1 2006).

'totalitarian' nature of GMOs because they deny the rights of farmers to resow their own seed or to go organic. They distribute leaflets at supermarkets defending the rights of consumers to choose GM-free food. They resist the incarceration of José in the name of the rights of the social movement, because José speaks in the interests of the public good and defends the rights of citizens to participate in political life. CUMS' charter, which I outline in Chapter 2, repeatedly emphasizes the centrality of rights in the struggle of the social movement. For Pierre, the social movement 'wants a society in which rights are primordial'.

In meetings for the preparation of Larzac 2003, rights were presented as the common thread linking the diverse political forums together. One meeting in Paris, involving twenty activists from a dozen associations, was devoted to deciding on themes for four or five large forums. The meeting was held in a prefabricated building behind the Confédération Paysanne's national offices. Those present, many of whom seemed to be acquainted, sat facing each other at tables arranged in rectangular formation around the room. Catherine and I were there to represent CUMS. José chaired the meeting, sitting up front under the blackboard with colleagues from the Conf. There was lively discussion in search of a 'common denominator' for the forums. Communication, one person suggested; repression, said another; the WTO, advanced a third. Then José announced, to much approval, that what was really important was the question of rights. He declared the gathering an effort to 'conquer new rights', a phrase subsequently adopted by others at the meeting and much repeated in public discourse (cf. Berglund 1998, 84). Finally, it was decided that two forums would 'give a strong emphasis to the conquest of rights'.

Activists tend to see rights as something the powerful observe in rhetoric but not in practice. This refusal to observe principles that elites themselves espouse – those to liberty and equality, for example – is seen to be at the root of their power. The refusal is what Gilles termed cynical:

> [Their] discourse [of rights] is totally demagogic, a hypocritical discourse, ... total cynicism. ... The discourse of the apostles of neoliberalism ... is about liberty, the eventual well-being of humanity ... [but] things only get worse ... [under a] neoliberal system. ... The gap widens between the North and the South, the gap widens between the rich and the poor. So you can see clearly ... that this discourse is totally false, demagogic, hypocritical and completely cynical.

A neoliberal economy is founded on a denial of rights. In José's words, 'all these rights are shattered by the logic of the market'. Water, the earth and other 'common goods' were becoming commodities, he said, 'so that now we find ourselves with a world which is structured by just one single logic which is that of the market. There are a huge number of fundamental rights that are completely denied'. In a neoliberal world, 'economic rights' – to private property, to money, to engage in business, to buy and sell, to profit – take precedence over rights that activists consider more 'fundamental'.[2]

---

2 Cf. Hastrup (2003, 26) on the 'rights economy' and how 'human rights have become the means of exchange par excellence'.

In the view of many, human beings thus find themselves 'in service of the economy' and not the other way around, as Claudine, a key member of CUMS, lamented over lunch one day. Indeed, their 'humanity' is almost denied as people are reduced to commodities. Gilles, who spoke passionately on the subject, put it thus:

> For me, the principal problem with the neoliberal system ... is that it ... includes *not a single human value*. ... There are some amazing examples from everyday language. ... Within the working world, a few years ago, one spoke of the director of 'personnel', now one speaks of the director of 'human resources'. So workers are no longer considered human beings but are considered a bit like natural resources. ... In the system in which we live at the moment there is a sacrosanct preponderance of the rights of business, the right to trade, the rights of high international finance ... over all the great international pacts, which, moreover, have been ratified by nation states, and which take into consideration the human being, ... the Universal Charter of the Rights of Man, the pacts on economic, social and cultural rights and even the right of the environment.[3]

The pre-eminence that neoliberalism gives to economic rights is considered a tool of domination allowing the powerful to deny others their rights. In resisting this domination, activists aim to invert what Bové calls a 'hierarchy of rights' and 'values'. 'Fundamental rights' and the 'human values' they express are the most important in the hierarchy, he told me, and ought to take precedence over economic rights. All political formations, agreements, decisions, social orders and economic systems should be based on a respect for such rights.

> We are rebuilding the world based on rights. And the market or the economy ... cannot exist unless it respects these rights. This means putting the economy in its place, a place with which it is currently unfamiliar. We need to ensure that when there is an economic agreement, that agreement can only function and is only legitimate from the moment it enters into this hierarchization of rights.

A hierarchy of rights is another expression of the idea that some rights are more fundamental than others.

Fundamental rights are thus seen to offer a tool of resistance and a means for controlling power. For Pierre, the WTO is the one organization whose international status puts it in an ideal place to control the workings of capital and the impact of multinationals on ordinary people. But, he pointed out, the WTO is both an instrument of regulation and of liberalization. By means of regulations it abolishes the regulation of trade and thereby allows capital to impinge upon citizens' rights. He considered this a contradiction to eliminate and favoured reforming the WTO to make it a truly regulatory body that acted in the interests of all and respected everyone's fundamental rights. While others would prefer the WTO's abolition, most seem to agree on the need for controls and regulations. 'There must be rules',

---

3 Activists speak of the rights of the 'environment' although, according to one, 'the notion is still vague' (Roux 2002, 110). Article 8 of the European Convention on Human Rights, referring to rights relating to family life, makes mention of the right to live in a healthy environment, Roux states.

Gilles suggested, 'precisely in order to protect the weakest'. For Christine rules, regulations and laws serve to

> limit the damage all these multinationals do. But what does the WTO do? ... Rather than restricting their rights ... it decreases their duties. It's the opposite of what we need. ... A regulation of business should move towards the respect of workers' rights and the respect of the environment in which the business sets up. ... Laws should limit [businesses] ... because we, simple citizens, are surrounded by a heap of laws, responsibilities ... a heap of things that limit us. I don't see why these companies don't themselves have limits on their economic development.

To counter neoliberal forms of power, one needs to institute a regime of control. Fundamental rights have great potential in this regard.

Most important are declarations of universal or human rights. The 1789 French Declaration of the Rights of Man and Citizen is often seen as France's great bequest to the world and its revolutionary spirit inspires activists today.[4] I sometimes saw the Declaration pinned up in poster form in people's houses and it adorned a wall in the restaurant at La Jasse on the Larzac. The rights originally codified in the Declaration, however, were applicable only within the French Republic. It was the Universal Declaration of Human Rights of 1948, ratified by the member countries of the United Nations, that first marked, as José told me, the extension of fundamental rights into an international realm. These rights were then augmented when the International Covenant on Economic, Social and Cultural Rights came into force ten years after being opened for signature in 1966. The rights enshrined in such declarations are, he said, 'effectively the international charter of relations between countries and between people and for the rights of individuals'. Pierre suggested that fundamental rights provide 'at all levels – at the French level and at the international level – an element of common reference'. They must, he said, be applied or 'concretized' universally.

Although they are perceived as a Western invention, activists consider the universalization of rights to be a good thing. At a weekend school on the Israel-Palestine conflict, activist academic Mohammed Taleb insisted that we must struggle for a 'globalization (*mondialisation*) and not a Westernisation of rights', an idea those present seemed to find persuasive. In a later conversation with Gilles, who had characterized globalization as the 'imposition' of the 'Western way of producing [and] consuming', I asked whether the extension of human rights to humanity as a whole did not involve the imposition of Western values.

> Yes, it's possible, it's possible. But it seems to me, all the same, that if, evidently, there is a diversity of cultures – and this is the reason we call not for 'another possible world' but for 'other possible worlds' – it's clear that ... there is also a unity of being. ... Human rights [are] claimed so that the 840 million people in the world currently suffering from hunger have something to eat each day. If that's a Western vision, I accept complete responsibility.

---

4 Activists tend to use the terms 'rights of man' and 'human rights' interchangeably. 'Man' is understood in its generic and not gendered sense. The notion of 'man' points to what Roux calls the 'two ends of this utopia under construction: the universal and the individual' (2002, 116).

What I accept a lot less is that we try to feed these people with GM food or with Coca Cola or with Big Macs.

Their universal applicability is precisely what is considered good about human rights and it is this that Gilles defends. He defends it against the private interests of Western multinationals who deny autonomy and rights by peddling food for profit and not for need. The whole thing about fundamental rights is that, in principle, they apply equally to all in virtue of our common humanity.

But activists often say that fundamental rights exist only 'on paper' – the paper of declarations – and are not necessarily observed in practice or 'applied' (*appliqué*) in law. Unlike the civic rights codified in the laws of nation states, or the European Convention on Human Rights (1950), the rights in the UN Declaration are not legally binding (Dembour 1996, 29). For activists, all laws should 'respect' the fundamental rights prescribed by declarations, and the more limited 'civic' or 'political' rights, pertaining to the citizens of particular nation states, should conform with universal principles. Rights, for the most part, do not need inventing, Gilles often asserted, because they already exist. They merely need to be respected in practice. 'A beginning', he told me, 'would be to try to use the tools that exist, to find legal means by which to have [existing rights] applied'. The movement, as he writes in GLL, tries to 'create a *rapport de force* with the aim of imposing the observation (*application*) of these rights' (Gesson 2003b, 7).

Rights 'on paper' exist as a positive set of ideas, values or principles and 'provide a base' for building a future, Gilles told me, adding that 'when you want to build, you need to build upon foundations'. A right is an idea that serves as a starting point for the whole process of building other worlds. Although there is an overwhelming emphasis on action within the alterglobalization movement, the concern with rights does demonstrate a certain idealism. The aim is to construct a utopian world that is somehow an inversion of the present one, where politics as power-seeking has been 'suspended' (Jameson 2004, 43). The fundamental ideas embodied in declarations of rights, but which are not applied in practice, provide a picture of what reality is not. They are the inverse of neoliberal political reality and ideology, for activists, the world turned upside down (Tucker 2002, 139–40). Those who are concerned with the 'application of rights' aim to construct reality after these ideas or principles. This idealism is the bequest of the French Revolution and the Enlightenment philosophers who first laid down the principles that were to become the Rights of Man (cf. E. Weber 1991[1974], 316). John Bowen (2003, 40) characterizes it as a general feature of French 'legal reasoning' in which 'values or norms are ... invoked in their legal incarnation' as the foundation of a good society.

In fighting for an application of rights, activists also struggle for a sort of 'coherence' (see Chapter 4). To apply a fundamental right is to create a relation of coherence because it implies that an idea or belief is put into practice or acted upon. The process resembles the conjoining of privately held belief and public action as the moral-political task of an activist. If acting coherently is the fundamental political act of an individual in the world, it is also one of the fundamental bases of a just society. The ideas of what is right and just are inscribed in declarations, and it is with these ideas, activists believe, that the actions of all and the organization of society must cohere. In this sense, it is the ideas that are fundamental. Activists affirm the power of an idea, that of rights. Their whole problem comes down to how to get fundamental rights applied and observed, how to make an idea into reality.

It is here that civil disobedience, in particular, has such an important role to play. A key assumption of much political activism is that it is fundamental rights, legally recognized or not, that justify protest and that the boundary between the just and the unjust, or the legitimate and the legal but illegitimate, can be expressed in terms of such rights. Injustice is often seen to involve a denial of rights. Civil disobedience – breaking the law – is considered a just and legitimate form of political activity if it is a defence of rights. 'Who will find it illegitimate to break a law that is contrary to the Declaration of the Rights of Man and of the Citizen?' Bové and co-writer, journalist Gilles Luneau, ask rhetorically (2004, 200, 216). And as François Roux, José's lawyer and rights activist, writes, citing the 'mythic' French Constitution of 1793: 'When the government violates the rights guaranteed by the Constitution, resistance in all its forms is the most sacred of rights and the most pressing of responsibilities' (2002, 24). A denial of rights gives cause for what, in the title of his account of his experiences as a lawyer, Roux calls a 'state of legitimate revolt'. He declares the necessity of 'moral conscience against the established order when the latter is unjust, the right of revolt when injustice makes itself law' (2002, 15).

Through protest, activists aim for what they call an 'evolution of laws', their gradual 'perfection' and incorporation of further rights. They aim, in the words of Roux, 'to expose (*faire éclater*) the injustice of a law so that eventually the law (*loi*) changes. So that the law (*droit*) evolves towards a more just world' (2002, 109). Rights, even those described as fundamental, are considered contingent, historical, social phenomena which have emerged through political struggle (see Tilly 1998; Wilson 1997, 23). 'Rights and law (*le droit*) don't come from some transcendental source', Bové and Luneau write,

> they are, in part, the expression of universal principles more or less recognized by human beings ... and partly the expression of *rapports de forces* between the social, cultural and economic interests of the members of a society. Rights and law are the product of the social contract at a particular moment of history. ... They are in a perpetual [process of] construction-deconstruction (2004, 209).

The struggle for rights may have known its finest hour in 1789 with the Declaration of the Rights of Man and Citizen, but the struggle is an ongoing one. At the time of the protests over the future of the public service, one activist spoke to me bitterly of the legal rights acquired through struggle during the twentieth century which were now threatened by neoliberalism: rights to strike, to social welfare, pensions, a 40 hour week. He considered the social movement's role to be to continue this struggle for rights. Gilles, similarly, told me that actions of civil disobedience offer

> the only solution to make the distinction between legality and legitimacy evolve. There are acts which were illegal but legitimate a few decades ago and which, due to the struggles of people at the time, became legal. The right to strike, for example. ... When we speak of legality, we must remember that the law always lags behind reality. ... The law (*droit*)

must evolve and it's in crossing the fictive boundary between legitimacy and legality that we can move things forward.

When Gilles says here that the law lags behind reality, he means that the law does not always recognize 'legitimate' rights. Protest must highlight the legitimate through illegal actions – GM crop neutralizations, occupations of land – in order to make its legitimacy visible to the public and to the law.

But what exactly makes a right 'legitimate'? It is precisely this question that Bové and Luneau pose in their book on civil disobedience (2004, 194): 'to which law (*loi*) and which superior rights (*droits supérieurs*) ... do nonviolent [activists] appeal' when they break the law? I should say here that English is exceptional amongst European languages in its separation of the concepts of 'rights' and 'law' (Pennington 1998, 237). The French word *droit* may, according to context, be translated by both these terms. It combines what in English are distinct notions into one, and it is this ambiguity, this richness, with which Bové and Luneau are somehow concerned. Any moral legitimacy, in their opinion, cannot be understood solely in terms of law but must make reference to *le droit*, which is always more than a mere 'legal' notion. They state quite explicitly that '*le droit* can't be reduced to the sum total of laws (*lois*)' and that 'legitimacy arises in the relation between the written and the unwritten law' (2004, 213, 195). This whole problem of the relation between the two is an old one, understood by thinkers such as Hobbes (1985), Locke (1960) and Montesquieu (1979) in terms of the relation between political rights and natural rights. In his *The Spirit of the Laws* of 1748, Montesquieu – whose 'legal programme still seems to govern present-day human rights thinking', according to Kirsten Hastrup (2003, 20) – distinguished natural from positive law, the former deriving from the 'constitution of our being', as Hastrup puts it (2003, 19), and the latter from our existence in society, from which stems political and civil right.[5] It was the Declaration of the Rights of Man, however, that in 1789 first codified in law what it called 'natural and imprescriptible rights'. For Bové and Luneau, these natural or, in their terms, fundamental rights do not have some transcendental origin, as I have noted, although they remain thoroughly legitimate. They derive from the way people everywhere live in society. Bové and Luneau insist, quoting jurist Dominique Rousseau, that '*le droit* is rooted where people live and in the forms they give to their lives' (2004, 212). Legitimacy, in other words, is more a question of life than law.

Human life, in all its diversity and complexity, thus seems to me to be at the centre of activists' concerns with legitimacy and rights. The society for which Christine fights is one in which everyone 'is able to live', as she put it. 'What revolts me the most is injustice. For me the biggest injustice ... is that not everyone is able to live'. The point of the rights for which she struggles is, at a most basic level, to protect what John Gledhill describes as the 'enjoyment of a fully human life' (1997,

---

5 Ideas of natural and inalienable rights have their origins in the writings of twelfth-century jurists whose concerns were taken up by later thinkers such as William of Ockham, with his ideas of subjective rights founded in reason and will, and Dutch jurist Hugo Grotius, whose concept of right as 'a moral quality of a person, enabling him to have or to do something justly' (Tierney 1997, 325) influenced Hobbes, Locke and others (Pennington 1998; Tierney 1997).

74). During my fieldwork, this concern with human life was embodied most clearly in demonstrations of solidarity with the Palestinians. At the Hour of Silence, as I have sketched above, the denial of Palestinians' rights to life and to live well was put on display in images depicting 'suffering', 'death' and 'destruction'. Leaflets spoke of 'violations of human life', and 'murderous raids' resulting in thousands of deaths, and the destruction of houses, plantations and social infrastructure. Several members of Palestine 12 were interested in going to Palestine as 'observers' during the olive harvest because, they said, Israeli soldiers aimed to disrupt the harvest and uproot trees as part of an attack on the Palestinian economy. The occupation, if it did not result in death, at least undermined the ability of Palestinians to lead ordinary and dignified lives. At a forum at the G8 counter-summit, one speaker described the checkpoint as 'the most powerful arm of the occupation' because of the way it 'cut up space and time' and 'made daily life impossible'. With people detained for hours at checkpoints as part of a routine of 'humiliation', social life came to a standstill. By such means, the Israeli occupation was seen to deprive Palestinians of an essential human dignity just as it deprived them of other rights. One of the leaflets handed out at the Hour of Silence described Palestine as having been made into 'a desert where the human has no place'.

For many Larzac activists, Palestine epitomizes the denial by the powerful of fundamental rights associated with 'human life'. I think it important that life and fundamental rights not here be understood merely in terms of basic human needs for food, resources or shelter. Activists, as the example of Palestine makes clear, are certainly concerned with what Giorgio Agamben (1998) calls 'natural', 'biological' life, but they are just as concerned with everyday social existence. Fundamental rights are rights to a normal, dignified life. Their 'fundamental' quality refers not to something 'natural' which precedes all social existence, but depends on the conjoining of natural and social (cf. Sennett 2002, 89). Fundamental rights always have both natural and social characteristics. The title of the Declaration of the Rights of Man and Citizen is here instructive. As Balibar notes (1994, 44), the 'rights of man' are natural, inalienable and independent of any social institution, while the 'rights of the citizen' are social, instituted, restrictive and 'founded' on natural rights. But the whole purpose of the Declaration, he continues, is to abolish the gap between the two: natural and social rights are the same. The natural life of man 'vanishes into the figure of the citizen', as Agamben puts it (1998, 127), naturalizing the French social order in the process.

Rights, like the sovereignty discussed by Agamben, also pose something of a paradox. Like the sovereign, rights exist both 'outside and inside the juridical order' (1998, 15). Agamben argues that the fundamental feature of modern sovereignty is the sovereign's legal power to suspend the law and thus to create a 'state of exception' to the law, one that is, however, simultaneously legal and extralegal, where law and non-law are indistinguishable. Sovereignty is marked by this 'zone of indistinction', where the sovereign resides both inside and outside the law and is included through his exclusion (1998). I want to suggest that the logic of fundamental rights is similar to this logic of sovereignty. Rights are simultaneously a legal and non-legal phenomenon. Activists draw on both legal and extralegal sources in justifying their right to resist: the legal sources are all those rights recognized in declarations that have been made binding in law; the extralegal sources are those rights that law and economic elites ignore or deny, but which activists recognize nonetheless as fundamental because concerned with human life. Activists affirm a certain sovereignty or autonomy in relation to politics and social life. Rights are an expression of a form of sovereignty, a justification for the autonomy of the social movement and for the illegal acts of civil disobedience considered a form of legitimate political activity. By appeal to rights, political resistance is naturalized as the right of sovereign human subjects.

Fundamental rights are thus ambiguous in relation to the meaning of the term 'right' (Dembour 1996, 32). The term refers both to legal rights and rights which are not yet legal. The ideology of human rights does away with the concept of the state and its laws to concentrate on the equal value of human beings, but the state and law always remain central to human rights practice (Dembour 1996, 29). This ambiguity is the source of a double authority and legitimacy, both legal and extralegal, social and natural. Fundamental rights form both the basis of social order, but only exist when socially recognized. Declarations of rights, which are considered by activists to be social phenomena, appeal to an authority that is 'natural' or 'human'. They refer to what is supposedly beyond all social formations – human birth, life, needs and natural rights, and not just citizens and their legal rights. The authority of rights draws on nature and a generic humanness, although without their codification in declarations, rights would have no authority at all, no broad social and political reality. It is the declaration itself – a political and social document – which confers authority and legitimacy. Rights lack efficacy when they no longer take the form of the rights of citizens (Agamben 1998, 126). Activists aim always to ensure that rights deemed to be natural, human and concerned with life enter into a political field. Human rights must become the rights of citizens, in Balibar's terms.

Truth

Rights point to a particular morality based on ideas of humanity and life. The truth activists claim to speak is similarly attuned to this moral concern with life and something profoundly human. In contrast, this moral dimension is thought lacking from the claims the powerful make to truth, allowing activists to speak of their 'counter-truths' and 'astounding lies'. The social movement and economic elites may be involved in a struggle over truth, both aiming to convince and to acquire the minds of the general public, but only 'we speak the truth', Gilles said, 'which is not the case [with the media and the powerful] in a general sense'. For Gilles, truth is objective and there are objective and yet moral facts which the powerful deliberately ignore in their own private interest, not the least being the facts of oppression.

The social movement is on the side of the oppressed and the powerless (cf. E. Weber 1991[1974], 301; Ross 2002, 167). The truly downtrodden are vividly confronted with the problem of life, of how to ensure their own continued existence and how to live with dignity. The examples activists cite of people face to face with 'bare life', in Agamben's phrase (1998), are many: the starving millions of the Third World; peasants forced off the land on which they depend to make their living;

the Palestinians whose Israeli oppressors destroy their crops and their homes, deny them access to land and resources, and make difficult the ordinarily simple tasks of shopping, farming or going to work. Oppression is often central to the truth activists aim to tell.

The condition of being oppressed is sometimes associated with a greater humanity. Oppression is imagined by some to reduce people to something truly human once the material trappings of existence have been stripped away. The oppressed are thought to retain a sense of community and solidarity with their fellow human beings that is essential to their continued existence as individuals and as a collectivity. One woman who had worked as a social worker with families 'in difficulty' spoke to me of people who are destitute and penniless (*les démunis*) who, unlike those who were comfortably off, she considered to possess truly 'human values', the 'essential values of humanity'. The most human of values reside with those who have little for they are forced to struggle for their very existence, she said, to 'develop an intelligence' not required of 'those who have everything', and in so doing to rely on others.

> The wealth of the most destitute is to have need of others in order to live. ... There is an enormous exchange between them ... a sort of reciprocity establishes itself. ... If I have everything, I have no need of others, I have nothing to receive from them because I have everything ... and I have nothing to give either. ... [But] in reciprocity there is a recognition of everyone [as a human being].

Amongst those who have nothing she saw a fundamental concern for the good of others and not just the good of self. There is, she insisted, a recognition of the solidarity of existence as integral to what is most truly human, in contrast to the individualistic creed of the wealthy in capitalist society.

If, for activists, the oppressed are most confronted with the truth of their basic humanity, the fundamental truth about the condition of their existence is also its injustice, an injustice the powerful consistently fail to acknowledge and deliberately attempt to conceal. Oppression is thought to involve lies or counter-truths for the very reason that it has as its aim the good of some at the expense of others. It is based on a partisan viewpoint whose goal is to justify domination. Israeli oppression of the Palestinians, for example, is considered to involve manipulation of the facts, a propaganda campaign and a withholding of information to hide the truth from Israelis themselves who, in the eyes of many in Palestine 12, would stand up to their government if only they knew the truth. Following a talk by a Palestinian in Millau, Christine expressed astonishment that, given this situation, Israelis did not have a greater curiosity about the truth. For her, the truth of oppression was so blindingly obvious: the occupation, the humiliation, the dehumanization, the control of Palestinians' movements in time and space, the checkpoints, the disruption to daily life, the killing and destruction, the denial of fundamental rights. Unless people are prevented from seeing it – and, for many, the Israeli public lives a sort of lie – the truth is there for all to see (J. Scott 1994, 365). As I have discussed above, this is a truth that is displayed in the Hour of Silence in the form of 'facts', in leaflets and in graphic illustrations. It is one in which the Palestinians are presented as having nothing to lie about and nothing to hide. They need only open themselves and their lives to outside observers to convince of the justice of their cause and the injustice of their plight.

The fundamental truth of oppression is thus considered something one can experience and communicate (see Fernández-Armesto 1998, 120ff.). Such a conception of truth is produced through particular social practices, the most salient of which are the information evenings, known as *témoignages*, that activists organize following 'civilian missions' to Palestine and which turn, as Robert Albro puts it, 'on the authority of lived experience' (2005, 261). Many from the Larzac-Millau area have been on these missions as observers, in order to express their solidarity with the Palestinians and to demand the 'protection of the Palestinian people' (see Cohen 2001, 256–7). The missions, the most well-known being the eleventh in 2002 in which Bové participated,[6] are organized in France by the Paris-based Campagne Civile Internationale pour la Protection du Peuple Palestinien. One of the key aims is to experience for oneself the conditions in which Palestinians are forced to live under Israeli occupation. Those who go consider themselves 'witnesses' (*témoins*). Their task is to observe, document and bring back information in order 'to make people aware' of what is really happening in Palestine. On returning, they 'testify' (*témoigner*) to Israeli oppression and Palestinian suffering at meetings of Palestine 12 or at specially arranged discussion evenings, attended mostly by other activists, where they present their testimonies or *témoignages*.[7] The immediate aim is to bear witness to something very concrete, something lived. Activists are motivated by the concrete suffering of people and in that suffering they consider the experiential truth of oppression to be revealed.

Témoignages, however, can only partly convey this suffering because the truth is really only revealed in personal experience. Agnès, who had been on a civilian mission, told me that 'as long as one doesn't meet for oneself the people who live these situations of suffering ... there is something that one cannot see and cannot understand'. My neighbour Valérie, speaking of her experiences in Palestine, said that what touched her the most was the humiliation that the Palestinians suffered at the 'mercy' of Israeli soldiers who could control at whim their every movement. That humiliation was something you could only really feel.

> Humiliation ... the feeling of injustice. For me it was unbearable. I think that theoretically you can understand the problem. ... Without going there you can understand that their struggle is just. ... But ... the humiliation, I think that is only something you can feel (*ressentir*). ... You can theorize it, but I don't think it has the same effect as when you feel it.

For many, injustice is something you feel, rather than something in need of intellectual explication. For Valérie, it was something she felt 'in the guts' and which, even as

---

6 See the book by Les Membres de la 11e Mission et José Bové (2002).

7 The verb is *témoigner*. The root is the same as the noun for witness (*témoin*) and as that for account, story or evidence (*témoignage*). A *témoin* testifies to the truth of something.

a child growing up in Millau during the Larzac struggle, she 'physically could not tolerate'. It was something that 'revolted' her.[8]

Like the confessional discussed by Foucault (1990, 58ff.), *témoignages* produce a truth in the process of creating activist subjectivities. Evenings in which people share their experiences help to create a realm of discourse in which participants, in speaking of what they have seen and felt, are seen, as activists, to speak the truth. Following what was dubbed the 'Larzac mission' to Palestine, such an evening was held at Le Cun and attended by residents of the Larzac and members of Palestine 12. Fifty people squeezed themselves into the dining hall for a slide show and to listen to the six witnesses who began by saying that they aimed 'to avoid abstractions' ('*sortir de l'abstraction*') and 'to show the life situation' ('*montrer l'aspect vie*') of the Palestinians. The truth of which they then spoke was one of suffering and humiliation, domination and oppression. It was one in which Israelis emerged, in terms frequently used in other contexts, as 'aggressors' and 'colonizers' and Palestinians as 'victims'. One man bore witness to the 'colonization of time' in which Palestinians' daily routines are constantly disrupted by Israeli check points. In response to a suggestion that a 'third force' was needed to act as mediator in the conflict, a man who had been on a previous mission asserted vigorously that you have, on the one hand, aggressors and, on the other, victims. We don't need mediation (as though the parties were equal) but a 'protection force', he protested.

Most agreed. Faced with Israeli aggression, Palestinians were cast as those who 'resist', reacting against their aggressors. All forms of resistance are 'understandable', one person offered during the ensuing discussion. You cannot condemn resistance. There was heated debate about suicide bombings, which, while not condoned, were 'understood' by some as the last resort of people suffering intolerably. The violence of a suicide bombing was presented during the discussion as clearly different from the violence of the Israeli army. It is 'resistance' to oppression. It is an effect of a 'cause' which is Israeli colonization and aggression, 'the fever and not the microbe', in one person's terms. But bombings were generally viewed as the work of an extremist minority which is sensationalized by a biased media. Most Palestinians were considered above such acts, 'noble' and 'proud', as someone put it. One witness spoke of how Israeli soldiers show 'no sign of humanity', treating the Palestinians like animals, and yet the Palestinians show, in turn, 'no hate'. He explained how he had seen Israeli settlers (the French term is *colons*, colonizers) wash their dogs in the wells from which Palestinians drew water. In response to this humiliation and dehumanizing treatment, he considered that the Palestinians only wanted to live in peace, to lead normal lives free of conflict, occupation and oppression. He affirmed their humanity, their desire for life, against the inhumanity and violence of the colonizer.

. There is not total agreement on the issues. Some disagree (often privately) with this man's denial of humanity to those on one side of the conflict and his attribution

---

8 It was also something she could define in terms of rights and inequality. Injustice emerged, she said, when 'certain sectors of the population appropriate rights that they refuse to others, appropriate riches that they plunder from others, and then these types of people manage to by-pass the law in order to escape [justice]'.

of it to those on the other. One person described it to me as 'racist'. At a forum
on the Palestine-Israel conflict in Marseilles, attended by hundreds, Leila Shahid,
from the General Delegation of Palestine in France and one of the most respected
figures of the Palestinian solidarity movement, affirmed that one must 'integrate the
humanity of one's own enemy'. Several activists with whom I spoke were impressed
by her recognition of the humanity of the Israelis, her ability to see the good in the
other side. At the evening at Le Cun, one person in particular, Didier, also tended to
downplay the opposition others see in the relation between Israelis and Palestinians.
He, too, said he had been able to see the humanity in Israeli soldiers. He suggested
the need to speak with Israeli settlers in an attempt to understand them. He accused
some activists of ignoring the Israelis killed by Palestinians. A death is a death, he
insisted, and we should be opposed to all killing, not just the killing of Palestinians.
When other activists reaffirmed that Israelis were 'aggressors', Didier replied that to
say that was racist. People are aggressors, he said, not whole peoples. He suggested,
using a chess analogy, that we must not fall into the trap of putting ourselves in the
place of the Palestinians. One sees the game of chess better from outside looking
in, although many activists put themselves on the board. He seemed to be appealing
for what Hervé from Le Cun, in a conversation I had with him, called 'non-partisan
solidarity'. Hervé considered activists did not help resolve the conflict by taking
sides.

Didier's desire for some form of non-partisan understanding largely fell on deaf
ears, and he often seemed to be arguing alone. Activists are very much partisan and this
conditions their understanding of the truth. Our objective, one person emphasized, is
the liberation of the Palestinian people. 'Action' in support of the victim, not further
'understanding', is what is needed, he said. For most, the Palestinians were self-
evidently victims of Israeli colonization, and the accounts of witnesses demonstrated
this. Didier's efforts, and the disagreement they provoked, only served to emphasize
how clearly, for others, the world was divided into a series of opposed categories:
oppressor and oppressed, aggressor and victim, power and counterpower, power and
resistance. People may disagree about the details but not, in general, the overall
'dichotomous' scheme (cf. Stoll 1997, 210). Rarely is a dichotomized view of the
world challenged in public. The most compelling evidence of this truth of oppressor
and oppressed is that presented by the witness. The publicly expressed experience
of the 'activist witness' – who emerges as the knower of a fundamental truth –
contributes to the lived human truth of this divided world. How can one disbelieve
what someone has experienced? Truth is obvious, self-evident to all who are willing
to 'open their eyes', to borrow the phrase of a couple who had more than once
been to Palestine. Experience – witnessing, seeing, feeling – contains truth, a truth
communicated within the activist network through display, discussion and debate.

A similar truth is also produced through the pedagogical forms I discuss above:
at demonstrations, in the media, at meetings, at the Hour of Silence where the 'facts'
are on display, in leaflets and books detailing 'domination' and 'oppression'. The
truth is not just known through experience. It is equally a matter of science and
rationality, argument and expert knowledge. The 'expert' (or, rather, counter-expert)
is as important as the witness in generating truth, as is the audience who reads or
hears that truth. At a workshop in Millau on Israel's occupation of Palestine, activists

listened studiously as scholar and activist Mohammed Taleb argued that Israel's actions are a form of 'colonial' domination and Israel a colonial society leading a colonial war. Israeli colonization is based on and justified by what Taleb called the ideology of 'Christian Zionism' whereby the colonization of new lands is viewed as a re-actualization of biblical history, the creation of a city of God in a land devoid of inhabitants, the founding of a new world. This ideology also justifies the existence of Protestant countries such as the United States and helps explain the support the United States gives to Israel given a 'profound identity' between the two nations. In addition, Israel is profoundly tied into the neoliberal global economy, and any peace will likely impose neoliberal domination as it takes away arms. An alternative form of globalization is really the only solution to the conflict.

Truth, one might say, emerges in the relation between the expert, the witness and an activist audience (Warner 2002). To participate in the network of knowledge – to read, to write, to listen, to talk, to bear witness, to demonstrate and display – is to participate in the production of truth. The complex truth for which Taleb argued, however, is premised on the more fundamental truth that in Palestine people are dying, their houses are being destroyed, their lives disrupted and their rights denied. It is the witness, armed with knowledge gleaned from experience, who contributes most convincingly this most fundamental activist truth. Concerned most directly with the experiential realities of oppression, the witness provides essential evidence of the immorality of the dominant and is instrumental in ensuring that the truth always has a moral dimension. This morality of truth is part of its objectivity, one demonstrated by observable facts. In contrast to what activists consider to be the fundamentally 'interested' truth of the dominant – that of Israeli colonizers or of a technoscience subservient to an economic domain devoid of morality – the activist truth is considered obvious and 'objective'. The truth proclaimed by the powerful is based on hiding otherwise self-evident facts, while activists aim only to reveal.

There is, perhaps, a tension here between the impartial, objective truth activists claim to know, and the partisan, moral truth that is on the side of the oppressed. But it would be wrong to oppose the objective and the moral (see Howell 1997, 8–9). The witness performs a normative role by making observed facts into facts of oppression and domination. The objective and the moral, the is and the ought, are thereby made to cohere. But it is the peculiar combination of objectivity and morality, the peculiar way in which an identity between facts and values is created, that is important. In the 'normative witnessing' in the Islamic court discussed by Clifford Geertz (1993), the truth is established upon the righteous moral character of the witness. Only those able to produce righteous judgements are deemed suitable witnesses. The facts must be 'reputable' and their reputation is not assured by knowledgeable individuals who stick to the empirical facts. In contrast, the truth of Millau and Larzac activists is thought to be there for all to see. It is an egalitarian and democratic, rather than hierarchical, truth. Witnesses merely report what they consider to be the objective facts of observable oppression, injustice and the denial of fundamental rights. Truth and morality are based on the facts, rather than the facts and truth being based on moral character. Like fundamental rights, both truth and morality are imagined to have their basis in facts of nature, life and humanity.

Chapter 8

Conclusion

My aim in this book has been to explore the 'political' world in which activists live. The politics in which they engage is multifaceted, complex and understood and enacted in diverse ways. For some, the political extends to all areas of their lives, while for others it is confined to the street. For no one should it be limited to the realm of parties and electoral politics.

The Larzac is, first of all, a political space. It is a place and symbol of resistance. The struggle against the military camp extension in the 1970s marked the Larzac out as somewhere special. It gained, for activists, an almost mythical status as a land inhabited by people with a political conscience and a desire to resist injustice and the power of the state. But if the Larzac's recent history is considered profoundly political, so is its present, as its current inhabitants attempt to ensure a continuity with the activist past. Larzac 2003, held thirty years after the first mass gathering on the plateau, served to proclaim the Larzac as the space of activism par excellence. The Larzac is also considered a place where people live their activism in daily life: in the communes that existed until recently; in the quest for simplicity and autonomy from consumer society; in the attempt to cut ties of dependency on Roquefort; in the de-intensification of farming and the rise of organics; in farmers' markets and direct selling. Everyday life, for many, is an expression of political commitment and awareness.

In a sense, the political is an attitude, a moral orientation, a felt obligation to act in the interests of the public good and in accordance with one's ideals. To act politically is to act consciously and critically as a 'citizen' and an 'individual'. It is to inform oneself and to become aware of injustice. It is to seek out and combat power in one's own life and to ensure a coherence between one's private and public existence. 'Activist', I argued, is a moral-political category. One ought, as an activist, to live coherently by putting one's ideals into practice. This moral-political obligation is one that must be self-imposed in reference to a norm against which people produce themselves as activist-individuals.

On the level of the 'collectivity', the political involves a particular type of organization that is enacted in meetings, associations and the activist network. If, on the Larzac, the political is somehow localized in space, the network is considered to extend activist politics across the globe. As an exemplary political space, the Larzac merges into the political more generally, the local is integrated into the global, the Larzac-Millau movement becomes part of a global social movement. Political activism has, for activists, a global orientation. Activists do not simply identify themselves with place or with a distinctive local form of politics, but with a non-localized global network. As an organizational form, the network is considered to allow for people's mobilization and for the participation of the powerless in political life. Along with activist associations and meetings, which ideally function on principles of solidarity and in a bottom-up, horizontal and egalitarian way, the network is thought to embody a participative type of politics in which citizens everywhere are free to contribute and where the common good is always the primary concern.

The political emerges with greatest force, however, as the autonomous collective actor of demonstrations, gatherings and media representations. The political is here embodied in the activist numbers who engage, and are seen to engage, in localized 'action' – the mass of citizens that turns out to form a crowd of protesters in order to demonstrate to power its discontent. Through such actions the social movement – a citizens' movement, a movement of civil society – constitutes itself as a counterpower, a movement of control. Its politics is enacted on the street and in the media, in 'public' space, as part of a struggle with the power of the state and of multinationals. This struggle is a struggle over knowledge and truth and involves an activist pedagogy.

A central feature of the political world of activists is its division in two. Not only do activists from the Larzac and Millau have a tendency to conceive of the world in terms of opposition between the forces of domination and oppression, power and resistance, they also enact this opposition. The forms of social action in which they engage serve to divide their world along oppositional lines. The way they organize collectively is oriented towards producing the social movement as a counterpower and force of resistance, one from which power in its various guises is absent. Thus they exclude from the movement all whose vision somehow threatens their own; they keep political parties and their power-seeking at bay; they endeavour to eliminate hierarchy and to function in a participative and horizontal manner; they aim always to increase the social movement's numbers and its strength – something reckoned in terms of a *rapport de force* – so that the movement may enter into a struggle with the forces of power; they demonstrate the counterpower of the movement in the street and present it to the world via the media. Similarly, activists aim to expunge from their own consciousness any vestiges of neoliberal thought, any misrecognition of injustice. By becoming aware their goal is to rid themselves of power in its ideological form and to live in a coherent way, keeping a certain distance from consumer society and the power inherent in it.

All these practices are concerned with producing some sort of autonomy. The thing that makes ongoing political action possible is the autonomy of individual activists and that of the social movement. Activists are much concerned, therefore, to ensure such forms of autonomy as part of a technique of resistance. They attempt to produce themselves as autonomous individuals, conscious of neoliberal ideology and of the truth of power and domination, because this is a condition of their activism. Similarly, they attempt to create an autonomous social movement, a counterpower capable of engaging in political struggle with powers whose autonomy is otherwise unconstrained. The ideal political subject, for activists, is an autonomous one. Autonomy, however, is highly problematic. It can't be taken for granted because power in the form of ideology always has a tendency to contaminate people's minds, and political and economic forms of power have a tendency to dominate their lives. As well as being defended, autonomy is something that must be won and increased in the process of resisting. The greater the autonomy of the social movement and of individual activists, the greater their potential for political action and for ongoing resistance. The struggle with power is thus a struggle over autonomy. Autonomy is what separates power from resistance, in a sense, thus dividing the world into two. The extent to which a space of autonomy exists is the extent to which power and resistance are opposed.[1]

It is interesting that autonomy has been made into an aspect of domination by scholars inspired, in particular, by Foucault. Foucault argued that modern forms of power produce persons as autonomous agents, individuals who internalize discipline and govern themselves (1977). More recently individual autonomy has been linked to the rise of neoliberal globalization and governmentality (Rose 1999). Of those working on the activist world, Sian Lazar writes that NGOs in Bolivia extend the power of government in their attempts (though not entirely successful) to 'create ... "empowered" individual, entrepreneurial, active citizens who will take responsibility for their own ... welfare, and who are prepared for the market rather than the state to provide for them' (2004b, 302). Barbara Cruikshank, similarly, discusses the 'technologies of citizenship' adopted by activists of various sorts, which, while they are 'aimed at making individuals politically active and capable of self-government', are actually 'modes of constituting and regulating citizens'. Their goal may be to create some form of autonomy and empowerment – 'self-help, self-sufficiency, or self-esteem' – but technologies of citizenship are in fact 'strategies for governing the very subjects whose problems they seek to redress' (1999, 1–2; see also Trouillot 2001).

For activists on the French left, however, autonomy is central to a discourse of liberation rather than domination. It seems to me that in the *idea* of autonomy, at least, is contained the idea of resistance – of not acting in accord with power and of not being touched by it. Autonomy does, in this sense, make resistance possible. But for resistance to then become effective, for it to emerge as a social force, autonomy must be increased and cultivated. So if autonomy is an effect of modern forms of power, it is equally the effect of resistance (cf. Mitchell 1999). It is created in the process of resisting. The autonomy of the French social movement and of the activist individuals who participate in it, and the opposition between power and resistance, are produced and reproduced through organizing, protesting, educating, attempting to live coherently, and critically reflecting on one's own existence.

I should make it clear that autonomy should not be understood in absolute terms, as something one either has or does not have. Steven Lukes, in a recent book on power, suggests that Foucault's 'ultra-radical' concept of power as all-pervasive and productive leaves little room for agency, freedom, rationality or autonomy. Indeed, he argues that the 'final Foucault' abandoned his earlier ultra-radicalism for just this reason (2005, 95–107). But I think the question here is not whether or not individuals or activists are 'really' autonomous or not in some ultimate theoretical sense. Anthropologists inspired by Foucault – and particularly by his rather cryptic claim that 'resistance is never in a position of exteriority in relation to power' (1990, 95) – have been somehow concerned with this question. In the past, they argue, power and resistance had been understood as things opposed – historical forces (capitalist and

---

1 I elsewhere take up this argument and the points which follow (Williams 2008).

working classes), or public and private transcripts (J.C. Scott 1990) – with resistance emerging from an 'originary space of autonomy beyond the reach of power' (Moore 1998, 352), 'from a space of "autonomous consciousness"' (Fletcher 2001, 48), or from an authentic and 'whole subject' (Kondo 1990, 224). But as part of an effort to 'eliminate the [false] dichotomy between power and resistance', as Robert Fletcher puts it (2001, 56), they insist that there can be no autonomous domain of resistance (see Abu-Lughod 1990; Mitchell 1990; Reed-Danahay 1993; Hegland 2003).

If the point is theoretical, then, in a sense, I agree. Activists can never be completely autonomous of the forms of power to which they are subject and which no doubt enter into their very being. The interesting question, however, is an ethnographic one. How precisely is autonomy an important social category, and what practices does autonomy involve? In this book I have been interested in autonomy as a social and historical phenomenon (as, indeed, was Foucault).[2] For activists, their autonomy as individuals and that of the social movement is variable and problematic. It exists, if I can put it this way, on a continuum, often more 'limited and partial' than 'integral', in Gramsci's terms (1971, 52; see Moore 1998, 352), and something to acquire as part of a political struggle, as it was for the 'subaltern groups' with which Gramsci was concerned (1971, 53). The more of it one has, the more able one is to resist, and the more one produces a dichotomy between 'power' (the state, the WTO, multinationals, neoliberal ideology, hierarchy) and 'resistance' (the social movement, activists, equality) as an ethnographic and empirical, rather than theoretical, fact.

I am not sure how the relationship between power and resistance could be understood in anything other than empirical terms, which is perhaps the point the anthropologists I cite above are trying to make. Forms of power and resistance are always historically specific and socially embedded. The degree to which subordinates demystify dominant ideologies, produce some sort of autonomous consciousness, or the ways in which they are subject to power and resist are all ethnographic questions. In the case I have considered in this book, I have argued that the relationship between power and resistance is usefully understood in terms of autonomy. Autonomy is something to struggle over, to increase, to cultivate, to win from the clutches of power. It is never something activists can assume given the

---

2 Foucault and those inspired by him historicize autonomy. They examine the rise of a new set of categories to think with, of a discourse and set of techniques by which autonomous domains are created – those of the individual, state, society, economy (Barry et al. 1996; Mitchell 1999). Other scholars have similarly elucidated the emergence of autonomy as a category of new historical import. Foucault's concern with the subject builds on an earlier French anthropological interest in the individual as a peculiar historical and social phenomenon, expressed in the work of Mauss (1985) and Dumont (1980, 1986). Berman (1980) examines the rise of the 'authentic individual' in Enlightenment thought; Schneewind (1998, 13) explores the moral philosophical tradition that culminated in Kant's development of the notion of morality as autonomy or self-government and his view of individuals as 'autonomous agents who impose morality on [them]selves'; Rosanvallon (1992, 13ff.) looks at the history of universal suffrage in France from the Revolution and how the right to vote was based on a new conception of political equality and individual autonomy (see also Heller et al. 1986; Taylor 1989).

political and economic forces that would deny it to them. The politics in which they engage thus involves a struggle over autonomy – over freedom, agency, the power to choose, to act independently, to be free of ideology, domination and dependency. Both dominates and subordinates are concerned with autonomy because it is a source of political action. An autonomy of mind and of action, in a sense, makes both domination and resistance possible, just as it emerges from certain practices of domination and resistance. To think in terms of power and resistance, if you like, is to think in terms of autonomy.

Autonomy is a very general notion, one which can be applied to all sorts of things. The importance of autonomy in the world of alterglobalization activism is indicative of the way activist politics has itself been generalized with the decline of Marxism and of 'old' social movements focused on class struggle. Domination in general is what concerns activists today, I have argued, as opposed to class domination in particular. Activists rarely reduce domination to a matter of the relations of production or class, but consider it to stem from an excessive neoliberal autonomy, an otherwise unconstrained power. Although Marx somehow lurks behind many of the ideas alterglobalization activists hold, the influence of Marxist thought has waned. What Larzac-Millau activists tend to share with Marx is an emphasis on the struggle between opposing social forces. For Marx, these forces are capital and labour; for activists, they are the powerful and the powerless, the rich and the poor, those above and those below (*d'en haut* and *d'en bas*). The terms, in the latter case, are much broader and more inclusive. Class domination has dissolved into domination in general, which is present whenever the rights of human beings are denied (see Engels 1954, 35–6; Hardt and Negri 2000, 256).

The paradigmatic political subject is similarly general and autonomous as far as activists are concerned. The figure of the worker has been generalized into that of the individual, the rights-bearing human being or the citizen. All have the potential to resist in truly meaningful ways if they can only free themselves from the ideology of neoliberalism or consumerism and from the political-economic constraints on their lives. Resistance is here a matter of individual and collective autonomy, whereas revolutionary potential from a traditional Marxist viewpoint was a matter of economic relations and class position. The working class had the privilege of making history. But the workers on whom intellectuals pinned so many revolutionary hopes were never quite autonomous individuals, rather they were always somehow subordinate to the vanguard within a party or movement hierarchy. Gramsci was concerned with the hegemony of a class in which an intellectual elite was to contribute the 'theoretical aspect' (1971, 334). The struggle for hegemony may have been a struggle for an autonomy of sorts (see Lukes 2005, 50), but for a limited autonomy, one sought collectively by subaltern groups as a whole as they battled to take control of the state. Individual autonomy had to be subordinated to that of the collective. Autonomy was not valued in the same way it is by alterglobalization activists today, where it is something sought at every level. The social movement must preserve the autonomy of the individuals and associations who participate in it, world trade policy must respect the autonomy of states and regions, the autonomy of individuals and communities everywhere is to be defended and fought for. Autonomy ought to be a ubiquitous and general feature of the world, and the fact that it is not is a consequence of all the forms of domination that deny it.

Even certain contemporary Marxist analyses, however, generalize the terms of the debate. John Holloway (2005) and Michael Hardt and Antonio Negri (2005), who have published influential books on power and resistance today, offer generalized understandings of autonomy, political subjectivity and class. For Hardt and Negri, '[m]ultitude is a class concept' (2005, 103). Class is something they define in terms of collective struggle rather than in relation to the means of production. The multitude is not the same as the working class because it is inclusive, constituted by all who struggle. Class, they write, is a political project, one that emerges from the unification of struggles (104). Likewise, the multitude needs a political project to bring it into existence (212). As the multitude emerges as a class, it simultaneously generates itself as an autonomous social subject, independent of power, capital and Empire. 'The multitude, in contrast to the bourgeoisie and all other exclusive, limited class formations, is capable of forming society autonomously', something absolutely 'central to its democratic possibilities' (xvii–xviii). And because the differences that constitute it are fundamental and 'cannot be reduced to sameness' (99), the multitude preserves the autonomy of the people who collectively make it up.

For Holloway, a class understanding of capitalism remains fundamental, but he sees class as a 'process' rather than an external antagonism (2005, 56, 142). 'Class struggle', he writes, '... is the unceasing daily antagonism ... between alienation and dis-alienation, between definition and anti-definition, between fetishisation and de-fetishisation'. As human beings, 'everyone is torn apart by class antagonism' (143–4). Capitalism, Holloway argues, exploits and oppresses by separating human doing from the done, by turning creative human doing into alienated doing, by converting human beings into mere workers. 'It is only in so far as we [are human beings and] *are not* working class that the question of emancipation can even be posed' (145, original emphasis). The struggle is thus 'against being classified ... in so far as we are human' (144). 'Class struggle is a conflict that permeates the whole of human existence, ... [that] exists within all of us', he states (147).

Hardt and Negri and Holloway thus generalize resistance to capitalism and Empire, making it the preserve of all human beings who struggle, rather than that of the working class. And they generalize class by making all who struggle somehow working class (in Holloway's case) or by locating any useful notion of class in relation to the struggle of an inclusive multitude. They also call for us to begin the process of resistance with our own experience as human beings. Struggle begins in daily life. This, I think, is a basic principle of alterglobalization activism, even if alterglobalization activists tend not to focus on class.

The most general solution to the problem of domination that activists propose is the principle of coherence. To live and act coherently is to ensure an accord, in everyday life, between thoughts and deeds, values and practices, private and public, individual and collective, ought and is. It implies seeking an autonomy from the hierarchical and oppressive forms of social relationship entailed by political parties, consumer society or commodity relations in general. Not only is coherence sought in everyday life but also in the way society, more broadly conceived, is organized. All social practices should cohere with certain fundamental ideas – ideas of rights, equality, autonomy. Coherence thus provides a principle for ethical individual action in the world, for creating a locally-based society autonomous of capitalism, and for reforming or constraining capitalist society so that it coheres with humanitarian ideals. Acting in the street in accord with your beliefs that the world needs to change, that the powerful need to be resisted, is also an expression of the value of coherence.

The notion of coherence is bound up with that of autonomy. Coherence implies some sort of autonomous consciousness, some desire to resist, in the face of a world of domination and oppression. Like autonomy, achieving coherence is problematic, given that activists are embedded in capitalist relations of power, production, consumption, and exchange. While ostensibly opposed to the global market economy, they have little choice but to participate in it. But the fact that reality contradicts the ideal provides activists with their starting point as they strive for coherence in daily life and to bring about a more coherent world. Any incoherence is not something to passively accept, but a problem on which activists must first reflect and ideally resolve through action.

Perhaps the contradictions between ideal and reality – the failure to produce enduring forms of autonomy – will mean that activists' efforts will eventually come to nothing and the alterglobalization movement will be incorporated into the general capitalist order (see Cerny 1982a, xiv). What I would like to suggest, however, is that contradiction may act as a creative force, a motor of change. Marx argued somewhere along these lines. He claimed that the contradictions of capitalism were key to its eventual dissolution. The contradictions of class, or those between private appropriation and socialized production, would lead to revolution and emancipation (Marx 1971, 21; see Giddens 1979, 131ff.). Marx, however, was concerned with contradictions intrinsic to capitalism. The contradictions between principle and practice that alterglobalization activists face emerge, in contrast, from the act of reflection and comparison that is required by the ethic of coherence. When actions don't cohere with ideals, they become objects of thought, criticism, debate, and further action. Contradiction means that activists don't lose themselves in impossible ideals and global utopian visions, their political project, while based on ideals, remains always practical, locally focused, centered in the here and now, and dynamic. Activists never quite have the 'solution', they always find more problems and contradictions to deal with through action. Their vision is never complete, but must be open to the contingencies and incoherences of the world.

Bibliography

Aarrg (2001) 'Règles de l'aarrg avril 2001', *Aarrg* [website], (published online) <http://www.aarrg.org/aarrguments.html>, accessed July 2004.

—— (2002) 'Article passant ordinaire janvier 2002', *Aarrg* [website], (published online) <http://www.aarrg.org/aarrguments.html>, accessed July 2004.

Abélès, Marc (1999), 'How the anthropology of France has changed anthropology in France: assessing new directions in the field', *Cultural Anthropology* 14:3, 404–8.

Abu-Lughod, Lila (1990), 'The romance of resistance: tracing transformations of power through Bedouin women', *American Ethnologist* 17:1, 41–55.

Agamben, Giorgio (1998[1995]), *Homo Sacer: Sovereign Power and Bare Life*, Daniel Heller-Roazen, transl. (Stanford: Stanford University Press).

Agulhon, Maurice (1992), 'Le centre et la périphérie', in Pierre Nora (ed.), *Les lieux de mémoire, vol. III, Les France, 1. Conflits et partages* (Paris: Gallimard), pp. 824–49.

Albro, Robert (2005), '"The water is ours, Carajo!" Deep citizenship in Bolivia's water war', in June Nash (ed.), *Social Movements: An Anthropological Reader* (Oxford: Blackwell), pp. 249–71.

Alland, Alexander (with Sonia Alland) (2001), *Crisis and Commitment: The Life History of a French Social Movement,* Revised Second Edition (Amsterdam: Harwood Academic Publishers).

Alvarez, Sonia E., Evelina Dagnino and Arturo Escobar (1998), 'Introduction: the cultural and the political in Latin American social movements', in Sonia E. Alvarez, Evelina Dagnino and Arturo Escobar (eds), *Cultures of Politics, Politics of Cultures: Re-visioning Latin American Social Movements* (Boulder: Westview Press), pp. 1–29.

Ancelovici, Marcos (2002), 'Organizing against globalization: the case of ATTAC in France', *Politics & Society* 30:3, 427–63.

Anderson, Benedict (1983), *Imagined Communities: Reflections on the Origin and Spread of Nationalism* (London and New York: Verso).

Appadurai, Arjun (1996), *Modernity at Large: Cultural Dimensions of Globalization* (Minneapolis: University of Minnesota Press).

—— (2000), 'Grassroots globalization and the research imagination', *Public Culture* 12:1, 1–19.

—— (2002), 'Deep democracy: urban governmentality and the horizon of politics', *Public Culture* 14:1, 21–47.

Arche (n.d.) *L'Arche: un mouvement et des communautés nés de la rencontre de Lanza del Vasto avec Gandhi*, Communauté de l'Arche (Brochure).

Arendt, Hannah (1959), *The Human Condition: A Study of the Central Dilemmas Facing Modern Man* (New York: Doubleday Anchor Books).

Aron, Raymond (1986[1964]), 'Macht, power, puissance: democratic prose or demoniacal poetry?', in Steven Lukes (ed.), *Power* (Oxford: Basil Blackwell), pp. 253–77.

Attac (2000), *Tout sur Attac* (Paris: Mille et Une Nuits).

Auteurs divers (2004) 'AGCS, démocratie en péril', *Construire un Monde Solidaire* [website], (published online 15 March 2004) <http://www.monde-solidaire.org/ spip/article.php3?id_article=1375>, accessed March 2004.

Baierle, Sérgio Gregório (1998), 'The explosion of experience: the emergence of a new ethical-political principle in popular movements in Porto Alegre, Brazil', in Sonia E. Alvarez, Evelina Dagnino and Arturo Escobar (eds), *Cultures of Politics, Politics of Cultures: Re-visioning Latin American Social Movements* (Boulder: Westview Press), pp. 118–38.

Balibar, Étienne (1994), '"Rights of man" and "rights of the citizen": the modern dialectic of equality and freedom', *Masses, Classes, Ideas: Studies on Politics and Philosophy Before and After Marx* (New York: Routledge), pp. 39–59.

Barral, Pierre (1966), 'Note historique sur l'emploi du terme "paysan"', *Études rurales* 22: June, 72–80.

Barry, Andrew (1999), 'Demonstrations: sites and sights of direct action', *Economy and Society* 28:1, 75–94.

Barry, Andrew, Thomas Osborne and Nikolas Rose (1996), 'Introduction', in Andrew Barry, Thomas Osborne and Nikolas Rose (eds), *Foucault and Political Reason: Liberalism, Neo-Liberalism and Rationalities of Government* (London: UCL Press), pp. 1–17.

Barthes, Roland (1957), 'Poujade et les intellectuels', in *Mythologies* (Paris: Seuil), pp. 205–12.

Beck, Ulrich (1992[1986]), *Risk Society: Towards a New Modernity*, Mark Ritter, transl. (London: Sage Publications).

Bellah, Robert, Richard Madsen, William Sullivan, Ann Swidler and Steven Tipton (1996), *Habits of the Heart: Individualism and Commitment in American Life* (Berkeley: University of California Press).

Berglund, Eeva (1998), *Knowing Nature, Knowing Science: An Ethnography of Environmental Activism* (Cambridge: The White Horse Press).

Berlan, Jean-Pierre (2001), 'Avant-propos', in Jean-Pierre Berlan (ed.), *La guerre au vivant. Organismes génétiquement modifiés et autres mystifications scientifiques* (Marseille: Agone), pp. 5–11.

Berman, Marshall (1980), *The Politics of Authenticity: Radical Individualism and the Emergence of Modern Society* (New York: Athenium).

Béteille, André (1983), 'The idea of natural inequality', in *The Idea of Natural Inequality and Other Essays* (Delhi: Oxford University Press), pp. 7–32.

Béteille, Roger (1979), 'Un réservoir d'hommes (1789–1978)', in Henri Enjalbert (ed.), *Histoire du Rouergue* (Toulouse: Privat), pp. 371–92.

Bonnefous, Pierre, Raymond Martin and les Paysans du Larzac (1984), *Alors la paix viendra* (Millau: Fondation Larzac).

Boucomont, Arnaud (2002), 'Riesel, le radical', *Midi Libre*: 19 Nov., 15.

Bourdieu, Pierre (1998), *Acts of Resistance: Against the New Myths of Our Time*, Richard Nice, transl. (Cambridge: Polity Press).

—— (2003[2001]), *Firing Back: Against the Tyranny of the Market 2*, Loïc Wacquant, transl. (New York and London: The New Press).

Bové, José (2000), 'Penser global, agir local !', *Gardarem lo Larzac* 230, 1.

—— (2001), 'A farmers' international?', *New Left Review* 12: Dec., 89–101.

Bové, José and François Dufour (2000), *Le monde n'est pas une marchandise. Des paysans contre la malbouffe* (Entretiens avec Gilles Luneau), Nouvelle édition augmentée (Paris: Éditions la Découverte).

—— (2002), *The World is Not for Sale: Farmers Against Junkfood*, Anna De Casparis, transl. (London: Verso).

Bové, José and Gilles Luneau (2004), *Pour la désobéissance civique* (Paris: Éditions La Découverte).

Bowen, John R. (2003), 'Two approaches to rights and religion in contemporary France', in Richard Ashby Wilson and Jon P. Mitchell (eds), *Human Rights in Global Perspective: Anthropological Studies of Rights, Claims and Entitlements* (London: Routledge), pp. 33–53.

Braudel, Fernand (1989[1986]), *The Identity of France. Volume 1: History and Environment*, Siân Reynolds, transl. (London: Fontana).

Brown, Wendy (1995), *States of Injury: Power and Freedom in Late Modernity* (Princeton: Princeton University Press).

Brush, Stephen B. (1999), 'Bioprospecting the public domain', *Cultural Anthropology* 14:4, 535–55.

Butler, Beverley (1996), 'The tree, the tower and the shaman: the material culture of resistance of the no M11 link roads protest of Wanstead and Leytonstone, London', *Journal of Material Culture* 1:3, 337–63.

Calderón, Fernando, Alejandro Piscitelli and José Luis Reyna (1992), 'Social movements: actors, theories, expectations', in Arturo Escobar and Sonia E. Alvarez (eds), *The Making of Social Movements in Latin America* (Boulder: Westview Press), pp. 19–36.

Calhoun, Craig (1992), 'Introduction: Habermas and the public sphere', in Craig Calhoun (ed.), *Habermas and the Public Sphere* (Cambridge, Mass.: MIT Press), pp. 1–48.

Canetti, Elias (2000[1962]), *Crowds and Power*, Carol Stewart, transl. (London: Phoenix Press).

Cassen, Bernard (2003), 'On the attack', *New Left Review* 19: Feb., 41–60.

Castelbou, Thierry (2002a), 'Les paysans ne sont plus ce qu'ils étaient', *Gardarem lo Larzac* 245, 1.

—— (2002b), 'La répression est en marche', *Gardarem lo Larzac* 245, 4.

—— (2002c), 'Encore non!', *Gardarem lo Larzac* 247, 1.

Castells, Manuel (1996), *The Rise of the Network Society. The Information Age: Economy, Society and Culture, vol. I* (Oxford: Blackwell).

—— (1997), *The Power of Identity. The Information Age: Economy, Society and Culture, vol. II* (Oxford: Blackwell).

Cerny, Philip (1982a), 'Introduction: The politics of protest in contemporary French society', in Philip Cerny (ed.), *Social Movements and Protest in France* (London: Francis Pinter), pp. vii–xxiv.

—— (1982b), 'Non-terrorism and the politics of repressive tolerance', in Philip Cerny (ed.), *Social Movements and Protest in France* (London: Francis Pinter), pp. 94–124.

Clarke, Richard W.J. (2003), 'Voices from the margins: knowledge and interpellation in Israeli human rights protests', in Richard Ashby Wilson and Jon P. Mitchell (eds), *Human Rights in Global Perspective: Anthropological Studies of Rights, Claims and Entitlements* (London: Routledge), pp. 118–39.

Cmiel, Kenneth (1999), 'The emergence of human rights politics in the United States', *Journal of American History* 86:3, 1231–50.

—— (2004), 'The Recent History of Human Rights', *The American Historical Review* 109:1, 56 paragraphs (published online) <http://www.historycooperative. org/journals/ahr/109.1/cmiel.html>

Cohen, Stanley (2001), *States of Denial: Knowing about Atrocities and Suffering* (Cambridge: Polity Press).

Coleman, Simon (2000), *The Globalisation of Charismatic Christianity: Spreading the Gospel of Prosperity* (Cambridge: Cambridge University Press).

Collier, George A. and Jane F. Collier (2005), 'The Zapatista rebellion in the context of globalization', *Journal of Peasant Studies* 32:3, 450–60.

Comaroff, John L. and Jean Comaroff (1999), 'Introduction', in John L. Comaroff and Jean Comaroff (eds), *Civil Society and the Political Imagination in Africa: Critical Perspectives* (Chicago: Chicago University Press), pp. 1–43.

Confédération Paysanne (2002), *Changeons de politique agricole* (Paris: Mille et une Nuits).

—— (2003), 'Victime de Monsanto et de la justice', *Campagnes Solidaires* 171, II.

Corbin, Alain (1992), 'Paris-Province', in Pierre Nora (ed.), *Les lieux de mémoire, vol. III, Les France, 1. Conflits et partages* (Paris: Gallimard), pp. 776–823.

Cowan, Jane K. (2003), 'The uncertain political limits of cultural claims: minority rights politics in south-east Europe', in Richard Ashby Wilson and Jon P. Mitchell (eds), *Human Rights in Global Perspective: Anthropological Studies of Rights, Claims and Entitlements* (London: Routledge), pp. 140–62.

Cowan, Jane K., Marie-Bénédicte Dembour and Richard A. Wilson, eds (2001), *Culture and Rights: Anthropological Perspectives* (Cambridge: Cambridge University Press).

Cranston, Maurice (1988), 'The sovereignty of the nation', in Colin Lucas (ed.), *The French Revolution and the Creation of Modern Political Culture. Vol. 2. The Political Culture of the French Revolution* (Oxford: Pergamon), pp. 97–104.

Cruikshank, Barbara (1999), *The Will to Empower: Democratic Citizens and Other Subjects* (Ithaca and London: Cornell University Press).

CUMS (2003) 'Charte du Collectif "Construire un Monde Solidaire"', *Construire un Monde Solidaire* [website], (published online, updated 18 Nov. 2003) <http:// www.monde-solidaire.org/spip/article.php3?id_article=19>, accessed Nov. 2003.

Cunningham, Hilary (2000), 'The ethnography of transnational social activism: understanding the global as local practice', *American Ethnologist* 26:3, 583–604.

Da Silva, Elian and Dominique Laurens (1995), *Fleurines et Roquefort* (Rodez: Editions de Rouergue).

Dagnino, Evelina (1998), 'Culture, citizenship, and democracy: changing discourses and practices of the Latin American left', in Sonia E. Alvarez, Evelina Dagnino and Arturo Escobar (eds), *Cultures of Politics, Politics of Cultures: Re-visioning Latin American Social Movements* (Boulder: Westview Press), pp. 33–63.

Della Porta, Donatella, Hanspeter Kriesi and Dieter Rucht, eds (1999), *Social Movements in a Globalizing World* (London: MacMillan Press).

Dembour, Marie-Bénédicte (1996), 'Human rights talk and anthropological ambivalence: the particular contexts of universal claims', in Olivia Harris (ed.), *Inside and Outside the Law: Anthropological Studies of Authority and Ambiguity* (London: Routledge), pp. 19–40.

Dilley, Roy (1992), 'Contesting markets: a general introduction to market ideology, imagery and discourse', in Roy Dilley (ed.), *Contesting Markets: Analysis of Ideology, Discourse and Practice* (Edinburgh: Edinburgh University Press), pp. 1–33.

Doane, Molly (2005), 'The resilience of nationalism in a global era: Megaprojects in Mexico's south', in June Nash (ed.), *Social Movements: An Anthropological Reader* (Oxford: Blackwell), pp. 187–202.

Donzelot, Jacques (1991), 'The mobilization of society', in Graham Burchell, Colin Gordon and Peter Miller (eds), *The Foucault Effect: Studies in Governmentality* (Chicago: University of Chicago Press), pp. 169–79.

Douglas, Mary (1966), *Purity and Danger: An Analysis of Concepts of Pollution and Taboo* (London: Routledge and Kegan Paul).

Dubofsky, Melvyn (1988), *We Shall Be All: A History of the Industrial Workers of the World*, Second Edition (Urbana: University of Illinois Press).

Dumont, Louis (1977), *From Mandeville to Marx: The Genesis and Triumph of Economic Ideology* (Chicago: University of Chicago Press).

—— (1980[1966]), *Homo Hierarchicus: The Caste System and its Implications*, Mark Sainsbury, transl. (Chicago: University of Chicago Press).

—— (1986[1983]), *Essays on Individualism: Modern Ideology in Anthropological Perspective* (Chicago: University of Chicago Press).

Durkheim, Emile (1933[1893]), *The Division of Labour in Society*, George Simpson, transl. (New York: The Free Press).

Duyvendak, Jan Willem (1995), *The Power of Politics: New Social Movements in France* (Boulder: Westview Press).

Edelman, Marc (1999), *Peasants Against Globalization: Rural Social Movements in Costa Rica* (Stanford: Stanford University Press).

—— (2001), 'Social Movements: Changing Paradigms and Forms of Politics', *Annual Review of Anthropolology* 30:1, 285–317.

—— (2005), 'When networks don't work: the rise and fall and rise of civil society initiatives in Central America', in June Nash (ed.), *Social Movements: An Anthropological Reader* (Oxford: Blackwell), pp. 29–45.

Eley, Geoff (2002), *Forging Democracy: The History of the Left in Europe, 1850–2000* (Oxford: Oxford University Press).

Elias, Norbert (1991[1987]), *The Society of Individuals*, Edmund Jephcott, transl. (Oxford: Blackwell).

Engels, Frederick (1954[1877/1892]), *Socialism: Utopian and Scientific* (Moscow: Progress Publishers).

Enjalbert, Henri (1979a), 'Déclin des notables et montée d'une nouvelle génération (1914–1978)', in Henri Enjalbert (ed.), *Histoire du Rouergue* (Toulouse: Privat), pp. 445–94.

—— (1979b), 'Une économie qui s'attarde (1789–1914)', in Henri Enjalbert (ed.), *Histoire du Rouergue* (Toulouse: Privat), pp. 345–70.

Escobar, Arturo (1992a), 'Culture, practice and politics: anthropology and the study of social movements', *Critique of Anthropology* 12:4, 395–432.

—— (1992b), 'Culture, economics, and politics in Latin American social movements theory and research', in Arturo Escobar and Sonia E. Alvarez (eds), *The Making of Social Movements in Latin America* (Boulder: Westview Press), pp. 62–85.

—— (2001), 'Culture sits in places: reflections on globalism and subaltern strategies of localization', *Political Geography* 20:2, 139–74.

Fabre, Magali (2000) 'La lutte du Larzac 1971–1981: Exemple d'une lutte sociale originale et novatrice', Master's thesis (Mémoire d'Histoire Contemporaine), Université de Versailles.

Faucheurs Volontaires (2003) 'Charte des faucheurs volontaires', *Construire un Monde Solidaire* [website], <http://www.monde-solidaire.org/spip/IMG/pdf/Charte_faucheurs.pdf>, accessed Nov. 2003.

FB (2002), 'René Riesel : "Je trouve répugnant de demander une grâce. Il est hors de question que je me renie"', *Midi Libre*: 22 Nov., 18.

Ferguson, James and Akhil Gupta (2002), 'Spatializing states: toward an ethnography of neoliberal governmentality', *American Ethnologist* 29:4, 981–1002.

Fernández-Armesto, Felipe (1998), *Truth: A History and a Guide for the Perplexed* (London: Black Swan).

Fletcher, Robert (2001), 'What are we fighting for? Rethinking resistance in a Pewenche community in Chile', *Journal of Peasant Studies* 28:3, 37–66.

Foucault, Michel (1977[1975]), *Discipline and Punish: The Birth of the Prison*, Alan Sheridan, transl. (London: Penguin).

—— (1990[1976]), *The History of Sexuality: An Introduction*, Robert Hurley, transl. (London: Penguin).

—— (1991[1978]), 'Governmentality', in Graham Burchell, Colin Gordon and Peter Miller (eds), *The Foucault Effect: Studies in Governmentality* (Chicago: University of Chicago Press), pp. 87–104.

Fox, Richard and Orin Starn (1997), 'Introduction', in Richard Fox and Orin Starn (eds), *Between Resistance and Revolution: Cultural Politics and Social Protest* (New Brunswick: Rutgers University Press), pp. 1–16.

Fraser, Nancy (2005), 'Reframing justice in a globalizing world', *New Left Review* 36, 69–88.

Galtier, Gérard (2000), *Larzac. Une terre qui dit non* (Sauveterre-de-Rouergue: Éditions de la Bastide).

Gandini, Jean-Jacques and members of Un Autre Futur de Montpellier (2002), 'La loi sur la sécurité quotidienne', *Le Monde Libertaire*: 13–19 June.

Garcés, Fernando Rosero and Sebastián Betancourt (2001) 'Les leaders sociaux au XXIe siècle : défis et propositions', paper presented at conference 'Formations citoyennes et formations de leaders sociaux', 10–12 June, organized by Institut d'Études Equatoriennes; Fondation Charles Léopold Mayer pour le Progrès de l'Homme; Programme Agricultures Paysannes, Sociétés et Mondialisation. (Available online) <http://www.alliance21.org/2003/article.php3?id_ article=458>

Gauchet, Marcel (1992), 'La droite et la gauche', in Pierre Nora (ed.), *Les lieux de mémoire, vol. III, Les France, 1. Conflits et partages* (Paris: Gallimard), pp. 394–467.

Geertz, Clifford (1993[1983]), 'Local knowledge: fact and law in comparative perspective', in *Local Knowledge* (London: Fontana Press), pp. 167–234.

Gesson, Gilles (2000), 'Les Aveyronnais en Amérique', *Gardarem lo Larzac* 230, 1, 7.

—— (2001), 'Un autre monde est possible', *Gardarem lo Larzac* 237, 1, 7.

—— (2003a) 'Alerte à l'AGCS', *Construire un Monde Solidaire* [website], (published online) <http://www.monde-solidaire.org/spip/article.php3?id_article=14>, accessed March 2004.

—— (2003b), 'À Porto Alegre, pour le droit', *Gardarem lo Larzac* 249, 1, 6–7.

—— (2004), 'Une autre Europe à Paris', *Gardarem lo Larzac* 255, 1.

—— (2005), 'La victoire du droit', *Gardarem lo Larzac* 261, 1.

—— (2006), 'Procès des Faucheurs, suite ...', *Gardarem lo Larzac* 267, 7.

Giddens, Anthony (1979), *Central Problems in Social Theory: Action, Structure, and Contradiction in Social Analysis* (Berkeley: University of California Press).

—— (1991), *Modernity and Self-Identity: Self and Society in Late Modern Age* (Cambridge: Polity Press).

Gildea, Robert (1996), *France Since 1945* (Oxford: Oxford University Press).

Gledhill, John (1994), *Power and its Disguises: Anthropological Perspectives on Politics* (London: Pluto Press).

—— (1997), 'Liberalism, socio-economic rights and the politics of identity: from moral economy to indigenous rights', in Richard A. Wilson (ed.), *Human Rights, Culture and Context: Anthropological Perspectives* (London: Pluto Press), pp. 70–110.

—— (2003), 'Rights and the poor', in Richard Ashby Wilson and Jon P. Mitchell (eds), *Human Rights in Global Perspective: Anthropological Studies of Rights, Claims and Entitlements* (London: Routledge), pp. 209–28.

Glenn, Vincent (2002) 'Davos, Porto Alegre et autres batailles', FilmO, Les Films Grain de Sable, Cityzen Télévision (Film).

GLL (1999), 'Spécial Anti Mac Do', *Gardarem lo Larzac* 228, supplement.

Goldman, Michael, ed. (1998), *Privatizing Nature: Political Struggles for the Global Commons* (London: Pluto Press in association with Transnational Institute).

Goodale, Mark (2006), 'Introduction to "Anthropology and Human Rights in a New Key"', *American Anthropologist* 108:1, 1–8.

Goody, Jack and Dick Whittaker (2001), 'Rural manufacturing in the Rouergue from antiquity to the present: the examples of pottery and cheese', *Comparative Studies in Society and History* 43:2, 225–45.

Graeber, David (n.d.), *Direct Action: An Ethnography* (unpublished manuscript).

—— (2004), *Fragments of an Anarchist Anthropology* (Chicago: Prickly Paradigm Press).

Gramsci, Antonio (1971[1929–1935]), *Selections from the Prison Notebooks*, Quintin Hoare and Geoffrey Nowell Smith, transl. (London: Lawrence and Wishart).

Green, Sarah F. (1997), *Urban Amazons: Lesbian Feminism and Beyond in the Gender, Sexuality and Identity Battles of London* (Houndmills: Macmillan).

Greenpeace (n.d.) 'The Greenpeace story: 1971 to 1974', *Greenpeace* [website], <http://www.greenpeace.org.uk/contentlookup.cfm?includeraw=slideshow&FirstResultParam=1&TLIDParam=14&MenuPoint=C&CFID=1455117&CFTOKEN=69887711&MenuPoint=C>, accessed Nov. 2004.

Grosser, Alfred (1966), 'France: nothing but opposition', in Robert A. Dahl (ed.), *Political Oppositions in Western Democracies* (New Haven and London: Yale University Press), pp. 284–302.

Guérin, Daniel (1998[1980]), *No Gods, No Masters. Book One*, Paul Sharkey, transl. (Edinburgh: AK Press).

Habermas, Jürgen (1989[1962]), *The Structural Transformation of the Public Sphere: An Inquiry into a Category of Bourgeois Society*, Thomas Burger, transl. (Cambridge: Polity Press).

Hannerz, Ulf (1992), 'The global ecumene as a network of networks', in Adam Kuper (ed.), *Conceptualizing Society* (London: Routledge), pp. 34–56.

Haraway, Donna J. (1997), 'Modest_witness@second_millenium', in *Modest_Witness@Second_Millenium.FemaleMan©_Meets_OncoMouseTM* (London: Routledge), pp. 23–48.

Hardt, Michael and Antonio Negri (2000), *Empire* (Cambridge, Mass.: Harvard University Press).

—— (2005), *Multitude: War and Democracy in the Age of Empire* (London: Penguin).

Harvey, David (1990), *The Condition of Postmodernity: An Enquiry into the Origins of Cultural Change* (Malden, Mass.: Blackwell).

Hastrup, Kirsten (2003), 'Representing the common good: the limits of legal language', in Richard Ashby Wilson and Jon P. Mitchell (eds), *Human Rights in Global Perspective: Anthropological Studies of Rights, Claims and Entitlements* (London: Routledge), pp. 16–32.

Hayes, Ben and Tony Bunyan (2004), 'The European Union and the "internal threat" of the alternative world movement', in François Polet (ed.), *Globalizing Resistance: The State of Struggle* (London: Pluto Press), pp. 258–71.

Hegland, Mary Elaine (2003), 'Shi'a women's rituals in northwest Pakistan: the shortcomings and significance of resistance', *Anthropological Quarterly* 76:3, 411–42.

Heller, Chaia (2001), 'From risk to globalisation: discursive shifts in the French debate about GMOs', *Medical Anthropological Quarterly* 15:1, 25–8.

—— (2004), 'Risky science and savoir-faire: peasant expertise in the French debate over genetically modified crops', in Marianne Elisabeth Lien and Brigitte Nerlich (eds), *The Politics of Food* (Oxford: Berg), pp. 81–99.

Heller, Thomas C., Morton Sosna and David E. Wellbery, eds (1986), *Reconstructing Individualism: Autonomy, Individuality, and the Self in Western Thought* (Stanford: Stanford University Press).

Herman, Patrick and José Bové, eds (2003), *Numéro d'écrou 20671 U. Lettres au détenu Joseph Bové* (Nantes: L'Atalante).

Hobbes, Thomas (1985[1651]), *Leviathan* (London: Penguin).

Hoffmann, Stanley (1974), 'The ruled: protest as a national way of life', in *Decline or Renewal? France since the 1930s* (New York: The Viking Press), pp. 111–44.

Holloway, John (2005), *Change the World Without Taking Power: The Meaning of Revolution Today,* New Edition (London: Pluto).

Holmes, Douglas R. (2000), *Integral Europe: Fast-Capitalism; Multiculturalism, Neofascism* (Princeton: Princeton University Press).

Holohan, Wanda (1976), 'Le conflit du Larzac: chronique et essai d'analyse', *Sociologie du Travail* 3, 283–301.

Howell, Signe (1997), 'Introduction', in Signe Howell (ed.), *The Ethnography of Moralities* (London: Routledge), pp. 1–22.

Humphrey, Caroline (1997), 'Exemplars and rules: aspects of the discourse of moralities in Mongolia', in Signe Howell (ed.), *The Ethnography of Moralities* (London: Routledge), pp. 25–47.

Ismaël (2003), 'Des racines et du zèle', *Gardarem lo Larzac* 249, 5.

Jacobson-Widding, Anita (1997), '"I lied, I farted, I stole ...": Dignity and morality in African discourses on personhood', in Signe Howell (ed.), *The Ethnography of Moralities* (London: Routledge), pp. 48–73.

Jameson, Fredric (2004), 'The politics of utopia', *New Left Review* 25: Jan–Feb, 35–54.

Jean-Klein, Iris (2001), 'Nationalism and resistance: the two faces of everyday activism in Palestine during the Intifada', *Cultural Anthropology* 16:1, 83–126.

—— (2003), 'Into committees, out of the house? Familiar forms in the organization of Palestinian committee activism during the first intifada', *American Ethnologist* 30:4, 556–77.

Johnston, Josée and Gordon Laxer (2003), 'Solidarity in the age of globalization: lessons from the anti-MAI and Zapatista struggles', *Theory and Society* 32:1, 39–91.

Jones, P.M. (1985), *Politics and Rural Society: The Southern Massif Central c.1750–1880* (Cambridge: Cambridge University Press).

Kasmir, Sharryn (2005), 'Activism and class identity: the Saturn auto factory case', in June Nash (ed.), *Social Movements: An Anthropological Reader* (Oxford: Blackwell), pp. 78–95.

Kedwood, Roderick (1971), *The Anarchists: The Men who Shocked an Era* (London: Library of the 20th Century).

Kertzer, David I. (1988), *Ritual, Politics and Power* (New Haven and London: Yale University Press).

Kondo, Dorinne (1990), *Crafting Selves: Power, Gender, and Discourses of Identity in a Japanese Workplace* (Chicago: University of Chicago Press).

Kumar, Krishan (1993), 'Civil society: an inquiry into the usefulness of an historical term', *The British Journal of Sociology* 44:3, 375–95.

Lacey, Anita (2005), 'Spaces of justice: the social divine of global anti-capital activists' sites of resistance', *Canadian Review of Sociology and Anthropology-Revue Canadienne de Sociologie et d'Anthropologie* 42:4, 403–20.

Laclau, Ernesto and Chantal Mouffe (1985), *Hegemony and Socialist Strategy: Towards a Radical Democratic Politics* (London: Verso).

Lambert, Bernard (1970), *Les paysans dans la lutte des classes* (Paris: Seuil).

Larzac Solidarités (2004), 'Après les forums sociaux', *La lettre d'information de Larzac Solidarités*: (Feb.).

Latouche, Serge (2002), 'D'autres mondes sont possible, pas une autre mondialisation', *Revue du M.A.U.S.S* 20: Second semestre, 77–89.

Latour, Bruno (1991), *Nous n'avons jamais été modernes. Essai d'anthropologie symétrique* (Paris: La Découverte).

Lazar, Sian (2004a) 'Citizenship and collective political agency in El Alto, Bolivia', (paper presented at Senior Seminar, Department of Social Anthropology, Cambridge University, 20 Feb.).

—— (2004b), 'Education for credit: development as citizenship project in Bolivia', *Critique of Anthropology* 24:3, 301–19.

Lebovics, Herman (1992), *True France: The Wars Over Cultural Identity, 1900–1945* (Ithaca: Cornell University Press).

Lebris, Michel (1975), *Les fous du Larzac* (Paris: Presses d'Aujourd'hui).

Lem, Winnie (1999), *Cultivating Dissent: Work, Identity, and Praxis in Rural Languedoc* (New York: State University of New York Press).

Les Membres de la 11e Mission et José Bové (2002), *Retour de Palestine. Campagne civile internationale pour la protection du peuple palestinien* (Paris: Mille et Une Nuits).

Letort, Solveig (2004), 'Oui, voter, c'est utile...', *Gardarem lo Larzac* 256, 1.

Levidow, Les (2000), 'Pollution metaphors in the UK biotechnology controversy', *Science as Culture* 9:3, 325–51.

Locke, John (1960[1690]), 'The second treatise of government', in *Two Treatises of Government* (Cambridge: Cambridge University Press), pp. 283–446.

Lukes, Steven (1986), 'Introduction', in Steven Lukes (ed.), *Power* (Oxford: Basil Blackwell), pp. 1–18.

—— (2005), *Power: A Radical View*, Second Edition (Houndmills, Basingstoke: Palgrave Macmillan).

Lukose, Ritty (2005), 'Empty citizenship: protesting politics in the era of globalization', *Cultural Anthropology* 20:4, 506–33.

MacIntyre, Alasdair (1984), *After Virtue: A Study in Moral Theory*, Second Edition (Notre Dame: Notre Dame Press).

Mageo, Jeannette Marie and Bruce M. Knauft (2002), 'Introduction: theorizing power and the self', in Jeannette Marie Mageo (ed.), *Power and the Self* (Cambridge: Cambridge University Press), pp. 1–25.

Mainguy, François (2005), 'K.O. social à Montpellier', *Gardarem lo Larzac* 261, 6.

Marshall, Peter H. (1992), *Demanding the Impossible: A History of Anarchism* (London: HarperCollins).

Martin, Didier (1987), *Larzac. Utopies et réalités* (Paris: L'Harmattan).

Martin, Jean-Philippe (2000), 'La Confédération paysanne et José Bové, des actions médiatiques au service d'un projet ?', *Ruralia* 6, available online <http://ruralia. revues.org/document142.html>

Marx, Karl (1967[1843]), 'On the Jewish Question', in Loyd D. Easton and Kurt H. Guddat (eds), *Writings of the Young Marx on Philosophy and Society* (New York: Anchor), pp. 216–48.

—— (1971[1859]), *A Contribution to the Critique of Political Economy*, S.W. Ryazanskaya, transl. (London: Lawrence & Wishart).

Mauss, Marcel (1985[1938]), 'A category of the human mind: the notion of person; the notion of self', W.D. Halls, transl., in Michael Carrithers, Steven Collins and Steven Lukes (eds), *The Category of the Person: Anthropology, Philosophy, History* (Cambridge: Cambridge University Press), pp. 1–25.

McDonald, Maryon (1989), *"We are not French!": Language, Culture and Identity in Brittany* (London: Routledge).

—— (2000), 'Accountability, anthropology and the European Commission', in Marilyn Strathern (ed.), *Audit Cultures: Anthropological Studies in Accountability, Ethics and the Academy* (London: Routledge), pp. 106–32.

McLuhan, Marshall (1964), *Understanding Media: The Extensions of Man* (New York: McGraw Hill).

Mellon, Christian (1998), 'Qu'est-ce que la désobéissance civile', *Alternatives non violentes* 108, 2–8.

Melucci, Alberto (1996), *Challenging Codes: Collective Action in the Information Age* (New York: Cambridge University Press).

Mendras, Henri and Alistair Cole (1991), *Social Change in Modern France: Towards a Cultural Anthropology of the Fifth Republic* (Cambridge: Cambridge University Press).

Mény, Yves and Yves Surel (2000), *Par le peuple, pour le peuple. Le populisme et les démocraties* (Paris: Fayard).

Messer, Ellen (1993), 'Anthropology and human rights', *Annual Review of Anthropology* 22, 221–49.

Mestrum, Francine (2004), 'The World Social Forum: a democratic alternative', in François Polet (ed.), *Globalizing Resistance: The State of Struggle* (London: Pluto Press), pp. 188–205.

Mitchell, Timothy (1990), 'Everyday metaphors of power', *Theory and Society* 19:5, 545–77.

—— (1999), 'Society, economy, and the state effect', in George Steinmetz (ed.), *State/Culture: State-Formation After the Cultural Turn* (Ithaca and London: Cornell University Press), pp. 76–97.

Montesquieu (1979[1748]), *De l'esprit des lois I* (Paris: GF Flammarion).

Moore, Donald S. (1998), 'Subaltern struggles and the politics of place: remapping resistance in Zimbabwe's eastern highlands', *Cultural Anthropology* 13:3, 344–81.

Moran, Jacques (2000), 'Un libertaire qui dérange...', *L'Humanité,* 17 March. http://www.humanite.presse.fr/journal/2000-03-17/2000-03-17-221881.

Mueller, Tadzio (2002), 'Gramsci, counterhegemony and the globalisation-critical movement', *Studies in Social and Political Thought* 6, 55–64.

Nash, June C. (2001), *Mayan Visions: The Quest for Autonomy in an Age of Globalization* (New York and London: Routledge).

—— (2005), 'Introduction: social movements and global processes', in June C. Nash (ed.), *Social Movements: An Anthropological Reader* (Oxford: Blackwell), pp. 1–26.

Nataf, André (1986), *Des anarchistes en France 1880–1910* (Paris: Hachette).

Navaro-Yashin, Yael (2002), *Faces of the State: Secularism and Public Life in Turkey* (Princeton: Princeton University Press).

O'Neill, Kate (2004), 'Transnational protest: states, circuses, and conflict at the frontline of global politics', *International Studies Review* 6:2, 233–52.

Ormières, Jean-Louis (1992), 'Les rouges et les blancs', in Pierre Nora (ed.), *Les Lieux de Mémoire, vol. III, Les France, 1. Conflits et Partages* (Paris: Gallimard), pp. 230–73.

Oyharçabal, Brice (2001) 'Le Larzac vingt ans après: les exploitations et exploitants agricoles et leurs évolution après la lutte', Master's thesis (Maîtrise), Université Paris 8.

Ozouf, Mona (1998), 'Liberty, equality, fraternity', in Pierre Nora (ed.), *Realms of Memory: the Construction of the French Past. Vol. III Symbols* (New York: Columbia University Press), pp. 77–114.

Pagis, Julie (2005) 'Conditions sociales du consensus dans un contexte d'action collective. Attac et la Confédération Paysanne. Enquête ethnographique sur deux configurations locales', paper presented at conference '"Cultures et Pratiques Participatives": une Perspective Comparative', 20–21 Jan., Paris: LAIOS et l'AFSP. (Available online) <http://www.afsp.msh-paris.fr/activite/diversafsp/colllaios05/txt/pagis.pdf>

Pennington, Kenneth (1998), 'The History of Rights in Western Thought', *Emory Law Journal* 47:1, 237–52.

Pichardo, Nelson A. (1997), 'New social movements: A critical review', *Annual Review of Sociology* 23, 411–30.

Polet, François (2004), 'Introduction', in François Polet (ed.), *Globalizing Resistance: the State of Struggle* (London: Pluto Press), pp. vii–xi.

Polletta, Francesca (2002), *Freedom is an Endless Meeting: Democracy in American Social Movements* (Chicago: University of Chicago Press).

Pons, Suzanne (2001), 'Agrochimie, semences, OGM et pillage des ressources génétiques', in Jean-Pierre Berlan (ed.), *La guerre au vivant. Organismes génétiquement modifiés et autres mystifications scientifiques* (Marseille: Agone), pp. 113–26.

Pratt, Jeff (2003), *Class, Nation and Identity: The Anthropology of Political Movements* (London: Pluto Press).

Prost, Antoine (1987), 'Frontières et espaces du privée', in Philippe Ariès and Georges Duby (eds), *Histoire de la vie privée, 5: de la première guerre mondiale à nos jours* (Paris: Seuil), pp. 12–153.

Purdue, Derrick A. (2000), *Anti-GenetiX: The Emergence of the Anti-GM Movement* (Aldershot: Ashgate).

Rabinow, Paul (1989), *French Modern: Norms and Forms of the Social Environment* (Chicago: Chicago University Press).

—— (2005), 'Midst anthropology's problems', in Stephen J. Collier and Aihwa Ong (eds), *Global Assemblages: Technology, Politics, and Ethics as Anthropological Problems* (Oxford: Blackwell), pp. 40–53.

Rawlinson, Roger (1983), *Larzac: A Victory for Nonviolence* (London: Quaker Peace & Service).

—— (1996), *Larzac: A Popular Nonviolent Campaign in Southern France* (York: William Sessions).

Raynaud, Philippe (1988), 'La déclaration des droits de l'homme', in Colin Lucas (ed.), *The French Revolution and the Creation of Modern Political Culture. Vol. 2. The Political Culture of the French Revolution* (Oxford: Pergamon), pp. 139–49.

—— (2006), *L'extême gauche plurielle. Entre démocratie radicale et révolution* (Paris: Éditions Autrement).

Reed-Danahay, Deborah (1993), 'Talking about resistance: ethnography and theory in rural France', *Anthropological Quarterly* 66:4, 221–229 (references pp. 240–46).

Riles, Annelise (2001), *The Network Inside Out* (Ann Arbor: University of Michigan Press).

Robertson, Roland (1991), 'Social theory, cultural relativity and the problem of globality', in Anthony King (ed.), *Culture, Globalization and the World-System: Contemporary Conditions for the Representation of Identity* (Basingstoke: Macmillan Press), pp. 69–90.

Rogers, Susan Carol (1987), 'Good to think: the "peasant" in contemporary France', *Anthropological Quarterly* 60:2, 56–63.

—— (1991), *Shaping Modern Times in Rural France: The Transformation and Reproduction of an Aveyronnais Community* (Princeton: Princeton University Press).

Rosanvallon, Pierre (1992), *Le sacre du citoyen. Histoire du suffrage universel en France* (Paris: Gallimard).

Rose, Nikolas (1999), *Powers of Freedom: Reframing Political Thought* (Cambridge: Cambridge University Press).

Ross, Kristin (2002), *May '68 and Its Afterlives* (Chicago: University of Chicago Press).

Rousseau, Jean-Jacques (1997[1762]), *The Social Contract and Other Later Political Writings*, Victor Gourevitch, transl. (Cambridge: Cambridge University Press).

Roux, François (2002), *En état de légitime révolte* (Montpellier: Indigène Éditions).

Sainsaulieu, Ivan (1998), 'La fédération Solidaires Unitaires Démocratiques des PTT (SUD-PTT): creuset d'une contestation pragmatique', *Revue Française de Science Politique* 48:1, 121–41.

Santos, Boaventura de Sousa (2004), 'The World Social Forum: towards a counter-hegemonic globalization', in François Polet (ed.), *Globalizing Resistance: The State of Struggle* (London: Pluto Press), pp. 165–87.

Sartori, Giovanni (1976), *Democratic Theory* (Westport: Greenwood Press).

Schneewind, J.B. (1998), *The Invention of Autonomy: A History of Modern Moral Philosophy* (Cambridge: Cambridge University Press).

Scott, Ian M. (2000), 'Green symbolism in the genetic modification debate', *Journal of Agricultural and Environmental Ethics* 13:3–4, 293–311.

Scott, James C. (1985), *Weapons of the Weak: Everyday Forms of Peasant Resistance* (New Haven: Yale University Press).

—— (1990), *Domination and the Arts of Resistance: Hidden Transcripts* (New Haven: Yale University Press).

Scott, Joan (1994), 'The evidence of experience', in James Chandler, Arnold Davidson and Harry Harootunian (eds), *Questions of Evidence: Proof, Practice, and Persuasion Across the Disciplines* (Chicago and London: University of Chicago Press), pp. 363–87.

Seidman, Michael (2004), *The Imaginary Revolution: Parisian Students and Workers in 1968* (New York and Oxford: Berghahn).

Sennett, Richard (2002[1977]), *The Fall of Public Man* (London: Penguin).

Sewell, William H. (1988), 'Le citoyen/la citoyenne: activity, passivity, and the revolutionary concept of citizenship', in Colin Lucas (ed.), *The French Revolution and the Creation of Modern Political Culture. Vol. 2. The Political Culture of the French Revolution* (Oxford: Pergamon), pp. 105–23.

Sklair, Leslie (1995), 'Social Movements and Global Capitalism', *Sociology* 29:3, 495–512.

Skocpol, Theda (1999), 'Associations without members', *American Prospect* 10:45, 66–73.

Spencer, Jonathan (1997), 'Post-colonialism and the political imagination', *Journal of the Royal Anthropological Institute* 3:1, 1–19.

Stjernø, Steinar (2004), *Solidarity in Europe* (Cambridge: Cambridge University Press).

Stoll, David (1997), 'To whom should we listen? Human rights activism in two Guatemalan land disputes', in Richard A. Wilson (ed.), *Human Rights, Culture and Context: Anthropological Perspectives* (London: Pluto Press), pp. 187–215.

Stone, Glenn Davis (2002), 'Both sides now: fallacies in the genetic-modification wars, implications for developing countries, and anthropological perspectives', *Current Anthropology* 43:4, 611–30.

Strathern, Marilyn (1996), 'Cutting the network', *Journal of the Royal Anthropological Institute* 2:3, 517–35.

Sud éducation (2001), *L'école face à la mondialisation capitaliste* (Fédération des syndicats Sud éducation, supplement to Le Journal, no.125).

Taylor, Charles (1989), *Sources of the Self: The Making of Modern Identity* (Cambridge, Mass.: Harvard University Press).

—— (2002), 'Modern social imaginaries', *Public Culture* 14:1, 91–124.

Tierney, Brian (1997), *The Idea of Natural Rights: Studies on Natural Rights, Natural Law and Church Law, 1150–1625* (Atlanta, Ga.: Scholars Press).

Tilly, Charles (1986), *The Contentious French* (Cambridge, Mass.: Belknap Press).

—— (1998), 'Where do rights come from?', in Theda Skocpol (ed.), *Democracy, Revolution, and History* (Ithaca: Cornell University Press), pp. 55–72.

—— (1999), 'From interactions to outcomes in social movements', in Marco Giugni, Doug McAdam and Charles Tilly (eds), *How Social Movements Matter* (Minneapolis: University of Minnesota Press), pp. 253–70.

Touraine, Alain (2001), *Beyond Neoliberalism*, David Macey, transl. (Cambridge: Polity Press).

Trouillot, Michel-Rolph (2001), 'The anthropology of the state in the age of globalization: close encounters of the deceptive kind', *Current Anthropology* 42:1, 125–38.

Tsing, Anna (2000), 'The global situation', *Cultural Anthropology* 15:3, 327–60.

Tucker, Philippa (2002) 'England's Antipodes: Early Modern Visions of a Southern World', MA thesis, Victoria University of Wellington.

Turner, Victor (1967), *The Forest of Symbols* (Ithaca: Cornell University Press).

—— (1969), *The Ritual Process: Structure and Anti-Structure* (Chicago: Aldine Publishing Company).

Ulin, Robert (1996), *Vintages and Traditions: An Ethnohistory of Southwest French Wine Cooperatives* (Washington: Smithsonian Institution Press).

Via Campesina (2005) 'Organization', *Via Campesina* [website], <http://viacampesina.org/en/index.php?option=com_content&task=section&id=31&Itemid=155>, accessed Jan. 2006.

Vree, Wilbert van (1999[1994]), *Meetings, Manners and Civilization: The Development of Modern Meeting Behaviour*, Kathleen Bell, transl. (London and New York: Leicester University Press).

Vuarin, Pauline (2005) 'Larzac 1971–1981 : la dynamique des acteurs d'une lutte originale et créatrice', Master's thesis (Maîtrise), Université Panthéon-Sorbonne (Paris 1).

Wallerstein, Immanuel (2003), 'Citizens all? Citizens some! The making of the citizen', *Comparative Studies in Society and History* 45:4, 650–79.

Warner, Michael (2002), 'Publics and Counterpublics', *Public Culture* 14:1, 49–90.

Weber, Eugen (1976), *Peasants into Frenchmen: The Modernization of Rural France, 1870–1914* (Stanford: Stanford University Press).

—— (1991[1959]), 'Left, right, and temperament', in *My France: Politics, Culture, Myth* (Cambridge, Mass.: Belknap Press), pp. 40–56.

—— (1991[1974]), 'Revolution? Counterrevolution? What revolution?', in *My France: Politics, Culture, Myth* (Cambridge, Mass.: Belknap Press), pp. 298–327.

Weber, Max (1991[1921]), 'The sociology of charismatic authority', in H.H. Girth and C. Wright Mills (eds), *From Max Weber: Essays in Sociology* (London: Routledge), pp. 245–52.

Weiler, Gershon (1997), 'Logos against Leviathan: the Hobbesian origins of modern antipolitics', in Andreas Schedler (ed.), *The End of Politics? Explorations into Modern Antipolitics* (Houndmills: Macmillan), pp. 40–56.

Weintraub, Jeff (1997), 'The theory and politics of the public/private distinction', in Jeff Weintraub and Krishan Kumar (eds), *Public and Private in Thought and Practice: Perspectives on a Grand Dichotomy* (Chicago: University of Chicago Press), pp. 1–42.

Weszkalnys, Gisa (2004) 'Alexanderplatz: An Ethnographic Study of Place and Planning in Contemporary Berlin', Ph.D. thesis, Cambridge University.

Wilder, Gary (1999), 'Practicing citizenship in imperial Paris', in John L. Comaroff and Jean Comaroff (eds), *Civil Society and the Political Imagination in Africa: Critical Perspectives* (Chicago: Chicago University Press), pp. 44–71.

Williams, Gwyn (2008), 'Cultivating Autonomy: Power, Resistance and the French Alterglobalisation Movement', *Critique of Anthropology* 28:1, 63–86.

Wilson, Richard A. (1997), 'Human rights, culture and context: an introduction', in Richard A. Wilson (ed.), *Human Rights, Culture and Context: Anthropological Perspectives* (London: Pluto Press), pp. 1–27.

Wilson, Richard Ashby and Jon P. Mitchell, eds (2003), *Human Rights in Global Perspective: Anthropological Studies of Rights, Claims and Entitlements* (London: Routledge).

Woods, Michael (2003), 'Deconstructing rural protest: the emergence of a new social movement', *Journal of Rural Studies* 19:3, 309–25.

WSF (n.d.) 'Charter of Principles', *World Social Forum* [website], <http://www.forumsocialmundial.org.br/main.php?id_menu=4&cd_language=2>, accessed July 2006.

WTO (n.d.) 'What is the WTO?', *World Trade Organization* [website] <http://www.wto.org/english/thewto_e/whatis_e/whatis_e.htm>, accessed May 2006.

Zaloom, Caitlin (2004), 'The productive life of risk', *Cultural Anthropology* 19:3, 365–91.

Žižek, Slavoj (1999), *The Ticklish Subject: The Absent Centre of Political Ontology* (London: Verso).

Index